therapy, coaching, and mediation that can transform conflict into creative potential. Vital reading for musicians, band managers, music industry professionals, mediators, and mental health practitioners working with creative individuals.

This really is an exciting and important book that will make a difference in the field and contribute to solving tensions and conflicts inherent to the music industry.

Joel Vos, *Metanoia Institute, UK*

Conflict is inevitable at some point in any meaningful creative partnership, and it can feel daunting and intractable. In *Musical Differences*, Monica Hanaway expertly guides you through the processes and benefits of mediation, equipping you with strategies to navigate disputes and potential pitfalls. I think her insights will be invaluable in helping me work through the more fractious aspects of my life as a musician.

Phil Selway, *member of the band Radiohead, UK*

This book offers incredibly valuable perspectives on conflict and mediation within the music industry and will be hugely valuable to any musician who works with other people. I certainly wish I'd had access to this when I was starting out with early collaborations! Monica writes with empathy and understanding in a way that is accessible and engaging for musicians. The book is focussed towards sharing tools, insights, and strategies for helping the reader to understand the psychological process and mechanisms involved around conflict and resolution which is entirely fascinating and hugely beneficial reading for anyone who works with others.

Adam Martin, *Huddersfield University, UK*

Monica has a global reputation as a mediator who brings psychological insight into the practice. In this new book, she continues to add to our understanding of mediation and its benefits, in a clear and well-structured way. The focus of this book is on how mediation can benefit those in the music industry both financially and, more importantly, psychologically. As with some of her previous books, she offers realistic and multi-layered case studies, showing in a practical way how mediation works. These are drawn from her considerable experience of mediations in the sector. She also offers some ways in which musicians can be proactive in reducing and tackling conflict themselves. I would highly recommend this book to all in the media industries and to all interested in finding out more about mediation.

Dida Mitchell, *mediator, psychotherapist and trainer, UK*

In my work with the charity Punk4MentalHealth, at the intersection between music and mental health, I've witnessed countless times first-hand how musicians navigate the complex terrain of mental health challenges alongside interpersonal conflicts. As an existential and meaning-centred therapist who has worked with many musicians throughout my career, I've seen how the industry's unique pressures create both internal struggles and interpersonal tensions. Monica Hanaway's *Musical Differences* addresses these crucial intersections with remarkable insight and practical wisdom.

What makes this book exceptional is Hanaway's existential framework that recognizes how musicians inherently choose their path because it feels deeply meaningful. Yet, as she expertly outlines in her introduction, this meaning-making project becomes complicated when commercialization shifts its purpose or when collaboration creates tension between individual visions. The book brilliantly explores what existential themes play beneath the musical notes – time and temporality, authenticity, freedom, and responsibility – all concepts that resonate profoundly with musicians struggling to maintain their creative integrity.

The exploration of how musicians cope when they cannot realize their meaning or when others block their meaning-making addresses a core existential question: how do we manage when we cannot fulfil the most meaningful musical ideals we have in life? This creates grounds for not only internalized frustrations but also externalized acting out that leads to polarized views and conflict – dynamics evident in many musical collaborations.

Hanaway's case studies, particularly those examining "what leadership means in a band and the paradoxical ambivalence" and cultural differences within groups, offer invaluable insights into how existential anxieties manifest in creative partnerships. She delves into the crucial questions of how musicians manage conflicting ideals and dreams within bands or orchestras, providing not merely theoretical perspectives but practical clinical examples that illuminate the path toward resolution.

The book's greatest strength lies in its practical approach to conflict resolution through mediation rather than litigation. Hanaway demonstrates through eight detailed case studies how mediation can address both the practical issues and the deeper psychological concerns that often underlie disputes in the music industry. Her framework for proactive conflict prevention in Part Three offers concrete tools that groups can implement before tensions escalate.

It's worth noting that Monica stands in a profound tradition that connects existential thinking with music. Following in the footsteps of R. D. Laing, who worked with the early punk movement and the Sex Pistols, I too have found myself working within this tradition. How I wish Monica's wisdom and this book had been available during my years working with musicians navigating their existential challenges! Her insights into what existential themes play under the musical notes and within their relationships, both one-to-one and in groups, would have been invaluable.

This important work doesn't just illuminate the hidden world behind the music and superficial smiles; it offers concrete directions for research,

Musical Differences

Musical Differences is the first book to focus specifically on resolving conflict among those working in the music industry using an existential perspective to explore the interpersonal and psychological nature of conflict itself.

It considers different ways of addressing conflict, compares litigation to the use of more creative methods such as mediation, and examines skills and strategies to prevent or resolve conflicts without resorting to a third party. As a mediator herself, the author presents a psychologically informed mediation approach through multiple case studies to illustrate how these techniques work in practice. By providing a route for taking musical disputes out of the long antagonistic litigation process, the book offers a way of dealing with conflict-based stress which has less negative impact on mental health and increases well-being while navigating a life in the industry.

This book is written for practising musicians and those working in the music industry, as well as for students of music and readers with a general interest in the stresses and challenges of those involved in the music world.

Monica Hanaway is a mediator, psychotherapist, coach, consultant, trainer, and author with a global reputation for her work introducing an existential-phenomenological approach in new contexts such as the corporate and business world, as well as for her work with individual clients, many of whom are from within the creative and media industries.

Musical Differences

Working with Conflict in the Music Industry

Monica Hanaway

Routledge
Taylor & Francis Group
NEW YORK AND LONDON

Designed cover image: Mikołaj Kołodziejczyk.

First published 2026
by Routledge
605 Third Avenue, New York, NY 10158

and by Routledge
4 Park Square, Milton Park, Abingdon, Oxon, OX14 4RN

Routledge is an imprint of the Taylor & Francis Group, an informa business

Library of Congress Cataloging-in-Publication Data
Names: Hanaway, Monica author
Title: Musical differences : working with conflict in the music industry / Monica Hanaway.
Description: [1st]. | New York, NY : Routledge, 2026. |
Includes bibliographical references and index.
Identifiers: LCCN 2025044334 (print) | LCCN 2025044335 (ebook) |
ISBN 9781041147473 hardback | ISBN 9781041147466 paperback |
ISBN 9781003675938 ebook | ISBN 9781040769270 adobe pdf |
ISBN 9781040769324 epub
Subjects: LCSH: Music trade | Conflict management
Classification: LCC ML3790 .H336 2026 (print) | LCC ML3790 (ebook) |
DDC 303.6/9–dc23/eng/20251223
LC record available at https://lccn.loc.gov/2025044334
LC ebook record available at https://lccn.loc.gov/2025044335

ISBN: 978-1-041-14747-3 (hbk)
ISBN: 978-1-041-14746-6 (pbk)
ISBN: 978-1-003-67593-8 (ebk)

DOI: 10.4324/9781003675938

Typeset in Sabon
by Newgen Publishing UK

Contents

Tables

Foreword

As soon as you enter a dressing room with a band, you become aware, in some way, of the dynamics of their setup. There are no ideal setups for relationships; there is no one correct way to be – it is just 'what works' or doesn't. It's about how things are or what is working right there and then. You might be greeted by a smiling, creative member – outgoing and charming – while other members hang back, sizing up the situation on their own. Some members might not speak at all until spoken to; others will be grilling you on your musical tastes or your 'top ten supermarkets'. A new addition (a visitor) will always change the dynamic and balance in the mix, but to walk into a dressing room or other media green room is always to have an encounter with the multi-dimensional; there is never just one thing going on at one time.

One might meet or have an idea of the 'collective' purpose, but there are also a series of very different individuals at play. Such an awareness of multiple motivations, memories, and emotions becomes a crucial factor when considering conflict. For a band working together on a daily basis, into this metaphysical environment constructed by the combined personalities of all the musicians will fall all manner of things, from a mundane offer of a gig to the dramatic departure of a band or crew member, the birth or death of a member's child, or falling sales figures. Yet there are implications for each, along a timeline that is always changing in its emphasis and relevance.

All manner of things, both personal and professional, will need to be dealt with and not just through the lens of the individual member's life and experience; they must, in some way, pass through (or by) the band's collective brain – usually an odd balance and counterbalance of relationships, perspectives, personalities, and a mixture of world views. The potential for the simplest of issues to cause tension is nearly always there the more frequently you work together. So much about making music involves collaboration. An idea like this might rightly lead you to believe that creativity within a band context involves cooperation, interaction, empathy, understanding, patience, and, most importantly, shared ideas and goals. Even with these in abundance, the business of creative production and all its shades of reciprocity may work for a while, and yet at some point, conflict is unavoidable. Although making the same play, everyone has an evolving script, everyone fundamentally ends up playing a different role than the one they imagined at the start, and so there will always be times when disagreement arises.

When it does arise, it is healthy to at least come to terms with conflict. A disagreement may come to light but then fade away, or it can build and build. By not dealing with the issues, the problems don't really disappear; they remain below the surface ready to erupt. Without recognising conflict, individuals may find that the only way they can stay true to themselves or express themselves fully is to argue (fight) or break apart the environment they created, perhaps ultimately just walk away from it (flight). What this book begins to map out are spectra of options between those two reductive poles of response. In essence, we begin to explore the space between stimulus and response, as noted by Viktor Frankl (in 1946), where we can discover our power to experience growth and freedom through choice.

This book is written with experience, expertise, and a genuine dedication and intention to help people's lives, to reinstate a form of clarity or sanity, and to help them 'get out of the hole' or break the deadlock of inevitable creative differences that may occur in a collaborative creative process. In the best possible cases, it may help to get the creativity flowing again among working collectives with powerful combinations of characters and personalities when things have become 'stuck'; emerging with a new form of cooperation and interaction, understanding of each other's fundamental (and perhaps originally inspired) positions.

Despite the romantic portrayal they usually are given, musicians and creatives deal with a lot of stressful situations. They are often self-employed, self-determined, and therefore self-reliant on all potential outcomes, good or bad, in situations that are qualitative, open-ended, and descriptive. The impact and implications for the projects they work on are real, but despite self-determination, they find themselves increasingly in situations that are reliant on others. They need tools to help facilitate good outcomes for all. This book is an attempt to begin to provide such tools which may help in such situations.

Mediation skills are becoming increasingly important in the workplace, and in many instances of conflict I have either seen or experienced over the years, the involvement of a neutral third party could have led to safer, easier, cheaper, and less emotionally draining alternatives. Mediation can be a transformative practice for everyone, including the facilitators. It is not a golden bullet; it is not guaranteed a first-time win in every situation within a limited time span, but it can work, and given a chance and time, it can move lives forward, release and renounce tension, and remove the restrictions that build on people's lives in conflict.

In essence, this book is focused on how mediation (alternative conflict resolution) can help resolve disputes in the music industry. The first part of the book explores the nature of conflict before moving on to look specifically at conflict in the music industry. In part two, the author introduces us, in a very practical way, to how mediation works, drawing on some real examples. Finally, in part three, the reader is offered some ways in which conflict can be reduced so that it doesn't escalate to the stage requiring mediation.

Monica Hanaway has extensive experience in the field, and as a result, her book will serve as key source material for mediators and those working with inter-relational issues, both experienced and aspiring. It will also be useful for musicians, managers, and industry operators in general looking to gain insight into managing potential pitfalls in creative situations or processes. It is my hope that the depictions of the situations and the reflections on various approaches within these pages resonate and may contribute to a world where conflict can be met with compassion yet still resolved with awareness and grace.

Dr Laurence Colbert
Lecturer in Popular Music at Huddersfield University
Professional Musician (drummer with RIDE)

Acknowledgments

I would like to thank and acknowledge all those musicians I have had the opportunity to work with and to learn from. They have given me access to both the good times and the bad times involved in being a professional musician and so inspired me to write this book.

I also owe thanks to my husband, himself a talented musician, composer, and performer. His continued patience and support provide me with the encouragement to continue with all my projects.

Introduction

My personal interest in conflict resolution focuses on the interpersonal and psychological nature of conflict. Indeed, I would propose that all conflict is psychological, emotional, and relational, and so linked to existential themes and challenges. This is the approach which I bring to all my work as an existential psychotherapist, coach, mediator and trainer, and so it will of course, be reflected throughout this book.

The focus of this book is on resolving conflict within the music industry and on the use of mediation to do this, as I believe that it is a more effective, cheaper, and more humane intervention than litigation. I believe that we learn best by doing and in the absence of being able to offer that experience in a book, I have devoted the second part of the book to some case studies which I hope will give a realistic picture of how mediation works. In part three I offer some approaches which may prevent conflict developing and some possibilities that can be tried to resolve a dispute without involving a third party.

Existential Issues for Musicians

In introducing the word existential here, I feel I need to give a little insight into how I am using the word, as it currently seems to be used in a very generic way. I am using the word as it is used in the existential writings of people like Sartre, de Beauvoir, Kierkegaard, Nietzsche, Merleau-Ponty, Buber, Heidegger, and others. They provide us with excellent but challenging and often inaccessible and difficult reading, but their thinking is based on a simple underlying framework of understanding, focused on the belief that that we are all unique individuals and have a human need for that individuality to be recognised and respected. Yet at the same time, we also have much in common and share a number of what are termed 'existential givens'.

DOI: 10.4324/9781003675938-1

These existential givens include the most fundamental one: that we are born and we die. Between these two points, which constitute our temporal existence, we all face the existential challenges of finding meaning, dealing with uncertainty, trying to remain authentic, being alone or finding ways of being with others, taking responsibility for our freedom to make choices with the full knowledge and acceptance of the implications that freedom of choice will have on others and on the world we inhabit. Even if we choose not to register, acknowledge, or work consciously with these existential givens, they are there, and by putting our heads in the sand, we are still using our freedom in our choice *not* to engage but instead *choosing* to behave in an inauthentic unreflective way.

Many of these existential themes provide the starting point for much art, including music. I do not intend to present you with a book heavy on philosophy, but these elements will be present in the conflicts I write about, and the existential flavour of my personal world view and my approach to my work will no doubt be evident. Looking at these existential givens is not just interesting theory, it is easy to see how they may come into play in navigating a life within the music industry.

Existential Givens

Time and Temporality

Musicians know a lot about time and timing. Each piece of music is set within time and also relies on everyone's timing interacting together to produce a work within which the changes in timing are an important part of its language, which develops the narrative and emotional ebb and flow of the piece. The world of music is also heavily influenced by and influential in the creation of the prevailing zeitgeist. When we think of recent decades, the 60s, 70s, 80s, 90s, 00s, etc., our thoughts are usually accompanied by an internal playing of music of the time, accompanied by the images of the art and fashion which are so closely aligned with that music.

The fact that we exist within a temporal space, in which we have to work with an understanding of time, presents many challenges. Some are quite basic – how do we work with different concepts and attitudes towards time in a group context. One person may become very anxious if anyone is even a few minutes late whilst another may operate under a personal time frame in which being somewhere for 1 pm is translated as getting there any time from 12–3. One dispute started when members of a band were boarding a plane and discovered one member was absent. He was located in duty-free, blindly unaware of time, searching for a present for a family member. This could be viewed as someone innocently not paying much attention to the time as they were wanting to do something nice for a person they cared about. It could equally be seen by other members of the band as a sign of disrespect and lack of care for them and their work. It certainly indicated a difference in attitude towards time amongst members of the group.

Having to work across geographical timelines can cause tiredness and disorientation, resulting in people missing meetings, flights, gigs, etc. or finding it hard to maintain any meaningful contact with families during touring. Negotiating ways of staying in touch with family and friends or even ensuring that the more basic tasks of life are completed, dealing with bills, maintaining a home etc., whilst they are on the other side of the globe is often an exhausting and not an easy task.

For those working in the popular music arena rather than the classical field, time is often tied up with fleeting success. Some types of music are popular for only a short period of time. A group or solo artist may be much in demand for a time, with days and months rushing by, only to find a sudden drop-off in interest, and therefore of work, leaving time hanging heavy, and issues of self-esteem, self-concept, identity, and self-worth come rushing to the fore.

For those who do manage to maintain success over a long period they must face the impact of time on their bodies. Touring is not easy on the body or the mind and can take its toll on health. Exercising regularly may be a well-established routine outside of tours, but it can be hard to maintain when one is constantly on the move and rushing from place to place or even from country to country or hemisphere to hemisphere.

Physical attractiveness may have been part of an artist's appeal. Equally the exuberance and the energy of their youthful performances may have marked them out as different and exciting. Although for most people time may be unkind and present them with personal bodily challenges and conflicts, we have examples of artists who seem to have a Dorian Gray relationship to passing time, a good example being Mick Jagger who, despite being in his 80s and having undergone non-invasive heart valve replacement surgery at the age of 75, continues to tour and gyrate. Time is not so kind to everyone.

Different attitudes to healthy eating and other lifestyle choices often change over time, if some members of a group embrace this whilst others do not, then conflict is likely. Constant visual reminders on the aging process are part of an artist's everyday experience and are often commented on publicly. It is not easy to go, in the public gaze, from a fit and attractive youth to someone who may be struggling through physical weakness, arthritis, etc. to play their instruments or finding they can no longer hit the top notes when they sing or get out of breath more easily.

Women are more often criticised about the natural physical changes which aging brings. Some make use of the insights that gives them, like

Viv Albertine who has used her experiences of being a woman over time as a focus of her work. Her album *The Vermilion Border* consists of songs about IVF, being fed up with life as a housewife, and being desperate to experience more out of life as she got older. Perhaps being a punk artist made it more acceptable for her not to project a glamourous image. By 2018, more musicians were giving more positive spins on aging, with Matty Healy discussing grey hairs and speaking of seeking enlightenment at 29, and Florence Welch in her 30s singing about getting over anorexia and wanting children and a space to watch things grow. We have Tracey Thorn singing about contraception and conception and being on the dance floor at 55 with a few drinks inside her and Robyn Honey writing about the need for human connection.

Other artists may seem to have tried to ignore time and been criticised as a result. Madonna is one artist constantly under scrutiny with people feeling they have the right to comment on her age and her changing body. She suffered many negative comments after an appearance at the Grammys in 2023, which caused her to feel the need to respond, stating,

> many people chose to only talk about close-up photos of me taken with a long lens camera by a press photographer that would distort anyone's face! ... Once again I am caught in the glare of ageism and misogyny that permeates the world we live in ... a world that refuses to celebrate women past the age of 45 and feels the need to punish her if she continues to be strong-willed, hard-working and adventurous.
>
> (Sun, 2023)

It is impossible as a musician to ignore the passage of time. As its impact varies from individual to individual it can cause tensions when some group members are more affected than others. Artists also have to deal with the external perspectives and discrimination about age.

Meaning

For many existential thinkers one of the main challenges in life is to find a project or projects to give meaning to our existence. The existential view as expressed by early writers such as Kierkegaard and Nietzsche, and built on by later thinkers such as Sartre, de Beauvoir, and others, is that we are individually free from any limitations in the way we think, act, or feel. Existentialists do not believe we can look to external guides such as religion for meaning as most do not believe there is a god. Camus, in his writings, popularised the idea of absurdism which focused on the meaninglessness of existence and the chaotic nature of the universe, encouraging us to embrace the nothingness, accept the absurdness of life, and find joy and freedom in creating our own meaning. Frankl, in his powerful book *Man's Search for Meaning* (originally published in 1946), describes the ways in which he found meaning while imprisoned in a concentration camp in the 1940s, whilst his mother and brother were murdered in Auschwitz and his wife died of typhus in Bergen-Belsen. His own individual meaning enabled him to survive these horrors, and he describes how it was those prisoners who found some aim or meaning who survived whilst those unable to do so descended into despair. From these experiences, Frankl centred his thinking on the belief that the primary force of each human being is the will to find meaning, through their actions, love, or suffering, stating,

> man should not ask what the meaning of life is, but rather must recognise that it is he who is asked ... Each man is questioned by life; and he can only answer to life by answering for his own life; to life he can only respond by being responsible.
>
> (Frankl, 2006: 113)

The belief that there is no universal meaning and that we must create our own brings a terrifying uncertainty which for some people is unbearable. They will seek high and low for a promise of 'the true meaning' which will give them clear guidelines by which to live their lives.

We all need to find meaning. For many people, we find that through our families and friends, our work, engaging in activities which hold meaning for us, and creating a legacy of some kind. The creation of art, professional or not, is a meaning-making project for many. Musicians often use their music as a meaning-making project in their lives.

Commercialisation of such art projects can cause a painful shift in their meaning. My first degree was in fine art. Before starting the degree, drawing and painting held a depth of personal meaning for me. Once I started producing work to fulfil university requirements, this meaning was lost. The original meaning was replaced by a need to produce art in order to meet certain course requirements and to be in line with what was fashionable at the time. Of course, this in itself gave the process meaning, but it reframed the reason for painting. It took some time after successfully obtaining my degree for me to find again the original meaning and enjoyment in my art.

Making music for pleasure can quickly be replaced by the need to make music to survive: buy food, pay the mortgage, etc., and so the meaning shifts. This can produce internal conflicts about authenticity and how to remain true to one's values, as well as external conflicts with those whose first aim is to make money rather than make meaningful music.

Uncertainty

Anyone seeking certainty would do well to stay away from the creative industries. Many artists can tolerate and may even welcome uncertainty and change because it is these elements which give birth to creativity. They understand the need to challenge the status quo and embrace the uncertainty inherent in starting with nothing and giving birth to something which never existed before, thus producing something which may burn brightly for a moment or have a long-term influence on many.

Choosing a life in any creativity industry is unlikely to bring much certainty. The uncertainty evidenced by a blank canvas inviting creativity is one thing, but dealing with the uncertainty of a life of almost constant change, in which many factors seem to be outside one's control, is quite another.

By its very nature, the profession provides precarious employment without a great deal of protection. Audiences can be fickle. What is popular one year may become 'naff' the next. An artist can be in great demand only to find that some bad publicity, old social media posts, or just a change in public preferences can cast them into the darkness where no one seems to want to know them.

The music industry is not isolated from everything which goes around it, and the economic pressures of the time impact on it in the same way as they do on other professions. People need money to legally stream or buy music, to attend gigs, or to buy merchandise. When a country is in recession and money is short, people have to make difficult decisions about prioritising their spending. We are currently living in a time when the economic value per unit of music has plummeted. On a very personal level, musicians may have made financial commitments in a time when things appeared more financially rosy and certain, which they are now finding very difficult to uphold.

It would have been hard to have foreseen some of the more recent events which have impacted on the music industry. Many artists had a healthy diary of gigs, recording sessions, and promotions lined up before the Covid pandemic suddenly struck. Venues were closed, members of bands were no longer able to meet together to rehearse or perform, festivals were cancelled. Life stood still. Before that the industry had needed to adapt to the impact of streaming on revenue.

Music is quite tightly associated with fashion; things come into and go out of fashion quite quickly. It is not just audience preference which can have an impact on success. A musician can feel 'certain' that they have made it and their work is in high demand. However, the uncertainty of life means things can suddenly change. A change in political power can make ways of being, even the use of certain words, suddenly unacceptable, and a musician and their work may overnight be seen as dangerous and to be silenced.

Certainty is an enemy of creativity, as what would be the point of engaging in a creative journey if we were to end up with something that had existed before? However, the practical uncertainty of life in the music industry creates tensions and challenges which can result in conflict.

Authenticity

Authenticity is a topic that comes up a lot in rock and popular music. Most artists want their uniqueness recognised. There is considerable philosophical debate about what authenticity is and whether one can ever be fully authentic. People often speak as though authenticity requires one to be the same in all contexts. This would seem to imply that to develop and change could be seen as inauthentic. Of course, this isn't and can't be the case – if I am talking with my partner, we have a shared history, understanding, and tolerance of the many aspects of our individual selves from the vulnerable to the strong, which means I can speak and behave in an uncensored way with him. If I am speaking with children, I may have just read something I am excited about and want to share but will not chose to share it with them in that moment as it would not be of interest or meaningful to them. I will not suddenly dance during a mediation, but I may do so in my kitchen and certainly at a party. We are multifaceted, rich, complex, and diverse individuals, and by not showing all aspects of ourselves all the time, we are not being inauthentic. I see being inauthentic as times when my behaviours or words do not match my values.

Musicians have to operate in a world in which their work is subject to the changing fashions and to audience demand. Many musicians have, at various points in their career, felt that they have needed to compromise on their authenticity. In order to maintain record contracts, and pay mortgages, they may have needed to compromise on their artistic integrity to deliver what was needed for economic and professional stability. This can often be seen where deals for more than one album have been struck, management will not wish a successful first album to be followed by a second which sounds significantly different, even though the artist will have been developing their ideas and skills between the two. It is not just around music development and changes in style that pressure is applied. There are several examples of artists, especially those from the LGBTQ+ community being pressured by management to conceal their sexuality or gender as they fear it would negatively impact on their marketability.

Maintaining an authentic self in any performance industry can be challenging. Some artists choose to make a clear distinction between their personal and professional selves using names which emphasise the difference, e.g. Lady Gaga. Gaga spoke of this in a recent interview with Zane Lowe (2025), stating,

> that is who Lady Gaga is to me. Maybe to someone else it might be the meat dress or something that I did that they remember as me. But for me, I always want to be remembered for being a real artist and someone that cares so much about a life of art.' The danger of course is that the art is not seen, just the materials in use.

This interplay between personal and professional self can act positively for some people by allowing them to adopt a persona which they can use effectively on stage, which they can leave behind when they head home, allowing them to retain a more authentic self, shared only with those who they care about and who care for them. Some seem perfectly in control of this and may move seamlessly between a number of personas, playing creatively with each one. Bowie had at least five personas including Ziggy Stardust, Aladdin Sane, Halloween Jack, the Thin White Duke, and the Blind Prophet. Bowies' art background and love of playing with ideas left him in control of how he portrayed himself. Although I perceive his changes in persona as being an integral part of his art, some critics have described him as inauthentic. I believe Bowie successfully and authentically managed to integrate aspects of his personal and professional life. He used (as most writers do) experiences from his personal life as inspiration for his writing. His album *Low* speaks of his recovery from cocaine, *Lodger* is inspired by his travels around the world, his wedding and marriage shaped *Black Tie White Noise*, *Heathen* expressed his worries about the future, and *Black Star* was concerned with his impending death.

Although some artists can effectively and healthily move between personal and professional selves, this is not always the case. The artist Anitta (real name Larissa de Macedo Machado) was able to leave Anitta on stage early in her career, but as she became more successful, this became harder and harder to do, and Anitta began to take over. In her September 2024 Netflix documentary *Larissa: The Other Side of Anitta*, the Brazilian artist is open about her struggles to balance Anitta and Larissa. In the documentary, she is seen in conversation with a producer talking about her Anitta persona, 'It's very complicated, man. It's really hard. As I said, it's like, I hear one side then the other side comes and "Boom!" Instantly. It's like my body doesn't know how to be at peace. And I can't take it anymore' (Avila, 2025). She describes moving from one personality to another, 'Every time I see somebody that knows who Anitta is, but I'm not close to that person, I become Anitta. That triggers me and I become the character,' she continued, 'I don't want to become the character all the time!' (Avila, 2025). Whilst in the early days she felt she had control of her persona, as time went on, she felt the persona was controlling her. She described, 'Now that everybody knows me, I don't have any control and I can't take it anymore. I can't stand not being able to control when I'm turning into the character' (Avila, 2025). Around 18 months earlier, Anitta told *People*, 'Larissa is very private, very relaxed, very low key and very quiet. Anitta is the opposite: outspoken, exposing myself … I think it's two completely different people and I used to struggle with that' (Avila and Hansen, 2023). She feels that she has now found ways of allowing the two voices to communicate.

Other artists, such as Ed Sheeran, appear to want to portray themselves on stage as being the same as if you met them in the pub. Some artists and their followers value 'staying real', whilst others see part of their function as offering an escape from day-to-day reality, leaving themselves open to criticisms of being fake.

Dealing with issues of authenticity can create mental health problems and can also lead to conflict with others in a band or with management if an artist wants to change the way they present themselves publicly.

Freedom and Responsibility

A key aspect of existential thinking is the acknowledgment of our freedom and the need to take responsibility for our decisions, which impact on the self, others, and the world environment. A number of people entering the creative industries do so from a desire to find a place where they can be free to explore their creativity. Of course, there are others who are seeking their fifteen minutes of fame or are hopeful of material riches.

Unfortunately, once any kind of commercial success is reached many artists may find their creativity stifled and feel anything but free. Most people are aware of some high-level disputes in the music industry which centred on the artist's loss of freedom. One was that of George Michael who took on Sony Music, his record company at the time, alleging that his recording contract was so restrictive that it was unworkable and that as a result he had lost the control of his own life and career. For the first time in a case like this, his lawyers cited European law, article 85 of the Treaty of Rome, which prohibits agreements affecting trade between member states. Effectively this meant that if Sony chose not to release his work in a particular country, he was forbidden to record for another company that would. One of the biggest prizes at stake in the case was the lucrative copyright and the back catalogue of his works currently held by Sony. If the contract failed, an issue then arose as to who retained the copyright. George Michael argued that as the money for recording costs, packaging, and some promotion was recovered from his royalties, he should retain the copyright to his own work.

A British judge rejected his case freeing him from his long-term recording contract with the Sony Corporation, a ruling welcomed by industry executives, who saw the case as a challenge to the traditional practice of signing artists to multi-album deals as a way to offset their heavy investments in discovering and promoting new acts.

However, this prompted George Michael, one of the biggest stars of the late 1980s, to call his situation 'professional slavery' that left him little control over his own work and career for up to 15 years. He testified that his discontent followed Sony's reaction to his 1990 album *Listen Without Prejudice, Volume I*. With that album, he had made a deliberate decision to play down the sultry, sex-symbol image he had cultivated during his days with the pop duo Wham, a decision he said did not sit well with Sony executives who were interested only in sales and not in his development as an artist. He felt Sony had sought to punish him by not promoting *Listen Without Prejudice* as aggressively as it should have, particularly in the United States. The album sold five million copies, a relative disappointment after his 1988 album *Faith* sold 14 million copies worldwide.

Sony executives testified that they had marketed the album to the best of their abilities and claimed that George Michael was well aware of the terms of the contract he signed in 1988 and that the deal was a considerable improvement over his earlier contracts with CBS Records, which Sony had acquired.

In issuing his ruling in the High Court in London, Justice Jonathan Parker largely accepted Sony's view of the matter, saying that the contract was 'reasonable and fair' especially in consideration of his access to expert legal advice, several renegotiations, and terms comparable to the industry standard for an artist of his commercial success. He stated,

> I am satisfied on the evidence that there is no substance in George Michael's claim of unfair conduct by Sony or in any of the detailed complaints which he makes ... I am satisfied that there was no such deliberate policy decision by Sony as George Michael alleges.
>
> (Stevenson, 1994)

At a brief news conference, George Michael said that he thought there were strong grounds for an appeal and that he would probably file one. Sony, clearly trying to avoid further damage to its relationship with him, restricted its official reaction to a short statement: 'We have great respect for George Michael and his artistry, and look forward to continuing our relationship with him' (Stevenson, 1994).

The case had been followed intently in the recording industry, not just because it was a rare instance of a spat between an artist and a label being aired publicly in great detail but because of the precedent it could have set regarding long-term contracts.

Another high-profile example is that of Prince. From his first album with Warner Music in 1978 to his untimely death, Prince had a 40-year history of battling for control over his music, comparing record contracts to slavery. As much as we can trace his artistic trajectory through his music, we can also track Prince's career through his tumultuous dealings with the music industry. He had deals with a variety of labels and refused to keep quiet when these deals turned sour. In an attempt to retain his freedom and remain authentic Prince set up his own label, Paisley Park Records, which was part funded by Warner.

However, the build-up to the release of *The Gold Experience*, saw Prince and Warner at loggerheads over both money and his music. He took the battle public, appearing with the word 'Slave' on his face. He changed his name to a symbol and was referred to, variously, as 'Symbol,' 'Squiggle,' or 'the Artist Formerly Known as Prince.' Unable to break free from his contract, Prince fulfilled the terms of his contract with a number of albums, some of which resorted to the use of studio tapes and offcuts just to make up the required number to fulfil his contractual commitments. His early attempts to sell direct to fans online were clearly an influence on Radiohead, then out of contract with EMI, when they released *In Rainbows* in 2007 as a 'pay what you like' download.

Nevertheless, it was not all joy for Prince in virtual land. In 2007, in an attempt to reclaim his art on the internet he announced he was going to take action against YouTube, eBay, and the Pirate Bay for unauthorised use of his music.

The growth of AI has been seen by many as another attack on artistic freedom and ownership. 2024 saw more than 200 high profile musicians, including Billie Eilish, Stevie Wonder, and Nicki Minaj, sign an open letter, issued by the Artist Rights Alliance advocacy group, calling for 'this assault on human creativity to be stopped'. The letter went on to say, 'We must protect against the predatory use of AI to steal professional artists' voice and likenesses, violate creator's rights, and destroy the music ecosystem.' When ChatGPT was asked to generate lyrics in the style of Nick Cave, the artist described the result as a grotesque mockery of what it is to be human.

Artists are not just having to contend with AI making use of the work but also with the spread of pornographic AI-created images, such as those of Taylor Swift. Not even deceased artists are safe. The estates representing several deceased artists were also signatories to the letter with likenesses of artists being used after their deaths and AI producing versions of those individuals for film, video, and television, thus raising a number of ethical issues.

Whilst many artists are very negative about AI, others such as Grimes have taken the opportunity to experiment and encourage others to make songs using their vocal likeness. Her track 'Basilisk's Lullaby' blended AI elements. Paul McCartney, Timbaland, Arca, and Holly Herndon have all incorporated AI in their creative projects, the most visible of which is perhaps McCartney using AI to separate John Lennon's voice from an old demo to create 'Now and Then,' which made number one in the UK Official Singles Chart in November 2023, breaking previous streaming records. Arca generates AI algorithms to create complex soundscapes, throwing her 2020 track 'Riquiqui' into an AI generator and creating 100 remixes. Herndon's 2019 *PROTO* was a collaboration with an AI named Spawn in which she analysed and mimicked her own vocal style. In 2023 Timbaland's use of AI to analyse the rapping of Notorious B.I.G. to create new verses mimicking his style caused a heated debate, with some fans excited and positive whilst others felt it deeply disrespectful and questioned the ethics of AI generated music impersonating deceased artists.

ABBA have taken some control and been more proactive, not waiting for their own deaths to present opportunities for others but choosing to create digital avatars of themselves as they were in 1979 (ABBAtars). They have enjoyed great financial success using them to create 'ABBA Voyage', a virtual concert.

Many artists seem to be more accepting of AI when the freedom lies with the artist to use it creatively rather than AI using what artists have produced. *The Sound of the Next Generation* report revealed that 47 per cent of young people believed that most future music will be AI generated, and 63 per cent of young creatives were embracing AI in their music making, but for others it is still a cause of unease (Youth Music, 2024).

Along with freedom comes responsibility, and the industry raises lots of questions about responsibility. Where does responsibility fit? Does the artist have a responsibility to their 'public'? Do they need to consider to what extent they are a role model, particularly for younger people? What responsibility does the industry and management have to the artist? There are many questions about the level of responsibility the industry has to artists but also that which the artist may have to the public.

In this time of cancel culture, we see attacks on freedom of expression and also criticism of the behaviour, political views, and lifestyles of musicians in the public eye. Glastonbury 2025 saw rapper Bobby Vylan leading chants of 'free, free Palestine' and allegedly 'Death, death to the IDF' and the band Kneecap, whose member Lian O'Hanna was already facing terrorist-related charges for a previous event, called on fans to 'start a riot outside the courts' but followed this with 'no riots just love and support'. It remains possible that legal action will be taken against them.

Previous generations recognised musicians for their revolutionary impact, including Hendrix, Dylan, Public Enemy, and many more.

It is often female artists who come under intense criticism for setting a bad example, in their clothing, language, overt sexuality, etc. We have witnessed the breakdown of Britney Spears, who was presented as the clean-cut virgin, an image it was impossible to maintain as she grew into womanhood. Another child Disney star, Miley Cyrus, at the age of 15, posed in a sheet for Vanity Fair and found herself facing headlines of 'Miley's Shame' in the *New York Post*, causing her to apologise to her fans. At the time of writing Sabrina Carpenter is receiving criticism for her latest album cover which some argue conveys misogynist fantasies whilst others say it is her owning her own sexuality.

Some artists, such as Taylor Swift, have responded directly to questions about being a role model. In an old TV interview (Dalla-Camina, 2025), Swift said,

> I mean, I think you have to be conscious of that. If you're choosing to put out music and to be there in the public, you have to be conscious of the fact that you're part of the raising of the next generation and you do have an impact on that so choose your outfits, words and your actions carefully because I think it matters. (Dalla-Camina, 2025)

As I mentioned briefly, when writing about authenticity, the rise of Tumblr and SoundCloud and the growth of Instagram, TikTok, and other social media platforms changed the nature of the relationship between fans and artists, leading to an expectation of greater intimacy in which greater access was given to artists' personal lives, thus increasing emotional investment which carries with it an expectation of accountability. In some cases, this has led to greater understanding and acceptance of behaviours which may not be deemed to be ideal. However, we can see how K-pop idols in particular come under intense ethical scrutiny and judgement, as they are considered not just as entertainers but as cultural icons and representatives of their country and its national values and so are expected to conform with expectations of 'normal' behaviour. We have recently seen incidents involving popular Korean K-pop singers Yeonjun of Tomorrow X Together and Felix of Stray Kids illustrating these high expectations. Yeonjun faced criticism for posting photos on Instagram taken in Japan on National Liberation Day, a day that commemorates the liberation of the Korean Peninsula from Japanese colonial rule on 15th August 1945. Some felt it was inappropriate to share images related to Japan on such an important day, leading to a swift backlash. He apologised on the global fan platform, The Straits Times reported that he had used the platform Weverse to apologize, 'I deeply apologize for my careless action on the day with such historical significance. I will reflect on my lack of awareness and be more cautious in the future.'

On the same day, Felix of Stray Kids received criticism when he mentioned a Japanese anime challenge for a short-form video on the fan app Bubble, leading to fans expressing disappointment over what they considered to be a lack of sensitivity. Felix too quickly issued an apology through agency JYP Entertainment expressing deep regret for his actions and acknowledging his lack of awareness.

South Korean musicians enjoy less leeway than peers in North America or Europe and are expected to be excellent role models, upholding their professional image while cultivating a strong sense of respect. This is particularly important in Korea, where the entertainment industry is closely tied to national identity. *The Korea Herald* (Jae-heun, 2024) quoted music critic Kim Do-heon, who while acknowledging the high expectations placed on K-pop singers, stressed that any blame did not rest solely on the idols,

> As celebrities, it's something that they need to handle to some extent. After all, it's true that they are held to higher ethical standards and sometimes they face criticisms that they deserve … . However, one might question whether it is ethical to excessively criticize an individual for their mistakes. If we delve deeper, we find that the root of the issue lies in the unique position, activities and power dynamics within the world of K-pop.

He made the more generally applicable statement that 'Idols are not creators and they are told what to say and how to act in public by their agencies'. This is not just true of K-pop singers.

Relatedness and Isolation

It is a truism to say we are born alone and we die alone. We may be surrounded by people at these life and death events, but the experience itself is unique and one in which we have to navigate ourselves through the most profound uncertainty. However, for most of our existence, we are in a state of relatedness to other people. For some people this is a welcome necessity, they thrive off being with others, whilst other people are more aligned with Sartre's feeling that 'hell is other people'! They may find being in the presence of others stressful.

Whatever the ethnic background and gender of those working in the music industry, the need for relatedness and the need for solitude often provide a challenge. The human desire to be seen as a social animal, accepted and respected by peers, and the need for self-sufficiency can be equally strong and so provide both internal and external tensions.

If we consider what it is like being in a touring band, living in close proximity to the other band members for long stretches of time, we can see how these two different approaches to being with others may cause stress, misunderstanding, and conflict. Some band members may seek out the company of others in the band to ward off the loss of intimacy with family and friends at home. Others find the general banter and group behaviour hard to cope with and seek solitude. Some may be committed to monogamous relationships despite the strain touring may put on this, others may choose a more polyamorous way of being or prefer to have more casual encounters. These different ways of meeting needs can cause tensions.

In addition to needing to relate to band members, families and friends outside the industry, and to other artists, it is also necessary to interact with others within the industry, such as managers, producers, and the audience. This may cause a clash in values and a challenge to the artist's authenticity. An artist may want to focus on innovation and creativity whilst the audience and management may want more of what brought them their initial success. This can lead to the artist feeling bored, frustrated, and angry if they are required to stick with their 'old hits', and it is equally frustrating to management if the artist wishes to play non-commercial innovative music and so lessen the possibility of financial success.

At a more macro level we need to consider whether everyone is treated equally and respectfully in the industry. There is indeed a relatedness between individuals and the industry itself. One might assume that the industry is one which thrives on difference and welcomes diversity but there is some evidence that this may not be the case.

It would appear that gender inequity is still a real issue. In March 2024, the findings of the first ever UK Musicians' Census, organised by Help Musicians and the Musicians' Union, showed that in the 2,526 female respondents, there was evidence of women being paid less than male colleagues, with the annual income of a female musician in 2023–2024 being £19,850 compared to £21,750 for males. This in turn means that women tend to have less career longevity than men, even when they are trained and educated to a higher level. Of the females, 51 per cent reported having experienced gender discrimination as opposed to 6 per cent of the male respondents. Thirty-three per cent of the women reported being sexually harassed whilst working as a musician, and 25 per cent said they had witnessed others being sexually harassed by people in the industry (Help Musicians, Musicians' Union, and Women in CTRL, 2024).

Roles within the industry continue to show some traditional divisions with 79 per cent of the women in the survey being performing musicians but only 29 per cent working as DJs, 24 per cent as producers, 15 per cent as live sound engineers, and 12 per cent as studio/mastering engineers. There were identifiable differences across genres with the largest gap reported in UK rap with just 8 per cent of women working in the genre. Research undertaken by the Musicians' Union (2020) highlighted the perception that women working in the technical side of the industry felt that their technical knowledge was often dismissed, and in studio, they were often ignored and referred to as assistants or girlfriends. One young female manager is quoted as saying,

> There is a dated perception in the industry of what an artist manager looks like. When people don't see a man in charge, they are often shocked to see it's me. I feel as though I have to work twice as hard as my male counterparts to get the recognition I deserve. Even then it feels everything I do is never good enough in the eyes of some of the powerful white men in the industry.
>
> (House of Commons 2024)

Nadia Khan, chief executive of CTRL Music, spoke of how she had personally experienced bullying and harassment:

> I have felt invisible when I have walked into rooms, been perceived or deemed to be just an assistant or a groupie. I have been kicked off festival stages while my artist is on stage performing because security does not believe that I could be the manager. I have been laughed away by bouncers at the front of shows who have not believed that I am the manager.
>
> (House of Commons 2024)

The House of Commons report on misogyny in the music industry (2024: 3) reported that

> 'Women working in the music industry face limitations in opportunity, a lack of support, gender discrimination, and sexual harassment and assault as well as the persistent issue of unequal pay in a sector dominated by self-employment and gendered power imbalances. Despite increases in representation, these issues are endemic and are intensified for women faced with intersectional barriers, particularly racial discrimination.

The report shows that this discrimination can be found where you would least expect and at a critical time in a female musician's career, starting with education and training. The researchers commented on the generalised assumption of there being certain instruments chosen by females and evidence of females who chose instruments more commonly used by males being the subject of casual misogyny or even direct bullying, sexualisation, and harassment and being held to a higher standard of performance and skills than their male counterparts. Deborah Annetts, the chief executive of the Incorporated Society of Musicians, is quoted in the government report (House of Commons 2024: 9): 'we saw inappropriate behaviours, started within those creative colleges, were learned and then went into the industry and there was no protection'. Sadly, the Musicians' Union (2020) reported female students being catcalled in rehearsals, made to feel uncomfortable by male lecturers, and even being told they couldn't play their instrument properly if they didn't sit with their legs open in orchestra rehearsals. These negative comments and behaviours are also expressed in the media and elsewhere, with the physical attractiveness of female artists being regularly commented on.

In addition to issues about gender-based discrimination, several black female artists spoke of being seen in an overtly sexual role. One explained how she was often told by men that she was only booked because of her ethnicity and gender and described how these repeated comments created internal doubts about her own ability as an artist.

Most women reported that misogynistic behaviours were often combined with evidence of ageism, racism, LGBTQ prejudice, and assumptions about women's capability to perform whilst pregnant or holding responsibilities for caring for families and others. The March 2024 Musicians census undertaken by Help Musicians reported that, not surprisingly, female musicians have a higher rate of primary caring responsibilities, 28 per cent compared to 20 per cent of other reporting genders, with 29 per cent of the women declaring that caring commitments were a barrier to career progression and success, whilst only 11 per cent of those of other genders reported this as the case (Help Musicians, Musician's Union, and Women in CTRL, 2024).

The UK Music *Diversity Report* showed that it was not just women suffering discrimination in the industry. Reporting on a recent Black Lives in Music (BLiM) survey carried out in 2024 amongst black musicians and music professionals, the report found evidence of individual discrimination and systemic and institutionalised racism in the UK music industry (UK Music, 2024). Sheryl Nwosu, a lawyer and chair of the Black Music Coalition, was quoted in an earlier 2021 survey as saying, 'We see black artists dominating the charts and making money, but (race and racism) still affects those artists' career and the careers of Black execs working in positions behind the scenes' (2021: 18).

The UK Music (2024) survey does not indicate much positive change, finding that:

- 86 per cent of all Black music creators agree that there are barriers to progression. This number rises to 89 per cent for Black women and 91 per cent for Black creators who are disabled
- 88 per cent of all Black music professionals agree that there are barriers to progression
- Three in five (63 per cent) Black music creators have experienced direct/indirect racism in the music industry, and more (71 per cent) have experienced racial microaggressions
- 35 per cent of all Black music creators have felt the need to change their appearance because of their race/ethnicity, rising to 43 per cent of Black women
- 73 per cent of Black music professionals have experienced direct/indirect racism in the music industry, and more (80 per cent) have experienced racial microaggressions
- 31 per cent of all Black music creators believe their mental well-being has worsened since starting their music career, rising to 42 per cent of Black women
- 36 per cent of Black music professionals believe their mental wellbeing has declined, rising to 39 per cent of Black women
- 38 per cent of Black music professionals earn 100 per cent of their income from music compared to 69 per cent of white music professionals
- 57 per cent of black music creators have seen white contemporaries promoted ahead of them despite being more qualified.

(UK Music Survey 2024: 24)

One might have thought that there would be fewer incidences of racism within the music industry than elsewhere. With music of black origin having a major influence on today's popular music and world music being embraced and influential. However, today, while there may be admiration for most black music, some aspects are under attack. Chapman (2021) offers us an overview of what he sees as the criminalisation of black music in post-war Britain, claiming that 'The emergence of Drill music over the last half-decade or so alarmed social institutions, especially the police, with its direct references to violence' (Chapman, 2021: 28). This together with the day-to-day racism encountered by non-white musicians and music professionals can cause additional stress and tension.

The BLiM reports found that although all genders experience racism there was evidence that women were most affected. One black female music professional is quoted as saying,

> As a Black woman in music, it's hard as you always have to prove yourself and be conscious of how you behave and interact with others. Being very male-dominated many men still struggle with being led

> or told what to do or what's required by a woman, let alone a Black woman. 99.8 per cent of the time, I'm the only Black woman in the room, so I feel a lot of tightropes have to be tread [sic] to be respected or considered great at what I do, which I am.
>
> (Black Lives in Music, 2021: 19)

Being female and black often went along with other areas of discrimination, with one respondent calling for collective support around the issues:

> Being a Black female and a working mum literally puts me at the bottom of the hierarchy. The industry consists of mainly white cliques at the top. There are subgroups that have a greater ratio of ethnic professionals, but if you've been caught in a white corporate bubble, you're not with the in-crowd in either scenario. Visibility for Black professionals is a priority, not only for progression and recognition but so we can connect and grow together. We need to champion each other.
>
> (2021: 28).

Some discrimination was direct and personal; other examples given showed a lack of awareness and sensitivity in general:

> In one creative meeting for a white female artist, the creative partner showcased a mood board full of Black women and afro-textured hairstyles. The artist and creative then proceeded to refer to hairstyles as 'rasta hair' and was not challenged or corrected.
>
> (2021: 15)

> In another scenario, during a meeting of a white male artist, a song containing samples of Jamaican patois (re-sung by said artist) was being played out loud. Everyone in that space had already heard the song except for myself. The lead colleague on the project asked for my opinion, and I shared that it should be sung by an artist of that heritage or be removed as it's not appropriate. I was met with the following response 'I did wonder if that is what you thought – that is why I was afraid to ask you.'
>
> (2021: 15)

Many welcomed recent initiatives such as mentoring schemes but highlighted the need for more such projects:

> At this moment in time, I see that there are some very deliberate attempts to specifically support Black music creators and professionals

> ... [who] have been in the industry a long time, and I can see that there is now something, whereas before there was very little. Saying that, I don't think [it] means it's all fine and we can sit back and be content with the status quo.
>
> (2021: 16)

Several well-known and successful female black artists have spoken publicly of their experiences. With Alexandra Burke revealing in a BBC documentary hosted by Little Mix's Leigh-Anne Pinnock that she had been told she would need to bleach her skin if she were to sell any records (Onafuye, 2021) and Beverley Knight telling ITV news in 2020 that a record company digitally lightened her skin tone on the cover of her first album so she would be more presentable to a non-black audience (White, 2020).

It can be hard to call out conflicts which have a racial or gender issue at their core, especially in a predominantly male and white industry. The intervention of a neutral third party, whilst introducing a further relatedness issue and additional dynamics to be managed, can be a productive way forward.

In addition to gender and race, physical disability is also an issue for the industry. In 2023, 5867 musicians completed a survey issued jointly by Help Musicians, Attitude is Everything, and the Musicians' Union. In the survey, 2593 respondents reported one or more conditions and/or impairments impacting their day-to-day lives, with 168 preferring not to say. Of those who considered themselves to have a disability, more than a quarter (27 per cent) reported having mental health or neurodivergent challenges. Three per cent of disabled respondents identified as trans, 46.8 per cent as female, and 49.5 per cent as male, with 1 per cent preferring not to say. Of this total group, 25 per cent identified as LGBTQ+ compared to 13 per cent of non-disabled respondents. This was broken down to show that, of the disabled musician sample, 53 per cent of neurodivergent musicians are LGBTQ+ and 59 per cent of musicians with mental health conditions were LGBTQ+ (2024).

The survey showed a disability pay gap of approximately £4000, with a further pay gap for those with mental health conditions of £1700. Musicians with disabilities also reported increased costs, with one female musician quoted in the survey as saying, 'I have a disability and access to appropriate training, cost of transport, cost of support to carry out admin to find opportunities and to get gigs has an enormous impact.' The industry itself can add to physical and mental disabilities, with one drummer I know having to pay large sums for regular massage and physiotherapy to cope with the physical demands of his job. It is well known that musicians are at a high risk of hearing loss. The Hearing Health Foundation in the US, looking to the work of Bauer (2023) found musicians were more than four times more likely to develop noise induced hearing loss (NIHL) and 57 per cent more likely to develop tinnitus than the rest of the population. Dr Paul Checkley of the Musicians' Hearing Service (https://www.musicians hearingservices.co.uk) pointed out that 'Musicians have a better and more in-depth relationship with sound than an average person, so any small change in their hearing has a much larger impact on their lives and livelihood.' (Crossley, 2023).

Several respondents to the 2023 survey, published in 2024, reported finding it harder than their non-disabled colleagues to remain in the industry. One woman wrote:

> I am autistic and my social difficulties negatively impacted my ability to keep work – I was regularly discriminated against and the impact on my mental health was traumatic. I am very, very happy working in education where I am treated with professional dignity and respect. I still enjoy facilitating community music and teach for my local music service as a Saturday morning music teacher, where again my relationships are valued and I am treated with positivity, respect and dignity. This was completely absent from my performing career and destroyed my love of my instrument.
>
> (Help Musicians, Attitude is Everything, and Musicians' Union, 2024)

Others left or chose not to work in the industry due to bullying, one reporting, 'I used to work as a freelance musician while pursuing my first degree. However, the bullying culture in the industry stopped me from making it my full-time career after I graduated' (Help Musicians, Attitude is Everything, and Musicians' Union, 2024:17).

A third of musicians with disabilities reported being subjected to gender-based discrimination (compared to 20 per cent of non-disabled colleagues), with 83 per cent believing that it impacted their ability to work or to advance their career. There was also an increased reporting of sexual harassment with almost a quarter of disabled musicians (23 per cent) reporting this, compared to 13 per cent of the other respondents (Help Musicians, Attitude is Everything, and Musicians' Union, 2024).

Those with disabilities also seem to experience additional levels of racism. Charlotte Beaumont, the chief executive of Black Lives Matter, reported that 65 per cent of black disabled music creators experienced discrimination due to their race, with 7 per cent experiencing discrimination due to their disabilities. (Help Musicians, Attitude is Everything, and Musicians' Union, 2024).

Being treated differently in ways that make it harder to pursue their profession is likely to bring disabled musicians into conflict with others and with the industry as a whole.

The final existential value I wish to introduce is concerned with the importance of values and beliefs. This focus interacts closely with authenticity and freedom, which I wrote about earlier.

Values and Beliefs

Living, as far as possible, in line with our values and beliefs, and therefore authentically, is an important aspect of existential thinking. I have already referred to some of the challenges this can place on musicians in some of the sections above.

If the musician is working in a band, they also have to negotiate how to stay true to their values if they differ from those of band members. I have worked with a number of bands who started off with the same values, hopes, and expectations but who found that these changed over time, with individuals in the same band holding different political, religious, and ethical values and beliefs. It could no longer be expected that they would all be 'singing from the same song sheet'. Whereas in the past, they could have guessed accurately how all members would respond to opportunities and challenges, this was no longer the case. When this happens, some members may want to pursue all opportunities that increase their visibility and/or are likely to be financially positive, whereas others may object to playing in certain countries whose laws and values differ from their own. Some people may want to 'reward' local fans by scheduling in local low-cost gigs, whereas others may see this as wasting time in which they could be making money. These differences can lead to major conflict.

Values about behaviours can also change. I have seen bands who initially thrived on the stereotypical lifestyle, with lots of sex, drugs, and rock and roll, change over time to become teetotal and advocates of physical and mental well-being practices of all kinds. This is fine if everyone in the band makes the same changes, but it can increase tension if some individuals are wanting an early night whilst others are wanting to take advantage of all the local nightlife has to offer.

People can feel divided loyalties. If an individual is choosing to remain faithful to their partner and sees another member of the band who is in in a long-term relationship engaging in casual sex at every venue, they may be able to just accept that they do not have the same values. However, if they are also friends with the colleague's partner, who believes them to be faithful, they are faced with an ethical dilemma of whether or not they tell the unknowing partner.

There are also ethical and value-led issues around financial remuneration. There are many questions which would ideally be talked through before they surface as a problem: Will any income be divided equally or will certain members, such as song writers, expect this skill to be recognised financially? If one person needs additional help due to a disability, is this something the band would want to take equal responsibility for, or would they expect that person to pay any additional costs themselves? If band members have different accountants do they have conflicting views about how income is split and declared? The questions go on and on and all are linked to how an individual sees the world and the values they wish to live by.

If there are different spiritual and religious beliefs within a group, attention has to be given to how these beliefs and associated behaviours may be respected. For example, when agreeing times and dates for shows, does the group take into consideration the needs of a member who may be observing Ramadan and fasting, one who needs to pray at different times, or whose beliefs prevent them from working on a particular day of the week?

In addition to the challenges presented by our existential existence and existential givens, we are confronted daily with conflicts small or large. Whatever the nature of the conflict, all conflict is emotional; if it were rational, logical, and concrete, it would be easy to determine the logical outcome. If people were logical beings, then they would quickly agree a logical solution. Fortunately, in my view, human beings are not robots and have a very complex and rich relationship with their personal world and those who share it, as well as a relationship with their hopes and dreams, their own bodies, their immediate environment, the material world, and indeed the cosmos. This richness of existence allows us to be truly creative beings, but it can make it harder to navigate our interaction with the world. Due to its emotional essence, its paradoxes and tensions, conflict can take its toll on our mental health and well-being or can be a force for creative engagement and enjoyment.

Existential Dimensions

Another existential concept, which may be equally useful, is that of existential dimensions. We have seen that the 'givens' provide tensions and paradoxes, which those in the music industry encounter. The contexts in which these givens are played out can simplistically be divided into five dimensions of human existence. Through these we can explore how a person is being in different contexts, making up what we may call a person's 'world view'. This is not an attempt to divide people into types or parts but to look to the different levels of experience and existence in which people operate; our ways of 'being-in-the-world' can be placed on a 'map of human existence' comprising five dimensions.

For those who like a bit of historical background, the first three dimensions were identified by Binswanger (1881–1966). He described identified three dimensions: the Umwelt, the Mitwelt, and the Eigenwelt (Binswanger, 1946). In 1984, van Deurzen introduced a fourth dimension: the Uberwelt (van Deurzen, 2001), and Hanaway introduced a fifth, the Unterwelt, in 2024.

The Umwelt is concerned with the physical dimension and the ways in which we relate to physical things, including our environment, our own body and bodily sensations, our health, and our own mortality. It extends beyond our own bodies to those of others and to the surroundings we find ourselves in, the landscape, climate, and the weather.

The Mitwelt, is focused on the social dimension in which we relate to and communicate with others in the public world, including our response to the culture we live in, including the class, gender, sexual orientation, and race we belong to (and, indeed, those we do not belong to).

The Eigenwelt is about the psychological dimension, the ways in which we relate to ourselves and create a personal world. It includes views about past experiences and future possibilities and facilitates the development of a sense of one's own character and identity. It contains within it our thoughts, memories, self-identity, and the similarities and differences we perceive there to be between ourselves and others.

The Uberwelt (the overworld) is that of the spiritual realm and how we relate to the unknown and create a sense of an ideal and meaningful world.

The Unterwelt, on the other hand, can be seen as the counterpoint to the Uberwelt. This 'underworld' can be one which encompasses our Jungian shadow world or equally those dimensions from which we seek to anesthetise or sedate ourselves. This can be the dimension in which we choose to ignore our values and beliefs or pretend that they do not exist or interact with those values, needs, and wants that we may feel would not be acceptable or understood by others. It is this world that is most private and that we may never give others access to, or to which we may restrict access to the very few who we believe will accept this part of us. Public expression of this dimension is often through art and music.

We can be in internal conflict in the ways we operate within each dimension, and we can come into conflict with others through the ways our understanding of these dimensions differs from theirs. This can lead to times when we are in direct opposition to others, as the way we wish to behave in a particular dimension is in opposition to the way another person feels they need to be.

I shall return to this later, when talking about mediation, to show how these concepts may be useful.

Mental Health and Well-being

Let us turn to look at the negative impact conflict may have on mental health and well-being. In my work as an existential psychotherapist, coach, and mediator, I have had the opportunity to work with many clients from the music, film, visual arts, and media industries. They are great clients to work with. I love their sensitivity, energy, creativity, and lateral thinking, all of which present interesting challenges in my work. However, it is this sensitivity and these creative ways of encountering the world that can put acute pressure on individuals.

Music is, at its core, an expression of emotion, and music can in turn exaggerate our emotions (Juslin and Sloboda, 2011). It impacts our bodies and our minds. Indeed, Sacks (2006: 2582), drawing on the existential writings of Nietzsche, claims we listen to music with our muscles: 'we tap our feet, we "keep time", hum, sing along or "conduct music" our facial expressions mirroring the rise and falls of the melodic contours and feelings of what we are hearing'.

Unfortunately, for many years it has been accepted, perhaps even expected, that those in the music industry would behave differently to most people. Creatives are perhaps expected to show their creativity through eccentricity, often encouraged by management and press who need to keep the 'celebrity' in the public consciousness. Unreasonable and irrational behaviour is taken as 'normal'. Indeed, UK music manager Chris Morrison claimed in his foreword to the first edition of *The Music Management Bible* (2003) that

> The best music comes from the heart, from inside. It tells of every aspect of human joy and pain. The people who write and perform it feel those emotions more intensely than others. So don't expect them to be easy to work with. They will on occasions be difficult, make bad decisions, blame you, be angry and even badly behaved. Without them, your job and those of everyone else do not exist. You are privileged. Try and remember this when nobody likes you and you're trying to make a square peg fit into a round hole.

My own personal experience of this was during my first year at art college. We worked in an open studio with small personal areas shielded off from one another by low screens. Sean, who was 19, worked in one of these studios and showed little interest in engaging with the rest of us, working away with passion at his abstract paintings. After a few weeks he began slashing at his arms with a Stanley knife and drawing blood which he would then use as 'paint' on his canvases. Several students brought this to the attention of the tutors, some were concerned but not sure what to do other than ask him to stop, others saw it as part of his creative expression. One day Sean didn't arrive at college, and we were told he had been sectioned and was in a psychiatric hospital. We never saw or heard of him again.

Whilst most of us wish to encourage innovation and self-expression this attitude can do a disservice to many individuals in the industry whose behaviour is not necessarily an expression of their creativity but more a cry for help.

From outside, the industries in which the artists work can appear glamorous, but on closer inspection, it can be a world of stress, tension, pressure (internal and external), and loneliness. This book focuses on the music industry, but similar challenges and tensions exist in all the creative fields. Indeed, recently, my daughter, who works in the film industry, was unable to work for many months due to the industry's dispute with film scriptwriters. From being in the middle of an exciting and extremely busy creative project, she was suddenly left with no work and no pay. This is an experience shared by many in the creative industries and those in the music industry suffered greatly in the Covid epidemic with the closure of music venues and studios, the cancellation of festivals, etc. Plans were paused or stopped completely, and people were under financial pressures that they could not have foreseen.

Trying to manage the demands of the industry and the demands of family and personal life can be hard. An individual may be able to live a frugal life without financial security, but it is hard to ask family members to embrace such uncertainty. Being away from family and friends at times chosen by 'the management' and audience demands, or the prioritising of business needs rather than personal needs, can put a huge strain on personal relationships. Being the charismatic superhuman performer who reaches transcendental highs during a performance cannot be maintained within the family. When away from one's professional persona, one is required to do one's fair share of the more mundane aspects of life: shopping, sorting finances, dealing with sick children, putting out the rubbish, etc.

The felt need to live the 'appropriate' rock and roll lifestyle can feel inauthentic and so create internal and external conflict. Although these tensions may be evident to the individual, who may also be aware of the damage the resulting stress causes, to choose a different lifestyle may cause problems with peers. If everyone else in the group wants to enjoy wild parties, casual sexual relationships, and fast food it can be difficult to be the odd one out who wants to retire back to the hotel early, phone the family, and then enjoy a quiet evening. Easy access to temptation, be it drugs, sex, alcohol, or something else, can prove hard to resist, often with long-term consequences. The damage done by such lifestyle choices are often very clear. Some people can manage and indeed blossom despite leading a 'wild' life, but for others, they can be caught up in a cycle that is hard to break.

Creativity and passion can often come up against the apparent consumerism and the bureaucracy of the business element of the music industry. There may be major cultural and values-related differences. Individual energy and ambition can cause clashes with others. Although we may think that most people in the industry are in it because they seek an avenue to express their creativity, there are others who are looking to it for financial gain or personal recognition. All may have equally strong ideas and goals, all acceptable and understandable, but which can often appear incompatible. Decisions may need to be made when it is difficult to address and balance both commercial and creative needs. This can put psychological stress on individuals, with some having to deal with extra pressure due to their race, gender, or sexual orientation.

Some artists have bravely drawn attention to this. Keisha Buchanan, a founding member of Sugababes, emotionally revealed that she went through a decade of therapy in the wake of her controversial departure from the group in 2009. She claimed that she was consistently labelled an 'aggressive bully' and stereotypically portrayed as an 'angry black woman'. This is not a one-off example of racial and sexual conflict. In the Black Lives in Music (2021) survey analysists reported that black female professionals are more likely than black men to say their mental well-being has worsened since starting their career in the music industry. Over one-third (36 per cent) of black music professionals were reported as believing that their mental well-being had declined since starting their music career. White professionals also highlighted this, with the report authors suggesting there should be a requirement for a sector-wide mental health and well-being support programme. Those people who reported having mental health challenges previously to their music careers now reported a further deterioration in their mental well-being. This seemed to be especially prominent for black female professionals, where two in five (39 per cent) said their mental well-being had worsened since starting their music career, ten points more in comparison to black men (29 per cent), and 16 per cent reporting that they had sought counselling due to racial abuse. Citing various reasons, including the barriers to progression and overt racial discrimination, the report also found that black women earn 25 per cent less on average than their white female colleagues, and 46 per cent earn less than half their revenue from music, creating extra pressure to find other routes to supplement their income.

Recently there has been growing awareness of the need to address the mental health challenges of all those in the creative industries. July 2011 saw the death of Amy Winehouse from alcohol poisoning. Amy's deterioration had been evident to all, and although concern was expressed by many people, it was not enough to save her. The death brought a significant moment of soul-searching in the consciousness of the London-based major label music industries. The 2015 award-winning documentary *Amy* which followed looked to who could be to blame and appeared to point the finger at many of those who had been involved in the management of her career and day-to-day life.

Artists began to speak out more openly about the psychological stress and subsequent damage involved in having a successful music career. In the same year that the film 'Amy' was released, Adele spoke out about the 'toxic' problems of touring (Bletchly, 2015). The following year, soul and gospel singer Laura Mvula opened up about her struggles with panic attacks, anxiety, and the trauma of being dropped from her recording contract (Lamont, 2016). Although female artists were speaking out, male artists were also struggling, and the following year saw the suicides of Chester Bennington, the frontman of the rock band Linkin Park, Soundgarden's Chris Connell, and K-Pop star Kim Jong-hyun. These were followed in 2018 by the death of South African rapper HHP, who for many years had suffered from depression, and the EMI producer and DJ Avicii, despite the fact that the film about his life *Avicii: True Stories* had been released the previous year, in which he is shown openly suffering under the pressures of heavy touring commitments. By the end of 2018, Music Business Worldwide suggested the music industry itself was facing a 'mental health crisis' (Dhillon, 2018).

This has led to a relative explosion of research examining the links between working in the field of popular music and the negative impact this might have on the mental health and well-being of artists. This built on previous work undertaken in the predigital age, primarily by Geoff Wills and Cary Cooper and written up in their 1988 book *Pressure Sensitive: Popular Musicians under Stress* and in the ground-breaking work of Susan Raeburn (Raeburn, 1987a; 1987b).

Much of the literature examining the links between the working lives of musicians and their mental or emotional well-being has been carried out with a focus on the existential element of uncertainty, a state in which all musicians have to live their professional lives (Lorey, 2011: 87; Vaag, Giæver, and Bjerkeset, 2014: 205). There has been a lot of discussion of this precarity and the idea of precarious labour, in relation not just to the working conditions for musicians but to all those involved in the expanding knowledge and gig economies. Standing (2011:18) uses the helpful concept of the 'the precariatised mind' which describes a psychological state brought about as a consequence of precarious work, such as musical work. This is linked to heightened levels of anger, anxiety, alienation, and his research draws on the work of Émile Durkheim and his notion of anomie.

Despite this research and many artists including Bruce Springsteen, Billie Eilish, Ariana Grande, and Lewis Capaldi, amongst others, speaking out about their own mental health struggles, we continue to see highly publicised tragedies like the recent death of Liam Payne and ongoing concerns about the mental health of Justin Bieber, Kanye West, and others being played out on social media. Musgrave and Lamis writing this year (2025) are still pointing out that suicide remains an occupational risk, with the concept of the '27 Club' (a group with a particular infamy and afforded an almost mythical status made up of musicians who all died at the age of 27 by suicide or other forms of violent death) continuing to reinforce stereotypes of musicians and early mortality. Empirical evidence has not found a spike in musicians' deaths at the age of 27, whilst there is evidence of elevated incidences of suicide amongst musicians of all ages. Unfortunately, this adds to the romanticisation of self-harm and suicide amongst musicians. Males are at greater risk of committing suicide (Bennett et al. 2023), but there is evidence that females attempt suicide more frequently (Canetto and Sakinofsky, 1998) *with female musicians dying by suicide at a higher level than their female counterparts in other industries*, (Windsor-Shellard and Gunnell, 2019; Sussell et al., 2023), and Kenny and Asher (2017, 547) noting, that 'unlike females in the general population, female gender did not bestow any protection against early death or manner of death by suicide, homicide or accident compared to male popular musicians'.

It is good to see a growing awareness and acknowledgment of the complex mental health challenges that musicians face. In addition to the well-publicised drug and alcohol problems, being a working musician potentially presents individuals with relationship problems within the group and within their families. The unique experience, described by one client as 'transcendental', when reaching a euphoric moment on stage, feeling the power over the audience and the love and adoration the audience offers, presents the artist with the recognition and love they crave, which is not replicated elsewhere. For many musicians the unsuccessful search for this experience in other spheres of their lives can destroy their self-esteem and result in anger at others and internal and external conflict. This is worsened when a successful band becomes 'unfashionable', and members must return to the 'ordinary' world where they may no longer be recognised and must seek more mundane jobs to cover such ordinary things as mortgages. This can be a shattering occurrence, which can happen virtually overnight, leaving the artist to question their self-concept and self-worth.

The focus of this book is specifically on dealing with conflict, and the benefits of mediation. However, as all conflict is emotional and therefore usually stressful, it felt important to include the previous short section on mental health and well-being. Others have covered it much more fully elsewhere (Jepson, 2019; Mardon and Schabert, 2021; Gross and Musgrave, 2020; Embleton, 2023). Tamsin Embleton, who is an attachment-based psychodynamic psychotherapist, who previously worked in the music industry in many roles, including festival booker, grants advisor, artist manager, and tour manager, has been influential in drawing attention to the psychological stresses encountered regularly by musicians. In addition to her psychotherapy work, she works for the Music Industry Therapist Collective (MITC; www.musicindustrytherapists.com), which provides presentations and workshops for the industry. In 2023, Tamsin published *Touring and Mental Health: The Music Industry Manual*, which helps musicians and those working in live music to identify, process, and manage difficulties that touring can bring. It includes sections on a wide variety of relevant areas which play an important role in maintaining good mental health while touring.

There are other mental health resources available for those working in the industry, which I want to mention before moving on to focus on mediation. These include Help Musicians UK (www.helpmusicians.org.uk) with a dedicated mental health helpline, called Music Minds Matter (08088028008); Tonic Music which is focused on substance use amongst working musicians (www.tonicmusic.co.uk); Key Changes which offers a recovery service (www.keychanges.org.uk); The British Association for Performing Arts Medicine (BAPAM) which connects musicians and others with free specialist health support (www.bapam.org.uk); Man Down which offers a programme for men primarily working in the music industry and providing a platform for supportive discussion (www.mandownprogramme.com); Music for Mental Wealth is dedicated to prevention measures including coaching and group workshops (www. musicformentalwealth.com); Music Support which provides support for those in the industry suffering from alcoholism, drug abuse, addiction, and/or behavioural, emotional, or mental health issues through direct referrals to a variety of specialists (www.musicsupport.org); Music and You who aim to offer a bespoke service (www.musicandyou.co.uk).

Where to from Here?

My interest in the mental health of those in the music industry and how conflict adds to their stress is longstanding. In a practical way, this was mainly limited to my psychotherapy practice and the occasional mediation. However, in 2013, I met Mirjam Buyteweg who, for many years, had worked as a lawyer within a high ranked global music company. We began to discuss the challenges of the music world, both for those on the 'creative side' and those at the 'business end'. We realised that to work together successfully, these two parties often must reconcile different ways of seeing the world and different sets of values. Despite those differing world views and needs, both sides needed to work together for it to succeed. The use of mediation or proactive behaviours to resolve, manage, or avoid conflict did not seem to be used much in the industry, with the automatic response being to look to the lawyers to sort out the problem. Lawyers are trained to resolve material, financial, and concrete issues and not how to deal with the emotional impact. They are trained to be adversarial and not trained to explore the emotional, collaborative, and joint needs or relational aspects. Both Mirjam and I felt there must be a better way of working with the inevitable conflicts which surface in the industry. So this led us to establish Mediation in Media in 2014 to provide mediation, coaching, consultancy, and training for those working in the media, film, and music industries.

I am not a lawyer. Any sections on the law in this book are not detailed or technical, as they do not come from a lawyer's perspective (although I have had Mirjam check them for accuracy!). If you want deep legal arguments, you are looking in the wrong place. Neither am I an academic, but a practitioner working with people in the music industry on a daily basis. I have included some theoretical sections to place the exploration of conflict within a wide framework, but I believe that we learn most through our lived experiences. For this reason, I have devoted a large section of this book to narratives presenting some real-life mediations, although names and any identifying features have been changed to retain confidentiality.

I am sharing my limited knowledge in order to hopefully set the context for change. My aim is to take most musical disputes out of the long, antagonistic litigation process and to explore other ways of resolving many of these issues. I believe we can offer a way of dealing with conflict which has less negative impact on mental health and increases well-being. I hope this book is a small step in increasing knowledge about mediation and so decreasing conflict-based stress in the music industry.

There will of course always be cases which require expert legal advice and may ultimately require resorting to the courts, but I believe they are far fewer than the numbers currently turning to litigation.

Part One

What We Mean by Conflict and Ways of Resolving It

1 What is Conflict and How Do We Address It?

The Nature of Conflict

Before focusing on conflict in the music industry, I want to say something about the nature of conflict in general. I have covered this in a similar fashion in previous publications and on courses, and so my apologies to readers or students who have already read or heard some of this before. For those of you who haven't yet given much thought to what we mean by conflict, why it exists, whether it has a positive aspect, or whether we need to eradicate it, I hope this chapter provides a little food for thought. It aims to give a brief overview of some thoughts and theories regarding conflict.

What Is Conflict?

There is no agreed definition of conflict. Please excuse me for a very brief dalliance with some of the philosophical thought behind conflict and feel free to hurry past this section if it is not of interest.

Douglas Yarn (1999) saw conflict as a state, rather than a process, with people with opposing values or needs being in a state of conflict, which may be latent or manifest. It is often this clash of values which is in play in ongoing music disputes. When we think of needs and wants, we tend to first think of material and financial ones, but quite often, the need is primarily an emotional or psychological one. People want and need fairness, respect, recognition, and other less obvious things for a resolution to be meaningful.

Early philosophers, such as Aristotle, and, to some extent, many contemporary lawyers approach conflict as if it were entirely logical, with the battle being between emotion and reason, where reason and logic are seen as superior to emotion. They believe that it is reason which makes humans 'human'. Indeed, Aristotle argued that human happiness depends on the exercise of reason and would like to have seen emotions obliterated.

DOI: 10.4324/9781003675938-3

This view has been challenged by later thinkers, with David Hume famously subverting Aristotle and asserting in 1739 in his *Treatise of Human Nature* (Hume and McCormack, 2004: 415) that 'Reason is … the slave of the passions'. A position modern neuroscience is now showing to be correct. Research on how the brain works indicates that there are certain regions of the brain associated with the emotions and others associated with intellectual reasoning. The amygdala, part of the limbic system which deals with emotions, motivation, and long-term memory, is located deep in the back of the brain near the top of the spinal column and has a primary role in processing emotional reactions. Antonio Damasio, a neurobiologist, studied people with damage to those parts of the brain where emotions are generated and found that their inhibitions were reduced and their ability to make decisions also damaged. They were able to describe the decisions they were supposed to make but couldn't find any basis on which to make those decisions: there were pros and cons on both sides, so how to decide? The importance of decisions being based on a moral stance was also considered to be limited, meaning that some people with such injuries could lie, steal, cheat, and ignore punishment with impunity. This research implies that the ability to experience emotions is essential to decision making, both logical and moral. I shall return later to the role of emotions in conflict but let us return briefly to look at how conflict itself has been thought about.

Psychologically informed mediation, coming from an existential and phenomenological approach, is more in line with the thoughts of Heraclitus (540–480bc) who suggested that everything is in a state of flux and opposition, constantly changing, meaning that you could not step twice into the same river twice as the water will have flowed, the pebbles beneath will have eroded, and everything will have changed. He believed that wisdom started with inward reflection. It was a prerequisite for him that we should know ourselves. As I hope will become apparent in this book, we need to know ourselves before thinking we are able to know the other side in a conflict. Heraclitus' view, which is in line with existential and phenomenological thought, suggests that all conflicts are unique, as every person in conflict is a unique individual with a different set of values, beliefs, and perceptions and will perceive the situation through their own lens. This leads us to understand that conflicts are never about facts but about an individual's unique perception of an experience and the narrative they build around it. If this is the case, then approaching a conflict as if it were subject to the same needs and wants as similar disputes is to miss the point and risk forming an agreement which fails to address the parties' deeper needs and so stands less chance of being sustainable. It also means that time can be wasted arguing about the 'facts' of past events. Facts (if they exist) cannot be changed, whilst perceptions can.

Many of us try our hardest to avoid conflict. Heraclitus' thoughts may help us to overcome our 'conflict allergy'. It is pointless to pretend conflict does not exist or that it can be eradicated from life, instead we need to see and acknowledge a conflict and the opportunity it offers for creative thinking as soon as possible. We should seek to unstick the conflict and let it flow freely, just as Heraclitus' river does, noting that time creates change; nothing actually stays the same. In saying this, I am not suggesting that we should seek conflict or that it is necessary for creativity but that we should understand that it is part of the very fabric of our lives and societies. Most people are uncomfortable with uncertainty and seek out a 'correct' black and white solution to a disagreement, in which one side is right and the other wrong. Human beings are much more complex than that. The potential creative nature of conflict, with the use of mediation allowing a safe place for this to be brought into play, makes it particularly attractive to creatives. Indeed, if we are too comfortable, we are unlikely to look to change things and make use of our creativity. The music industry has survived by continually challenging the status quo which often acts as a block to creativity.

We need to be imaginative if we are to move conflict from something negative to something creative. We can draw on Hegelian dialectics (1800s) for a model in which a person offers up their thinking on a topic (a 'thesis') and another person offers their opposing thought (an 'antithesis'). This provides the potential for these two opposing theories to generate a new creative perspective ('a synthesis') through the combination of elements of both approaches, to form a connected whole. This is essentially the movement one is hoping for in a mediation. Of course, this can then set off a new cycle in which the new combined thesis is challenged by a new antithesis. In this way the whole conflict of ideas is experienced not negatively but as a creative act. It requires a willingness to listen to and engage with the other person's point of view and a trust that they in turn will give your views a fair hearing.

When considering more recent thoughts on conflict, we can look to Louis Coser's (1913–2003) theory of social conflict. He looks at conflict in terms of interactive processes and depicts conflict as a form of socialisation. As we know through our own lived experience, it is not possible for a group (of any kind, not just the musical variety) to remain entirely harmonious. If it did, it would lack process, flow, creativity, and structure. Group formation is a result of both association and dissociation, so that both conflict and cooperation serve a social function. A degree of conflict is an essential element in group formation and can have a unifying function as it creates strong associations and cohesiveness within the respective groups. A theory you may recognise as being at the heart of many team building programmes. This potential creative role can be lost, and conflict can result in dysfunctional groups where there is insufficient toleration or institutionalisation of conflict. Highly intense conflicts that threaten to tear apart groups (and indeed societies) tend to arise only in rigid structures. Although musicians are often seen as laid-back and valuing freedom and self-expression, it is far from unusual to find that they have built rigid structures within the group and around them, with individuals being unconsciously ascribed roles and expected behaviours which cause tensions when they try to step outside these expectations.

Coser (1964) suggests that social conflict creates two opposing responses. If resources are limited, we want them for ourselves and those 'special people' we care about. This has the effect of binding these people together. At the same time, it also requires us to perceive those who disagree with us as existing outside that special group of people who are deemed 'correct' because they share our views, experiencing them as 'others' or 'alien', that is people who are unlike us, separate from us, and therefore those who we will fight against to protect resources. So, paradoxically, when faced with limited resources we both bond and separate. Importantly, we also need to limit our empathy if we are to sustain the line between us (the OK/correct/normal side) and the 'other side' who we are required to dehumanise in order to maintain our difference from them.

Morton Deutsch (1920–2017) is perhaps the best-known modern writer on conflict. He held a positive and constructive view, believing that all those involved in a conflict have the capacity to gain from the experience. This is where the term 'win–win' outcome originates, where it is not necessary that one side 'wins' and the other 'loses'. It is the basis of what is termed 'transformational mediation' in which the knowledge of the other and self has the potential to change the individuals involved in the process. He suggested that those in conflict usually have a mixture of cooperative and competitive motives, and that conflict may be positive and productive, or negative and destructive (Deutsch and Coleman, 2000). Those of us who have been involved in many mediation processes can recognise that this holds a truth but is not always the case. Some people agree to mediation not to cooperate but as an arena to be heard and proved right and so can resist agreement even when they see the sense in it. Deutsch (1948) did not hold unrealistic aims for conflict resolution, seeing the goal as being to make conflicts productive, not to eliminate all conflict. This would be an impossible dream. People do not generally skip hand in hand from a mediation, but they may be able to drop the burden of the conflict they have carried for some time, hold a greater understanding of the other's point of view, and explore how to move forward within that reality.

Deutsch (Deutsch and Coleman, 2000) offered us four basic conflict resolution skill sets, useful to both participants in conflict and third parties. These skills are still at the core of mediation today. The primary and most important skills are those needed to establish an effective, open, trusting working relationship between the parties and any involved third parties such as a mediator. Without this trusting working alliance, it is hard to find an authentic sustainable resolution. Secondly, once this is established then cooperative problem-solving approaches are brought into play. Thirdly, he saw skills in developing effective group and decision-making processes as being needed. Deutsch's fourth skill set is concerned with holding substantive knowledge of the relevant issues. I would question what is meant here by 'relevant' issues. I have successfully mediated many disputes in fields of which I have no deep knowledge. The knowledge I bring as a mediator is not factual (if it were, I may be tempted, for the sake of my ego, to prove the depth of my knowledge), but the interpersonal skills, the ability to work with uncertainty, the desire to maintain neutrality, and to listen to all sides actively and equally. I would argue are the most important skills for a mediator.

The 20th and 21st century saw a growth in the study of psychological aspects of conflict. John Burton (1990) distinguishes between conflict and dispute by time and issues involved. He suggests short-term disputes are relatively easy to resolve whereas long-term conflicts may contain seemingly resistant non-negotiable issues involving moral or value differences, vulnerability of ego state, and domination of one party, in addition to more concrete material matters. He warned that attempts to suppress conflict will only lead to exponential increases in conflict, as conflict is always at some level about unmet human needs. There is often an instinct to calm the waters and move on, which may contain the conflict for a while, but the likelihood is that, like a boil, it will erupt elsewhere unless it is deeply examined and excised. So often a minor short-term dispute develops into a longstanding conflict as a quick and easy solution was reached which failed to address the underlying psychological causes. One could liken it to taking a paracetamol which works well to temporarily remove the symptoms by getting rid of the headache, but does not explore what is causing the headache, which could be anything from poor lighting (easily fixed) to a brain tumour (with more lasting implications).

This psychological approach puts emphasis on unearthing the value systems, emotional language, and world views of disputants, which are key elements for such an approach to encounter and work with conflict. It invites us to look deeply into our own motivations and perceptions and to do the same in relation to the other party. This can feel unsettling and potentially threatening. In exploring another's world view there remains a need to seek to preserve or enhance self-esteem through working with the fundamental human psychological needs for identity, security, and recognition. Strasser (a psychotherapist) and Randolph (a barrister), both of whom I was fortunate enough to work with, developed and championed this approach in mediation, and they see these elements as present in both short-term disputes and longer-term conflicts. In their 2004 book they emphasise the need for a mediator to facilitate the parties in exploring not just the overt reasons for the dispute but, perhaps more importantly, the covert reasons, as inevitably 'parties will have developed rigid belief systems as their overall strategy for survival in an uncertain world...' (Strasser and Randolph, 2004: 27).

Although many of those exploring conflict have come from a philosophical or legal background, psychologists and psychotherapists also recognise it as a central challenge we constantly face in life. The question of whether it is always negative and potentially aggressive is picked up by Totton (2006), who suggests psychotherapeutic debate on conflict has centred too much on questions of aggression, asking whether aggression is an innate human trait or the product of specific conditions? Whether it is wholly negative or has positive aspects and expressions? Interestingly, as a psychotherapist myself, in that role, I haven't spent much time on that, being more concerned with the underlying issues motivating and fuelling the aggression and exploring less aggressive ways to express these issues so that people are not too scared to listen and there is more chance of engaging, leading to people getting what they need.

The same question applies to mediation. If we try to mediate by ignoring or suppressing any aggression or negativity, it will not be an authentic dialogue, and we will not be fully doing our job. The mediator must provide a safe place for exploring these aspects and must be ready and skilled to deal with the heightened emotions that all conflict brings.

Freud writing in 1930 in *Civilisation and Its Discontents*, saw aggression as innate and characterised it as dangerous: 'men are not gentle creatures who want to be loved ... they are, on the contrary, creatures among whose instinctual endowments are to be reckoned a powerful share of aggressiveness ... In consequence of this primary mutual hostility of human beings, civilized society is perpetually threatened with disintegration' (1930: 302). This may be true, although much of his writing, and indeed his behaviour, might indicate a reluctance to engage with conflict. An important aspect of contemporary therapy is to provide the opportunity to explore these seemingly 'dangerous' aspects of what it means to be human, especially what it is to feel conflicted. These aspects cannot be ignored in mediation either although obviously they would not be explored as deeply as they would in therapy. If we ignore these deeply held emotions the person will feel unseen, unheard, and not understood and would find it hard to trust the mediator.

Not all early analysts avoided exploring conflict and aggression. Another analyst, Reich (1967) disagreed with Freud, seeing human beings as essentially possessing natural decency, spontaneous honesty, mute and complete feelings of love, and seeing aggression as the life expression of the musculature, or the system of movement. Suttie (1936) claimed that hate and destructiveness were secondary reactions to threatened primal love, and Melanie Klein (2017) based her theoretical approach on an innate conflict between love and hate which was dealt with by projecting our destructiveness into others and adopting the depressive position to address the task of reparation. Personally, I accept that the complexity of being human means we have both positive and negative elements which we can choose to draw on. In any mediation both these elements will be present.

Today, most therapists and psychologically informed mediators would agree that aggression and conflict are essential parts of our internal human nature. Samuels (1993) also pointed out that aggression often masks the deepest need for contact, dialogue, playback, and affirmation. This provides us with a more positive approach to conflict, in which the more 'negative' or challenging aspects are accepted as a precursor to growth and change. When working on the streets with people, offering street therapy, I always felt that aggression was a secondary reaction, with the first being fear. For some people, being considered as aggressive and dangerous is preferable to showing any vulnerability as they believe they would completely fall apart if they let someone in.

My work as a therapist had already alerted me to the central role conflict can play in a person's mental health. However, when first entering the field of conflict resolution, I had to change my personal stance from the desire to be a peacemaker, acquired in childhood, growing up as the eldest child, to a more enquiring and curious response, respectful of the individual perceptions which disputants expressed. Initially, when reading Mindell (1995: 241), a key writer on conflict with his clarion call of 'Value trouble. Accept nature. Make peace with war', and the psychotherapist Totton's call to 'affirm aggression, support conflict, speak up for competition – while also affirming, supporting and speaking up for the victims of alienated and destructive expressions of these qualities' (2006: 30), I was at a loss as to what they meant and was not initially drawn to their way of seeing things. On reflection, I came to understand that they were challenges to me as a mediator (and as a therapist) to respect the party's experience of what was 'trouble' and their felt experience that it was like being in a 'war'. If I tried to downplay it or ignore it, I was being disrespectful and would never understand the real nature and meaning of the dispute, and so I would be unable to facilitate a meaningful resolution. I came to understand that I needed to go deep and look at what the conflict had raised for the individuals at a psychological level whilst not getting lost in it and remaining aware that they desired a resolution in a short, fixed amount of time.

Individual Response to Conflict

On training courses, I often ask participants just to respond to the word 'conflict', what it brings to mind and body. People generally come up with nouns such as 'competition', 'war', 'hate', 'destruction', 'fight', but they also report emotional responses – 'fear', 'anger', 'shock'. Some describe physical sensations 'freezing', 'stomach pain', 'trembling legs', 'dizziness', etc. What we can be sure of is that conflict, even just the naming of it, creates a response. We are not generally indifferent to it. We feel something about it, even if what we feel is 'boredom'.

We all have different responses to conflict, and these will come into play in mediation. In the past I had the misfortune of working in an open-plan office. I was fascinated by what tended to happen on a Monday afternoon. Monday mornings usually passed uneventfully, with people feeling refreshed after the weekend. Some people would recall stories of the weekend events before settling into the routine of the working week. However, by midafternoon, there was often the growing realisation that the weekend was now well and truly over, and they had another four full days of work to survive. Those who enjoyed their work might feel energised, but for some, the working week was more something to be endured than to be looked forward to.

I would watch curiously to see how people behaved. One person might respond to their growing boredom by looking round to see who they could goad into an argument, loving the adrenalin rush that comes with conflict. They may look around to find someone they can provoke, perhaps someone whose football team suffered a heavy loss at the weekend, and so they head over to confront them.

Another person may see this happening and know exactly what is going on. As someone who cannot cope with conflict, they may head for the door, announcing that they are going to make coffee and asking if anyone would like one, thus giving an invitation to others who may also wish to avoid the situation. By doing so, they are hoping that the process will occupy them and keep them safe until after the argument is finished and they can safely return to the shared space.

Others can tolerate remaining in the room while hoping to ignore what is going on by lowering their head, banging away at their computer keyboard, and trying to become invisible in the hope they will not be drawn into the argument. Another may watch on with interest, enjoying the conflict, but only as a spectator sport. A different person may be bored by the whole thing, as it seems to happen every Monday, and so they just carry on with their work as though nothing is happening, even if by now the two disputants are yelling at one another.

Our responses to conflict and our different levels of tolerance. will depend on our personality, historical and family responses to conflict, the context of the dispute, the level at which it personally impacts, and how we feel about the individuals involved. Indeed, what one person defines as conflict and can be deeply affected by, another person may barely notice.

To work effectively with conflict, we need to be insightful about our own instinctive responses. We rarely get into conflict about something we do not care about. It may not be about the surface 'factual' dispute, but it may happen when arguments, disagreements, or competition threatens something which is important to us by connecting with or challenging our self-esteem, values, and beliefs. This may concern something external, like our job, family, or friendship, or may be internally affecting our self-concept or self–esteem. It can be a very uncomfortable process raising questions about just how in control I am: am I really being listened to and understood? Am I getting the respect I deserve? Am I being perceived as stupid or vulnerable? Are they trying to exclude or humiliate me? When we are feeling this vulnerable any questions may feel like attacks and be seen through the lens of the need for self-protection. All such questions impact on our self-esteem and how we see ourselves. We may perceive an attack whether it is there or not and experience physical responses to the perceived attack, linked to the built-in flight, flight, freeze instinctual reaction triggered by our amygdala. Our response is not logical; it is emotional and embodied. In this movement, our emotions take precedence over our actions. In a moment of perceived threat, the emotional part of the brain, the amygdala, overrides the thinking part of the brain, the neocortex, and compromises the ability to think logically. This is often referred to as an 'amygdala hijack'. When this occurs, the working memory becomes less efficient, blood pressure, adrenaline, and hormone levels rise. The body prepares itself to deal with the perceived threat through running away, standing its ground, even freezing, or fighting. This response served us well in prehistoric times, when it was an essential tool for survival for those living in wild and dangerous places where life or death threats from others, animals, and the environment were always a risk. In today's 21st century the response is still active, but the threat is not usually of bodily extinction but may be more likely to be a threat to our psychological well-being, self-concept, and self-esteem. When in this state of stress, we are more prone to impulsive thinking and behaviour which we may regret later. Even after the threat is removed, it can take three to four hours for adrenaline to clear the system.

Despite the physical and psychological discomfort being in conflict may cause, artists know that conflict is the very essence of existence (often the subject of songs and works of art) and the tension and conflict we encounter by being human beings interacting with other human beings cannot be truly avoided. We may choose to try to pretend there is no conflict or that we are not affected by it, but this would be inauthentic. It is impossible to go through life without conflicts. For many of us, these will be minor and easily sorted, yet for others, conflicts can be life changing – for better or worse. Our conflicts may be internal when we are faced with conflicting desires or needs or know that the consequences of our actions may be both positive and negative. Artists, in their work, use conflict creatively creating tension and interest and so encouraging the listener/reader/observer to stay with the narrative. The fact that the conflict is one step removed from their lived experience, even if they identify very strongly with it, can make the conflict safe to explore. However, certain kinds of conflict can also block creativity and destroy lives.

2 Creative Conflict

As stated, most people's first instinctive thought about conflict is that it is negative, disruptive, and potentially destructive. However, without conflict, it could be argued that we would have died out as a species – without some grit in the oyster, we would have not needed to develop and innovate. For Darwin, it is the competition between species which resulted in one dying out and another developing which was more suited to survival.

So, conflict could be seen as necessary and a catalyst for growth, development, change, and creativity, sowing the seeds for the generation of new thinking and ideas. It does not need to be destructive and hostile. We can approach difference, including differences of opinions as potential opportunities to learn, develop, and be creative, leading to innovative solutions, breakthroughs, and co-created ideas.

It is the process by which we approach and deal with conflict which makes it creative. It isn't the nature of the conflict itself; whatever the dispute is about, it is possible to transform it into creative conflict.

Often, in a conflict situation, we feel fearful or angry, and our first instinct is to defend ourselves and our views. People may mask their fear through anger, so the angriest and most aggressive person in the room may well be the one who feels most threatened. The threat is unlikely to be physical, but a threat to our self-esteem, a denial of our beliefs and values, or someone else's needs placing an obstacle in the way of our getting our own needs met that carries long-standing implications. This can feel like a greater threat than a physical attack which is likely to be over quickly.

For conflict to be creative, it requires that individuals or groups with different viewpoints, experiences, or goals find a way of openly and authentically engaging in a constructive dialogue in which they cultivate curiosity about the other's perspective, knowing that listening with curiosity does not equate to agreeing with. To have a respectful exchange of ideas and a willingness to explore differences through open and honest debate requires

DOI: 10.4324/9781003675938-4

bravery and commitment, plus a trust in the process, even when there is little trust in the individuals.

This will allow for a safe but thought-provoking exchange of ideas aimed at challenging the status quo, stimulating critical thinking, and considering alternatives. In creative industries like music, design, writing, art, or product development, creative conflict is often acknowledged and seen as essential for pushing boundaries and coming up with innovative concepts. As trust is usually compromised when we are in dispute with someone, creative conflict has to be well managed by all involved.

For such a dialogue to be well managed and successful, a number of things need to be done:

- Agree ground rules
- Use active listening
- Challenge assumptions
- Encourage open and authentic yet respectful interaction
- Encourage critical thinking
- Promote collaboration
- Give birth to innovation

It requires everyone involved to enter into the process with a willingness to:

- Listen with curiosity to others (though not necessarily agree with them)
- Show others they have heard through reflecting back, paraphrasing, and summarising
- Remain open to being told that in the other person's view they are wrong
- Be open to re-evaluating their own assumptions
- Consider new perspectives
- Be open to exploring their blind spots and any sedimented assumptions and values
- Be open to seeking new explanations that may challenge their own perspective
- Be excited by the possibility of finding new viewpoints and potentially new solutions
- Present and defend their own ideas whilst being open to constructive questioning and critique
- Willingly listen to others present their ideas and offer them constructive questions and critique
- Be open to changing their mind

Creative conflict could be seen as a natural fit for the creative industries as it is crucial for cultural evolution and the development of art, literature, and music. Artists, writers, and musicians often challenge established norms and conventions, push boundaries, and introduce new ideas that have ramifications not just within their artistic context but that may also be influential in reshaping societal attitudes and values.

In addition, creative conflict approaches have much to offer in a wide range of contexts. They are used in sociopolitical contexts where there is conflict due to diverse political perspectives and ideologies and perceived different needs and interest in societies. It can be called on to encourage and facilitate democratic discourse and participation, enabling people to engage in debates and discussions regarding public policies, social norms, values, and acceptable behaviours, exchanging diverse opinions and beliefs and fostering critical thinking, potentially leading to compromise of actions without compromise of values. We can see evidence of such an approach in the civil rights movement and the calls for gender equality and environmental protection, where the tensions between those advocating for change and those resisting it can be safely discussed, leading to significant legislative reforms, cultural shifts, and advancements in human rights.

As creative individuals, those working in the music industry can bring their creativity into dealing with conflict. In Part Three, I shall say more about what individuals and groups can actively do to promote a creative conflict approach.

Instead of creative conflict approaches, litigation is often the first thought when people consider ways of dealing with conflict. However, litigation is perhaps the opposite of creative conflict, in that it offers a linear model based on perceived logic and reason in which emotions are considered irrelevant or counterproductive, and which sees all those involved as pawns in a game focused on defeating the opponent, rather than using creative, lateral thinking to find a solution suited to the unique individuals involved in the dispute. If a third party is to be involved in resolving conflict, then a more bespoke and creative response is offered through conflict coaching or psychologically informed mediation.

Before I go on to look at what these are and what these interventions can offer, let us look at the more common areas of conflict within the music industry.

3 The Nature of Conflict in the World of Music

My personal view is that all conflict is psychological and emotional and therefore has an impact on the mental health and well-being of all involved. Having written *Psychologically Informed Mediation* in 2021, in which I offered an introduction to mediation and presented some cases I had mediated, it was suggested to me by some of my clients that I might write a similar book focused on disputes within the music industry. They had continually drawn my attention to news of high-profile music disputes, mainly concerned with copyright issues and the varied challenges that working in the music industry brought. Several of the dilemmas they brought to coaching and therapy involved dealing with conflict, either within the band, within their personal relationships, or in what may at first appear to be the more transactional aspects of the business such as contracts, intellectual property etc.

In the introduction, I have already referred to some examples of such conflicts in the context of writing about the existential challenges confronting musicians. However, I think it is worth taking a look at some of the more common conflicts which occur in the industry. In most of these cases, the dispute was not mediated but went through a long, drawn-out, and expensive (both financially and emotionally) litigation process. In my view, mediation would have been a more suitable way of addressing many of these conflicts.

People are rightly very proud of their creations and can be very hurt and angry when allegations are made that the work is not authentic but draws too fully on the work of others. Unfortunately, this is not a rare situation in the industry. To be accused of stealing another's ideas, and its implication that one's own creativity is more limited than might appear to be the case, is a threat to one's self-esteem. For those who believe their work is stolen and not recognised, there can be feelings of disrespect and lack of acknowledgement, which then may result in them feeling small

DOI: 10.4324/9781003675938-5

and worthless. Working with these emotions is never part of a legal solution but would form a focus of exploration in a psychologically informed mediation.

One high profile case concerned the allegation filed in 2017 by songwriters Sean Hall and Nathan Butler that Taylor Swift had 'stolen' lyrics from their 2001 song 'Playas Gon' Play', written for the R&B group 3LW, and used them in her hit 'Shake It Off'. Laura Snapes (2022) writing in *The Guardian*, reported that Swift's lawyers argued that lyrics like 'plays' and 'haters' were too common to be monopolised under copyright law. The case was due to go to trial in January 2023 but suddenly settled in December 2022. I have been unable to discover whether there was a mediation and/or out of court settlement leading to the dropping of the case, but after six years, I am sure all parties would have been exhausted and losing money by the day.

March 2022 saw a similar case, in which Katy Perry won a copyright ruling at a federal appeals court when it was declared that her 2013 chart-topper 'Dark Horse' hadn't infringed an earlier song, 'Joyful Noise', by rapper Marcus Gray. The ruling was seen as a clear rejection of similar infringement cases over songs, stressing that simple common musical 'building blocks,' like the short 'ostinato' in Perry's song, cannot be owned by a particular songwriter. To do so would limit future song writing creativity.

This could be seen as part of a move away from earlier decisions, such as that over Robin Thicke's 'Blurred Lines,' in which a judgement was made in favour of Marvin Gaye's estate which had claimed Robin Thicke's and Pharrell Williams' song included elements of Gaye's work. Gaye's estate received $7.4 million in damages, the largest amount ever granted in a music copyright case. This judgement was heavily criticised by some for expanding music copyright to more basic elements.

In April 2022, Ed Sheeran also won his case over his 2017 hit 'Shape of You,' when a judge ruled that he didn't copy the song from a little-known track called 'Oh Why' and awarded Sheeran and his song writing partners £916,200 in legal costs. Following an 11-day London trial, the judge ruled there was no evidence Sheeran had intentionally or even 'subconsciously' copied any of the earlier material. However, in October of the same year, a federal judge in New York ruled that Sheeran should face a jury trial in a separate case where he is accused of borrowing key elements of his 'Thinking Out Loud' from Marvin Gaye's iconic 'Let's Get It On'.

Such long, drawn-out, and expensive cases are emotionally draining for all concerned. In a Twitter post on 6th April 2022, following the success of the first case, Sheeran, drawing attention to the very personal and upsetting nature of such allegations, wrote,

> I don't want to take anything away from the pain and hurt suffered by both sides in this case, but I just want to say that I am not an entity. I'm not a corporation. I'm a human being. I'm a father. I'm a husband. I'm a son. Lawsuits are not a pleasant experience and I hope with this ruling it means in the future baseless claims like this can be avoided.
>
> (cited in Khomani, 2022)

His words reflect the way in which artists often feel as though they are seen and treated as commodities rather than people. Sheeran's powerful statement lays a claim for a new approach to tackling disputes which puts a more psychological approach at its heart, recognising not just the financial cost but the human costs involved in disputes.

Unfortunately, his words do not seem to have brought about much change, with Dua Lipa currently facing two separate lawsuits claiming she copied earlier songs when writing 'Levitating.' Artikal Sound System, a Florida reggae band claim Lipa lifted the hook for her song from their 2015 song 'Live Your Life.' Subsequently, she has also been accused of copying both a 1979 song called 'Wiggle and Giggle All Night' and a 1980 song called 'Don Diablo.' Both cases remain pending at the time of writing with emotional as well as financial strain on all involved.

These cases can take a heavy toll on the mental health of those involved. One example is that of Megan Thee Stallion who was quoted in *Rolling Stone* (Miers, 2022) as saying she needed to take a break because she was 'so tired, physically and emotionally' following her legal battles with her former record label, 1501 Certified Entertainment, which had escalated when she accused the company of purposefully mislabelling an album to keep her locked into the deal. This saw 1501 countersuing, and in August of the same year, Megan presented new allegations and demands for damages. It is easy to see how such disputes escalate, become Kafkaesque, and cause damage to mental health. On 20th October 2023, BBC News reported that a settlement had been reached with Megan and her record company amicably parting ways and reaching a mutually confidential settlement to resolve their differences (McLaren, 2023). It is the aim of mediation to facilitate such a confidential agreement to disputes. The case highlighted the naivety of many young artists when, in 2020, 28-year-old Megan said on an Instagram Live post in 2020, quoted by BBC News on 20th October 2023 that she 'didn't really know what was in [her] contract' when she first signed it, stating, 'I was young. I think I was like 20, and I ain't know everything that was in my contract' (McLaren, 2023). It is worth pointing out that these legal proceedings were taking place at the same time as she was embroiled in a criminal case against Tory Lanez over charges that he shot her in the foot during a July 2020 altercation in Los

Angeles. This would not be a case for mediation. At the trial in that case, the toll it had taken on her was apparent with her tearfully declaring, 'I wish he had just shot and killed me.' on an Instagram Live in 2020 (cited in McLaren, 2023).

Where emotional aspects are very clear, I would suggest mediation should always be the first port of call. Having said this, I also wish to emphasise that mediation can also work well where the financial and business aspects are more prominent as we can be very emotional about our business and finances. Most resolutions are achieved by a large degree of common sense and through understanding what the deeper needs of the disputants are. Sometimes they are quite transactional. It is not unusual for parties in mediations to be accompanied by their legal representatives, but a mediator would wish to give most space to hearing from the disputants themselves. I would argue that most disputes can be resolved through mediation, but there may be some which are better served through legal process.

In 2022, the case of Young Thug and Gunna arose, where a debate over lyrics was also the focus of a criminal case when the band were indicted as part of a gang case against members of the Altana rap crew YSL. The charges included references to Young Thug and Gunna's music, claiming lyrics were the kind of 'predicate acts' that contributed to the overall criminal enterprise. This case was based on a criminal law judgement but does shows the vulnerable position of any musician in relation to how their work can be interpreted.

Social media is an active platform for disputes to be played out in the full force of the public gaze. Cardi B won a $4 million defamation case against Tasha K, a gossip blogger who made salacious false claims on YouTube about drug use, STDs, and prostitution. She also won a case filed by a California man whose back tattoos were unwittingly photoshopped onto the 'raunchy' cover of her 2016 mixtape *Gangsta Bitch Music, Vol. 1*. At the trial Cardi spoke of the pain of being defamed and the ways lawyers treat people.

The case that prompted me to get on and write this book stemmed from hearing, yet again, about the ongoing, seemingly never-ending, dispute between David Gilmour and Roger Waters, which seemed to have taken much time from individuals' lives. At the same time, I read an article written by Vanessa Thorpe (2023) in *The Guardian* which described the hurt and anger of Louie Duffy, the 19-year-old son of Martin Duffy, the late keyboard player with Primal Scream.

In the Gilmour/Waters dispute, we see two grown men engaged in a battle which has lasted longer than the time they spent working together in the band Pink Floyd. Following the release of *Dark Side of the Moon* in 1973 and *The Wall* in 1979, in which Waters drew on his own life experiences, tensions in the band grew, and Waters finally left the band after their 1983 album, *The Final Cut*. Bandmates David Gilmour and Nick Mason wanted to continue the band without Waters, which resulted in Waters taking them to court in 1986 because they thought the band was a spent force. After two years of fighting and litigation an agreement was reached, but it didn't end the feud between Waters and Gilmour, despite them being able to reunite for a one-off charity event in 2005. This is an example of a dispute where we can see common power struggles and group dynamics playing out which led to members of the band feeling disrespected and aggrieved. In a *Rolling Stone* interview on 10th December 2018, Nick Mason quoted Gilmour as saying, 'It's really disappointing that these rather elderly gentlemen are still at loggerheads' (Greene, 2018). Despite Gilmour now being 77 and Waters 80, the dispute continues! As recently as 2023, Gilmour's wife, Polly Samson, took to Twitter/X to call out Waters for antisemitism, being a Putin apologist, and being a 'lying, thieving, hypocritical, tax-avoiding, lip-synching, misogynistic megalomaniac,' all of which Waters has denied stating 'I call myself a humanist, a citizen of the world. And my loyalty and respect belong to all people regardless of their origin, nationality or religion' (cited in Donaldson, 2023). In thinking about the deep feelings and anger which have lasted decades I was struck by the clear existential themes which are so evident. Themes which would never be explored through litigation but may have been through psychologically informed mediation. The dispute goes on and no doubt continues to cause pain to all involved.

The hurt expressed by Louie Duffy, regarding the way he considered his father was treated after leaving Primal Scream, is another case in which I feel early mediation could have prevented many years of ill feeling. Martin Duffy joined the band in 1989 and contributed to all their albums, including the award winning *Screamadelica*. He was dismissed from the band at a time when his son considered that his father was vulnerable and in need of support, due to his struggles with alcoholism, which had led to him making mistakes in his final Primal Scream gig in Glasgow. Following his dismissal, Duffy became depressed and his alcoholism worsened, putting the family in debt. Martin Duffy died in December 2022 from a brain injury, following a fall at home in Brighton, after drinking two bottles of wine. His son Louie believes that his father should have received a share of the profits from Primal Scream's tours and back catalogue, including a £5 million rights deal with BMG. Louie wrote:

> I am well aware that the financial reward may not have saved dad from himself … But I do know that while the band were reaping the rewards from touring 'Screamadelica'… he was having to live month to month – just being paid session fees to perform it – when in fact he had played

> an important part in creating it. I know dad found this insulting and not right.
>
> (Duffy, 2023)

His concern was partly about money, but also that in his view, his father had been shown little respect or given little credit for all the work he had done. At the coroner's court it was reported that the band did continue to pay Duffy's wages even after removing him from the tour, and that band members Andrew Innes and Bobby Gillespie, both of whom had undergone their own battles with substance abuse, hoped that showing 'tough love' to Duffy might have been a way to make him face the self-destructive path he was on and that might result in him changing his behaviours and saving his career and life.

Although some blame was levelled at the band, Louie placed some of the responsibility on the music industry and the way it treated performers. Vanessa Thorpe's (2023) article in *The Guardian* quoted an unnamed music promoter as saying,

> the duty of care in the music industry in the mid-80s and early 90s was absolutely terrible. The business was reckless and there was little understanding of mental health. Drinks were on every performer's rider. Once you are well known, everyone buys you a drink … It was a different time back then.

In *The Art of War*, Sun Tzu (2009) counselled military leaders to build a golden bridge for an opponent to retreat across as, without an escape route, your opponent will engage in battle and fight like a caged and cornered tiger. By providing Sun Tzu's golden bridge, it may have proved possible for a way to be found for Duffy to leave the band with dignity, even if it couldn't have repaired the band relationships sufficiently for them to continue working together. Mediation is not about providing a happy ending, in which conflict is obliterated and everyone becomes friends, but about finding a way in which everyone can resume their lives with the least cost both financially and emotionally.

This example speaks clearly to some of the central themes in psychologically based mediation: self-concept and self-esteem, real and perceived power dynamics, ego states, freedom and responsibility, temporality, uncertainty, identity, loneliness, and relatedness, of which I shall write more throughout the book.

Although the promoter quoted above seems to imply that things have got better, I am not too sure. Certainly, there is better understanding of mental health issues, with agencies such as MITC and others working hard to improve things, but the pressures are still there. In this book, I am not focusing on the broad area of mental health but specifically on conflicts that occur in the industry. These are always emotional and affect mental health.

Having already worked with individual musicians as a therapist, when I qualified as a mediator in 2000, my thoughts turned to how some of the issues which had been brought to therapy stemmed from stresses caused by disputes and conflicts which could perhaps have been quickly addressed through early interventions including mediation.

Other Common Disputes in the Industry

Disputes between Artists and Recording Companies

Many disputes arise out of complaints from the artists. These cover many different things, including what they believe to be inequitable recording contracts which saddle them with poor royalty returns, dictating how much they will receive for sales, and accounting policies which may also disadvantage them. Intellectual property and other ownership issues that may arise after the official relationship has ended are also all fertile ground for disputes. Most of these disputes spring from the original recording contracts, which are often painfully long and complex. There is probably no subject in the music business more frequently discussed, yet more misunderstood, than the subject of recording contracts, and so, not surprisingly, the content of a record deal is a key potential source of many artist complaints. Most artists have spent many years dreaming of the day when success arrives and they land their first contract. Often naively, the artist believes the record company is there to help them, but these companies are not charities or patrons of the arts, they are businesses that need success for themselves as much or more than they need success for their artists. Of course, their success is intimately connected with the commercial success of the artist. Although there are many legal aspects of such disputes, such as the term or length of the contract; commitment versus options; territory (the geographical area in which the record company is allowed to sell the artist's records); the exploitation period including the ownership of masters and licensing agreements; pre-recording restrictions tying the artist to the label; creative control; use of name and likenesses and the whole area of royalties, advances, and recoupment. Many of these would need to be dealt with by lawyers but disputes in these areas could be avoided by time being given to discussing all aspects with the artists, not just their managers, and ensuring that artists know what they are signing. History has provided us with some high-profile examples of disputes in this area.

Michael Jackson disputed ownership of masters. In October of 2001, Michael Jackson released his album *Invincible.* The release of the album coincided with a dispute between Jackson and his record label, Sony Music Entertainment. The dispute originated from Jackson's inability to obtain the masters to his original albums despite the fact that he believed that he possessed this right in his contract with Sony. If Jackson owned the licences, he would have been able to promote his own material and receive the profits from these original works. However, due to concealed clauses in the contract, Sony owned the masters to his original albums for several more years. After launching an investigation, Jackson discovered that the attorney who represented him also represented Sony, creating a conflict of interest. Jackson also voiced concern that Sony was pressuring him to sell them his music catalogue. He was hesitant to take this action because if his career began to fail, he would be forced to sell his share of the catalogue at a low price, thus benefiting Sony and therefore providing Sony an incentive for Jackson's career to start failing. In 2002, Jackson revealed details of his dispute with Sony and his strong dislike for the head of Sony, Tommy Mottola. Jackson claimed that Sony had purposely stopped promoting *Invincible* five months before the release of the album and that Tommy Mottola was the devil because of his past history of exploiting artists, especially African American performers.

Copyright reversion, or the return of master recordings and publishing to the creators when copyrights run out, is an issue that is finally reverberating throughout the music industry. In perhaps the most high-profile music reversion to date, Paul McCartney and Sony/ATV reached a settlement over the ownership of many of the Beatles' back catalogue. In January 2017, Paul McCartney sued Sony/ATV Music Publishing, claiming copyright ownership of multiple masters. He sought to reclaim copyright ownership over the band's iconic catalogue using a reversion right provision established by the Copyright Act of 1976. Under the terms of the act, songwriters could reclaim copyright of their catalogue from music publishers after a 35-year term, or 56 years for songs from before 1978. After long and expensive litigation, McCartney and Sony settled, releasing the statement that, 'The parties have resolved this matter by entering into a confidential settlement agreement and jointly request that the Court enter the enclosed proposed order dismissing the above-referenced action without prejudice,' (*MusicWeek*, 2017). The details of the settlement remain undisclosed.

Although these examples may feel like ancient history to some readers, such disputes continue today, with current disputes revolving around ownership of masters, royalty rates, and the impact of new technologies such as AI on copyright and fair use. Recently, we have seen Taylor Swift concluding a long-standing battle over the ownership of her music by buying back the master recordings of her first six albums.

Although many of these disputes may appear to be about money or ownership, it is clear that there are personal elements at their core. It is possible to mediate all such disputes, but the mindset of the industry needs to change for due consideration to be given to mediation before litigation.

Disputes between Band Members

Being in a band can bring the same kind of intimacy and tension which occurs when adult children need to remain in the family home for financial reasons. An individual may have 'outgrown' the band and the group behaviours associated with it, or members may never have got on, even when knowing they could make 'sweet music together.' The psychoanalyst, Michael Jolkovski (2007), in an article for Atlas Plugged in July 2007, (republished on his own blog) noted

> A newly formed band has the life expectancy of a mob informer in prison. If you are involved with bands, you know how hard it is to keep them together. The brutal economics and Darwinian pressures of the music life are often the cause.

He suggested that

> It might actually be a good thing for some bands to die quickly so the members can learn from their mistakes and go on to form new bands. Besides, if some bands didn't die, the entire surface of the earth would soon be covered in bands.

He likened joining a band to a 'combination of marrying them, fighting alongside them in a war, and being trapped in an elevator with them.' Whilst acknowledging that bandmates do not need to be best buddies, he does warn that any dislike a person may have for another member of the band is likely to intensify when on the road together and often having to share confined spaces.

Music is a passionate business, and if we are passionate about something, it often leads to disagreements with others who are equally passionate about their own differing point of view. Without basic respect for differing perspective, strengths, and behaviours, coupled with trust for the individuals, it is likely the band will tear itself apart.

Not all musicians are collaborative in nature; some are fiercely competitive, and many don't like the idea of traditional authority relationships. There may be positioning for leadership roles in the group, whilst not liking the idea of leadership in theory. However, as Jolkovski (2007) reminds us, 'a good group is full of leaders, who can inspire the group to be effective in different ways at different times.' Attempts to share leadership can highlight personality differences which may be hidden until decisions need to be made. We all have egos, and for most of us, they are quite vulnerable to criticism or feelings of being put down. 'Musicians who claim to have no ego or narcissism are either dishonest or naïve. Anyone who pursues a career that is performed on a raised platform, with spotlights and amplifiers and expects applause is seeking attention – ergo – ego.' (Jolkovski, 2007). He also claimed that there is a fair amount of narcissism in the industry, claiming that it often goes with creativity. If this is the case, then communication is particularly difficult as 'extreme narcissists don't listen' (Jolkovski, 2007);, they will not be genuinely interested in the views of others and will be unable to take criticism. Such narcissism tends to grow with fame.

In his how-to guide, *Making Money Making Music*, (1989: 78). James Dearing recommends that when aspiring Liams and Damons audition new recruits for their bands, they get them to fill out a Musician Personality Test. Among the suggested questions: Were they naturally friendly? Who was the most positive person? He claimed that if everyone used this test, it seemed unlikely that Pink Floyd, Nirvana, and Oasis would have hired Syd Barrett, Kurt Cobain, and Noel Gallagher, respectively. Or that the guitarist Johnny Marr, looking for a lyricist partner, would have formed the Smiths with insecure miserabilist Morrissey. Although it may have made relationships easier, there would no doubt have been a creative loss.

It is unusual for these tensions to be proactively acknowledged and worked through in any positive way. In Part Three I explore some ways in which this could be done.

Having stated earlier that being in a band is like being in a family, it is not surprising to find problems when band members are from the same biological family.

Sibling Rivalry

> Happy families are all alike; every unhappy family is unhappy in its own way.
>
> *Anna Karenina* by Leo Tolstoy

According to Your Child Team (2011) from the University of Michigan, each child in a family competes to define who they are as an individual and wants to show that they are separate from their siblings. Children may feel they are getting unequal amounts of their parents' attention, discipline, and responsiveness. Children fight most in families where there is neither any understanding that fighting is not an acceptable way to resolve conflicts nor any alternative way of handling such conflicts; in families in which physical fighting is forbidden, but no method of non-physical conflict resolution (e.g., verbal argument) is permitted, the accumulation of everyday disputes and their conversion into long-simmering hostilities can have an effect that is nearly as corrosive. Stress in the parents' and children's lives can create more conflict and increase sibling rivalry.

Alfred Adler (1937) saw siblings as striving for significance within the family and felt that birth order was an important aspect of personality development. In fact, psychologists and researchers today endorse the influence of birth order, as well as age and gender constellations, on sibling relationships. However, parents are seen as capable of having an important influence on whether they are competitive or not.

David Levy introduced the term 'sibling rivalry' in 1941, claiming that for an older sibling, 'the aggressive response to the new baby is so typical that it is safe to say it is a common feature of family life.' (Levy, 2010: 53). Researchers today generally endorse this view, noting that parents can ameliorate this response by being vigilant to favouritism and by taking appropriate preventative steps. Researchers say that the ideal time to lay the groundwork for a lifetime of supportive relationships between siblings is during the months prior to the new baby's arrival.

Given the above, it is not surprising that when siblings are in the same band there is often trouble. Being in a band requires the same sharing of limited space and competition for attention. There are many examples of sibling rivalry in famous bands, as outlined in the following examples.

THE EVERLY BROTHERS

With their intertwined harmonies, no brothers could have sounded closer. Indeed, Linda Ronstadt, who scored one of the biggest hits of her career in 1975 with her recording of 'When Will I Be Loved,' written by Phil Everly, told Randy Lewis (2014) of the *Los Angeles Times*, 'They had that sibling sound ... The information of your DNA is carried in your voice, and you can get a sound [with family] that you never get with someone who's not blood related to you ....' However, as their career faded in the 1960s, the tension between the brothers steadily grew, not helped by their addiction to speed. They finally parted ways during a 1973 show at the Knott's Berry Farm amusement park in Buena Park, California. After Don turned up drunk, Phil destroyed his guitar and stormed off the stage. Don told the flabbergasted crowd that the duo had broken up and finished the show by himself. 'We give each other a lot of space,' Don Everly told the *Los Angeles Times* in May 1999 (Boehm 1999) when they played a couple of shows in the Southland. 'We say hello, we sometimes have a meal together .... Everything is different about us, except when we sing together. I'm a liberal Democrat, he's pretty conservative.'

They remained estranged for much of the last two decades. 'Don and I are infamous for our split,' Phil told Time magazine in 1986, 'but we're closer than most brothers. Harmony singing requires that you enlarge yourself, not use any kind of suppression. Harmony is the ultimate love.' (Lewis, 2014) When they played a few shows in the 1990s, the tension was still in play.

THE KINKS

The battles of the brothers, Dave Davies (the Kinks' founder and lead guitarist) and Ray Davies (the principal singer and songwriter) are legendary: onstage, offstage, in the studio, in the backs of cars. Ray throws curry at Dave to emphasise a point; Dave gets into a heated argument with Ray and then ends up with a black eye when he tells off the drummer for not taking his side. 'Nothing good ever happened without a fight of some kind,' Dave said (Let It Rock, 2024).

As the years wore on, the struggles became greater, the battles more brutal, the mind games more intense, weirder, and the lows much lower. Dave was quoted in *Rolling Stone* (2011) as saying, 'Ray's an asshole ... you've heard of vampires, well, Ray sucks me dry of ideas, emotions and creativity. It's toxic for me to be with him. He's a control freak.' Whether or not the two can put aside their differences for a reunion tour has been the subject of dozens of news stories over the past few years. The brothers haven't performed together since 1996.

THE BEE GEES

The Bee Gees were one of the longest-running family bands ever, with a career that lasted from 1958 to 2003. In an article in the *Daily Express* (2014), the band's frontman (and eldest brother) Barry declared, 'Robin was really competitive with me.' In the early years of the group, the two competed for the role of lead vocalist; when Barry won that battle, Robin left the group for a solo career.

Robin ended up releasing six solo albums before his death in 2012 but achieved his greatest success singing backup to Barry. Ironically, the sudden death of Maurice Gibb (Robin's twin), in 2003, bonded the brothers after years of dissension, with the brothers being with him when he died. 'When we lost Mau, Robin and I gravitated back towards each other a little bit,' Barry said (*Daily Express*, 2014).

CREEDENCE CLEARWATER REVIVAL

Tom Fogerty was the band's original lead singer. But by the time it was called Creedence Clearwater Revival, his little brother John was the sole singer and songwriter. The fact that John was vastly more talented than Tom didn't stop the demotion from rankling. 'It's an unnatural situation having your younger brother lead the group you're in,' Tom said. In an angry letter to John, he wrote, 'You have never given me (or Doug or Stu) credit in public' (Hann, 2025). The bitterness only grew after Tom quit the band decades later; friends had to plead with John to visit Tom's deathbed.

THE ALLMAN BROTHERS BAND

For decades, Gregg Allman played in the Allman Brothers Band as the singular Allman brother. His older sibling, Duane, had died in a motorbike accident in 1971. Their relationship had not been good before this. Duane never let his little brother forget who was boss. Gregg tells stories of when they were kids with a lemonade stand and how Duane got him to do all the work. It is not surprising that this type of strained relationship continued when Gregg was reluctant to join a band with Duane. Duane knew how to push his buttons: 'You can snivel on out of here,' Duane challenged him, 'If you don't try, don't call yourself my brother.' (Paul, 2014: 22) This set the tone for the relationship.

THE JACKSON 5

Jermaine Jackson always felt like the superstardom achieved by his little brother Michael could and should have been his. The culmination of that resentment: Jermaine's 1991 single 'Word to the Badd!!' where he attacked Michael for his extensive plastic surgery.

'Michael and I have never feuded,' Jermaine claimed. 'The only reason I wrote this song – and it came from the bottom of my heart – was to help my little brother get a grip on reality.' (Citron & Cerone, 1991). For his part, Michael apparently sabotaged Jermaine's solo career. According to record executive Clive Davis, when Michael found out Kenneth 'Babyface' Edmonds was going to produce a Jermaine album, Michael deliberately kept Babyface too busy to do it.

THE BLACK CROWES

A rift between the two brothers, Chris and Rich Robinson caused the break-up of The Black Crowes. Rich blamed his brother, singer Chris Robinson, for the dissolution of the group that has sold more than 35 million albums.

> It is with great disappointment and regret that after having the privilege of writing and performing the music of The Black Crowes over the last 24 years, I find myself in the position of saying that the band has broken up … I love my brother and respect his talent but his present demand that I must give up my equal share of the band and that our drummer for 28 years and original partner, Steve Gorman, relinquish 100 per cent of his share, reducing him to a salaried employee, is not something I could agree to.
>
> (*Uncut*, 2015)

Chris's response was to say the band had become a 'very tedious scenario' and the band was 'not going to turn around and be something that I think is super amazing again and fun and vibrant with the energy I'm looking for'(*Uncut*, 2015).

Childhood stories tell of Chris buying hundreds of records growing up whilst his brother Rich Robinson said he never had to, because he could just steal Chris's. The brothers successfully wrote dozens of songs together, but sometimes they had to ride on separate tour buses. 'We could sit in the same room, but all you'd get out of Rich would be "fuck you,"' On 1st June 2015, Chris told *Rolling Stone* magazine 'Brotherly love, you know?' Rich's take was, 'Chris and I have one unwritten rule – we can't hit each other in the face' (Edwards, 2015).

THE NATIONAL

The National is made up of five members, with two sets of brothers: guitarists Aaron and Bryce Dessner and drummer Bryan Devendorf and bassist Scott Devendorf. Singer and songwriter (and moody) Matt Berninger is the group's odd man out, musical sibling-wise. But he, too, has a brother: Tom Berninger, a sort of amiable, slightly doughier version of Matt who is nine years younger and still lives at their parents' home in Cincinnati.

It might be inevitable for a band with two pairs of brothers in it to be a hotbed of sibling rivalry. The Tom Berninger (2013) documentary *Mistaken for Strangers*, however, was a portrait of a different axis of fraternal tension: the National's lead singer Matt Berninger invited his brother Tom to come on tour with the band to work as a roadie and to make a movie. Tom proved hapless as a roadie and got kicked off the tour after he forgot to get on the bus. But as a filmmaker, he got great footage of his brother!

KINGS OF LEON

The three Followill brothers in Kings of Leon – Nathan, Caleb, and Jared – spent their childhood on the road. Dad was a Pentecostal preacher. The brothers sang hymns at revival meetings. They were home-schooled, and they faced strict rules (no movies, TV, or secular music), made few friends, and shared a handful of clothes.

The Kings of Leon documentary *Talihina Sky* (Mitchell, 2011) offers us many insights into the brother's relationship: 'We didn't think, "We're dirt poor," ' said Nathan. 'Struggles came with our dad doing the Lord's work. We thought we'd have more stars in our crown when we got to heaven.'

The documentary shows how their world changed in the late 1990s when their parents divorced amidst their father's battles with alcohol. 'The divorce shattered our world,' says Nathan. 'We saw that preachers, people we held in the highest regard, fail like everyone else. We realized we won't go to hell if we have some beers.' Jared added, 'When you're super-religious, a level of fear is instilled in you. But I grew out of it' (Mitchell, 2011).

It has been suggested that the Followill role models were, apparently, Cain and Abel. After singer Caleb left the stage halfway through a Kings of Leon concert in July 2011, bassist Jared said fans should 'hate Caleb, not us.' Nathan (the band's drummer) and Caleb can get into a fight over a game of pool; one drunken night in 2007 climaxed with Nathan dislocating Caleb's shoulder, breaking a $7,000 mirror, and stabbing Caleb's bed with a kitchen knife. Their form of brotherly love was captured in the documentary *Talihina Sky*, which showed Nathan screaming at Caleb: 'You get drunk, and you talk shit' and 'Your band cannot stand you!' Caleb shrugs off tensions, saying, 'I'd fight anyone who touches him (his brother). We love each other like that'(Mitchell, 2011).

The director of the Kings of Leon documentary *Talihina Sky* confirmed everyone's belief of tension between the brothers in the band, saying,

> Those two [Caleb and Nathan] have notoriously gone at each other over the years. I mean broken shoulders, pulled hair, trying to stab each other. Those two are like twins almost. They're so close but they're too close, if that makes sense.
>
> (Mitchell, 2013).

THE JESUS AND MARY CHAIN

The Scottish band, founded by the brothers Jim and William Reid, was fuelled by alcohol, cocaine and conflict, earning the brothers a fiery reputation. *Rolling Stone* (Edwards, 2015) reported Jim Reid as saying, 'We do fight, and there's no getting around it.' On their 1998 US tour, a Los Angeles gig that lasted just 15 minutes featured Jim knocking over microphone stands and the brothers arguing with each other – 'Play anything but that,' Jim said – and ended with William quitting the tour. Reportedly, the band's tour manager even considered calling the Reids' mother back in the UK to see if she could get them to settle down. Despite the feuding and the loss of several drummers and other band members along the way, the names of whom the brothers claim not to remember, the band are still touring in 2025. Ironically, their book *Never Understood* (Reid and Reid, 2024) coincided with the news of the Oasis reunion. In the book, William Reid jokes that the Gallagher brothers were the 'Hollywood remake of our little indie film about sibling rivalry' (Reid and Reid, 2024: 27).

OASIS

Indeed, the Gallagher brothers of Oasis have come to symbolise sibling rivalry, re-enacting the primal brotherly conflict of groups like the Kinks with constant insults and punch-ups.

They stopped doing joint interviews because they got into fist fights in front of reporters. One of their in-studio arguments was even released in 1995 as a single in England, entitled 'Wibbling Rivalry' (cheekily, under the name Oas•s). All it consists of is an audio recording of an interview the brothers did with NME's John Harris in early 1994, before *Definitely Maybe* was released; basically, it's fourteen minutes of bickering and insult-flinging, with Noel comparing Liam to a football hooligan, and Liam telling Noel that 'You can stick your thousand pounds right up your fuckin' arse 'till it comes out your fuckin' big toe.'

By their own admission, the brothers have been at each other's throats basically since Liam was born. Noel used to mess with Liam, who is apparently afraid of ghosts, by moving furniture around and making him think spirits did it. They continued their fights throughout the life of Oasis with Noel quitting the band on a number of occasions. In *NME* (2000) Noel stated, 'If I wasn't related to him (Liam), I'd have sacked him fucking four years ago.' By 2005, Noel admitted that he was resorting to mental manipulation to get Liam to do what he wanted. 'I've kind of learnt that instead of arguing stuff out with him and ending up in a fight, I work on his psychology, and he's completely freaked out by me now … I can read him and I can fucking play him like a slightly disused arcade game' (*NME*, 2000).

Oasis famously broke up in 2009, following years of threats, and the estranged brothers continued to trade barbs in the press and on social media. It started in 2009, when Liam tweeted, 'what a pair of old housewife's [sic]' about Noel and Russell Brand's short-lived comedy radio show. From there, he went on to make fun of Noel's new band calling Noel, 'Noel Katie Hopkins Gallagher' and describing his music as 'beige' (Renshaw, 2015).

Liam's goading of Noel took a more serious turn in the wake of the 22nd May 2017 terrorist attack during an Ariana Grande concert at the Manchester Arena. Liam made a surprise appearance at the One Love Manchester Benefit Concert on 4th June that year, performing a few Oasis songs, including a poignant rendition of 'Live Forever' with Coldplay's Chris Martin. However, the day after the event, he took to Twitter to chastise Noel for not showing up to support Manchester, calling his brother a 'sad fuck.' (Beaumont-Thomas, 2017) Noel performed at the reopening of the Arena in September 2017, shedding tears while playing 'Don't Look Back in Anger,' a song the Manchester public had taken as an anthem to declare their defiance to terrorism and their determination not to live fearfully.

At the time of writing, Oasis is embarking on the 'Oasis Live 25' tour after an unusually quiet reconciliation. Liam has been sharing updates on rehearsals expressing sadness at time lost and excitement for the future, declaring on X 'You know what it's spiritual but I can't help think about all those wasted years, what a waste of PRECIOUS time.' (Gallagher, 2025). Noel has been less active on social media, so we watch and wait to see what will happen.

You Don't Have to Be Related!

Although being from the same family seems to cause lots of problems you don't have to be a family member for inter-band conflict. There are plenty of examples of band members who were not related but who couldn't stand one another and yet seemed to be able to continue and forge success. Let's start by looking at one such band, whose longevity shows that even when there are conflicts the band can play on.

ROLLING STONES

Bill Wyman (1990) famously said that the Stones was made up of blokes who were not the sort he would have chosen as mates if he hadn't joined them in a group. The band is notorious for occasional discord and intrigue, stretching back to their early years, when guitarist Brian Jones floundered in his attempt to take the band's leadership as Jagger and Richards emerged as the Rolling Stones' creative force. Things were alleged to be so bad that in 2013, Jan Bell, the daughter of Frank Thorogood, Jones's builder-cum-minder (who it has been rumoured murdered Jones) who was present at Jones's farm on the night of his death (3rd July 1969) claimed that Mick Jagger and Keith Richards had a blazing row with Jones on the day he died, culminating in Richards drawing a knife. The row was about who owned the rights to the group's name.

Jones drowned at the age of 27 under suspicious circumstances, only weeks after being fired by the Stones following two years of drug and legal problems. Richards, speaking about Jones in an interview with David Fricke for *Rolling Stone* magazine (2010), said,

> I enjoyed his company, and I tried incredibly hard, in 1966, to pull him back into the group. He was flying off. But my attempts to bring Brian back into focus were a total failure. After that ... [long pause] He did some despicable things. The man was failing. He had been a strong man, but he was wiping himself out. Brian demanded, you have to understand. And in a band like this, you also have to be supportive and giving. Having to deal with his jealousy, with Mick and me writing the songs, when you're working 300-odd days a year — it becomes intolerable, and you can get really nasty about it. I tried to be fair to him. But to be honest, he was a bit of a bastard. And it doesn't surprise me that he came to a sticky end.

Speaking in 2015, former Rolling Stones bassist Bill Wyman accused Mick Jagger and Keith Richards of stealing Jones's glory over the years. During an interview with ClashMusic.com, Wyman was asked about the fact that Jagger and Richards both stayed away from Jones's funeral. Wyman lashed out at the 'Glimmer Twins' for not paying the proper respects to Jones, who created the band and was the architect of its original vision, saying,

> The only ones to come were me and Charlie (Watts). There were a lot of peripheral people around the Stones that never turned up. No, it was disgusting. It really was disgusting. It was awful. It showed guilt. It showed the guilt by them of the way they treated him. Do you know that in Dartford Railway Station where (Mick and Keith) met, they've just put up a plaque now saying they created The Rolling Stones, which is totally out of order. Brian Jones created the Rolling Stones, not Mick and Keith. They were invited into his band at later times, and they completely ignore it, because they want the accolade for Dartford.
>
> (Marsbar, 2017)

He went on to say: Mick and Keith should stand up and say

> No, this is wrong. We didn't create the Rolling Stones, Brian Jones did. Brian Jones chose the name the Rolling Stones, Brian Jones decided what music we would play, and Brian Jones enlisted every member into his band in 1962 and '63. That's what they should say, but they ain't going to, are they?
>
> (Marsbar, 2017)

Jones, although uncredited, co-wrote and played the recorders and cello on 'Ruby Tuesday,' sitar and tambourine on 'Paint It, Black,' dulcimer on 'I Am Waiting' and 'Lady Jane,' the lead guitar riff on 'Get Off My Cloud,' harpsichord on 'Yesterday's Papers,' the trumpet and trombone on 'Something Happened to Me Yesterday,' the marimba on 'Under My Thumb,' and the autoharp on 'You Got The Silver.' It was acknowledged that he was able to walk into a studio and play whatever instrument was lying around, even though he'd never played it before.

As part of his agreement to quit the Rolling Stones, Brian Jones was offered a settlement, which gave him a lump sum of nearly $200,000, as well as a yearly salary of $40,000 for as long as the band stayed together. He was also allowed to issue a statement saying that he had quit the band.

Within the Stones. the arguments were not confined to those involving Brian Jones. As their success grew, it became evident that Jagger and Richards no longer always saw eye to eye about the band's purposes, and Richards' legendary keenness for heroin and alcohol threatened to spoil the band's chances.

In 2010, Jagger and Richard's relationship was strained to the brink following the publication of Richard's autobiography, *Life*, in which he said some brutal things about Jagger, including describing Jagger's 2001 album *Goddess in the Doorway* as *Dogshit in the Doorway*. He portrayed Jagger as a changed man who had moved from being beguiling to someone who was cold, ambitious, and controlling. Richards saw the change as starting in the 1980s, and he began to refer to Jagger as 'Brenda' or 'Her Majesty', 'We would be talking about that Bitch Brenda with him in the room and he wouldn't know' (Richards, 2011, 52). He also claimed that Jagger has 'a tiny todger' and was not a good lover (Richards, 2011, 56).

Not surprisingly, Jagger was hurt and angered which didn't surprise Richards:

> As I told Mick, 'You should have seen what I left out! ... I know exactly what you did. You got the book, you went straight to the index – Jagger, M – and that's what you read. You didn't take it in context.
>
> (Parsons, 2012)

Despite this, they have found ways of continuing working together. 'So, yeah, we had a bit of a doo-dah, but I expected it. We resolved it, in our own way, you know.' Richards, anticipating the arrival of the Stones' 50th anniversary, contacted the band's members and said, 'Hey, boys, I'm getting itchy. Anybody feel like it?' This led to a meeting resulting in what Richards termed 'a gentlemen's agreement or something like that.' In an interview, it seems Richards did apologise, 'I said that I regret if I caused you any, you know, inconvenience or pain, or something,' but added 'I'd say anything to get the band together, you know? I'd lie to my mother' (Gilmore, 2013).

The history of the Stones encompasses decades, and so it is not surprising that their history shows most of the types of conflict experienced in bands.

THE RAMONES

Despite taking on the same last name in the mid-1970s, Jeffrey and Johnny weren't biologically related. Joey was born Jeffrey Hyman, and Johnny was born John Cummings. Their history includes the legendary feud over a woman, Linda Daniele, who had dated Joey and ultimately married Johnny. The dispute was so bitter it basically proved that they really saw themselves as brothers. In most families, this would have meant loud arguments every Thanksgiving, but for the Ramones, it meant decades of high-octane gigs where the band's two main members weren't speaking to each other.

THE SMITHS

A band which did not last quite as long as the Stones yet managed to throw up a considerable amount of controversy and conflict is The Smiths. The Smiths was one of the most influential bands of the 1980s, renowned for Morrissey's doom-laden lyrics and mournful Mancunian delivery. Hit singles included 'Heaven Knows I'm Miserable Now' and 'Girlfriend in a Coma.'

One cause of conflict was the perception, eventually exposed in High Court, that Stephen Morrissey treated the less well-known members of the pop band The Smiths as 'mere session musicians as readily replaceable as the parts of a lawnmower' (Taylor, 2021). This statement stemmed from a legal dispute, in 1996, with the Smith's ex drummer Mike Joyce. Morrissey termed Mike Joyce 'Joyce Iscariot' after he famously won the 1996 court case over unpaid earnings. In his 2013 autobiography, Morrissey claimed that when Joyce's 'finances frittered away, Joyce decided to turn to those who had served him generously in the past … a flea in search of a dog … Each man kills the thing he loves, and Joyce killed The Smiths' (Morrisey, 2013: 163).

Joyce brought the case, having discovered that Morrissey and Johnny Marr, the lead guitarist, each took 40 per cent of the profits whilst he and Andy Rourke, the bass player, received 10 per cent. Nigel Davis, QC, for

Joyce, said it was not until after the bestselling band split up in 1987 that his client discovered he was getting only 10 per cent of the profits.

> It may be that some will say this claim is a cynical piece of opportunism prompted by the dissolution of the group. We submit that's not fair. Mr Joyce's case is that it was only when the group dissolved, that he went to see his accountant and was told that he'd been getting only 10 per cent.
> (Hackworth, 1996)

Joyce's legal team claimed that Joyce's share of past profits could amount to as much as £1 million, which they believe was owed by Morrissey and Marr. Joyce also claimed a 25 per cent stake in royalties from any future sales instead of the 10 per cent he was offered (Hackworth, 1996).

Rourke, who gave evidence in the four-day hearing, settled with Morrissey and Marr in the late 1980s for £80,000 and 10 per cent of future royalties. He said that Morrissey, who wrote the lyrics for the songs, and Marr, who wrote the music, were 'clearly entitled' to the royalties from the group's songs and there was no dispute over that. But royalties for the recordings and profits from concerts by the group were paid to a company called Smithdom Limited, and Joyce claimed that as a partner he was entitled to a quarter share. 'Now that it is admitted there was a partnership agreement between the four members of the band, the presumption is one of equality' (Hackworth, 1996). Mr Davis said it was 'wrong to rubbish' Rourke and Joyce's contribution (Hackworth, 1996). The court was told that after Joyce raised the matter with Morrissey in 1988, they subsequently received £270,000.

After a seven-day hearing, Judge Weeks found in favour of Joyce, ordering that he receives approximately £1 million in back payments and 25 per cent henceforth. Morrissey, without Marr, unsuccessfully mounted an appeal to the Court of Appeal (Civil Division) in November 1998. Inspired by Joyce's success, Rourke reportedly considered legal options to continue the suit, although no further action was taken, presumably due to the earlier lasting renouncement of all further claims.

During legal proceedings, Morrissey revealed that Joyce had received £215,000 each from Marr and Morrissey in 1997, along with Marr's final back payment of £260,000 in 2001. Morrissey failed to make his final payment because, he said, he was overseas in 2001 and did not receive the paperwork. Joyce obtained a default judgement against Morrissey, revised his outstanding claim to £688,000, and secured orders to claim the singer's income and assets in the UK. This was a source of ongoing inconvenience and grievance to Morrissey, who estimated that Joyce had cost him at least £1,515,000 in recovered royalties and legal fees up to 30th November 2005.

Member Leaving

If differences cannot be resolved, whether family members or not, common disputes can feel overly personal and end up with someone leaving. When a member of a band is dismissed or choses to leave the record company will reserve the right to terminate the contract. The label may also try to obtain a clause allowing them to sign any leaving member as a solo artist, and if the group break up before releasing a record, but after spending their advance, they will probably be sued for breach of contract and return of the monies they have received. There are very clear commercial aspects which are important here, but it is very rare for there to be any process that tries to address what it feels like for both sides when someone leaves a group that they have been a part of for a long time. Being in a band is very like being in a family, you find some members easy to get on with and others irritating and difficult but there is a long-standing bond and some degree of co-dependence; for the band to succeed you all have to find ways to create and work together. So, when someone leaves, voluntarily or not, it is a loss like any other and may require grieving, or possibly celebration if it is a form of 'conscious uncoupling.' It is rare that every person in a group will feel the same when a person goes. For some it may be pure relief; others may feel guilty and haunted by the question of whether they could have done more to make it work or question whether the person is leaving because of them. There is no built-in exit report process as there may be in some professions where the leaver has an opportunity to feed back what has been good and what has been difficult about being in the group. In many industries, when a crisis happens there is often a 'debriefing' and checking of how those who remain are feeling. A band member leaving is often a crisis, but I have never seen a reflective process being used to help people move on. Instead, the hurt of individual band members can lead to desires to get revenge. A common tactic can be to dispute who thought of the band name. Examples of bands, across music genres, who have ended up arguing over who can continue to perform and record when a founding member leaves include Yes, ELP, Marillion, Wishbone Ash, Camel, Hawkswind, The Animals, Frankie Goes to Hollywood, Buck's Fizz, Fleetwood Mac, Sugababes, Rubettes.

It is not just disputes over names which occur following a band member leaving. For example, New Order were at loggerheads for years after bassist Peter Hook quit the band in 2007. In 2015, Hook sued the rest of New Order for continuing without him, although the seeds for the whole debacle were sown as far back as 1991. It is a long way from their days in Joy Division, the group from which New Order was born. In fact, *NME* looked to the band history to list 11 easy steps to kill a friendship, with every example being something one of the band members had done that had upset the others. The article presents a wonderfully clear example of how no communication, poor communication, or petty communication worsens a dispute. An early intervention could have prevented such escalation (Bassett, 2015).

Disputes between Artists and Publishing Companies

In the past, one or two persons would write songs and jointly enter into songwriter agreements under which they are obliged to provide a pre-agreed number of songs. Having said this, these days nearly all songs are co-written by far more than one or two people and a publisher only has a part of a song in their catalogue (in EDM, hip-hop, rap). How much each gets depends on negotiations between the parties and can result in big disagreements.

Disputes with Managers and Artists

The relationship between manager and artist is an extremely important one. The manager needs the artists but also exercises considerable power and control. There are many allegations about powerful managers ripping off the bands who employed them. These include some very famous examples. We only have to look to Elvis and Colonel Parker. Parker, who came from a circus background, had learnt the two secrets of getting people into a tent; always have a gimmick and always appeal to the lowest common denominator. Initially he worked with country music stars such as Eddy Arnold and Hank Snow before moving on to manage Elvis Presley. He was not willing to settle for the standard 10 per cent fee, instead demanding 25 per cent rising to 50 per cent. He wanted total control and demanded his fees up front. Although Parker blamed security issues for the reason Elvis never performed overseas, the truth lies with the Colonel's status as an illegal alien. If Parker left the country, he may have found it very difficult to return. He dominated and largely controlled Elvis' life.

Another major figure was the cuddly yet grizzly Albert Grossman who, in the 1960s, was known to intimidate record companies and artists. Although Dylan terminated his bitter relationship with Grossman in 1971, Grossman trailed Dylan for more than a decade, filing a multimillion-dollar lawsuit for back loyalties. In Martin Scorsese's *No Direction Home* (2005), Dylan said, 'He was kind of like a Colonel Parker figure. You could smell him coming.' At the time of his death in 1987, Grossman was still pursuing the money.

There are lots more such examples including Robert Stigwood who, when trying to control the Beatles, was told by Paul McCartney 'If you somehow manage to pull this off, we can promise you one thing. We will record "God Save the Queen" for every single record we make from now on, and we'll sing it out of tune' (Wall, 1998). Stigwood was also sued by the Bee Gees in 1980, claiming that Stigwood had withheld $75 million in royalties. Stigwood countersued, and they settled out of court, trading barbs in the press.

A former accountant, Allen Klein, became perhaps the most infamous manager of the rock and pop era. Once dubbed the 'Robin Hood of Pop,' he made an early name for himself by reaping millions in misappropriated royalties for clients such as Bobby Darin and Sam Cooke. A notoriously brash character and tough negotiator, Klein invented the role of business manager but his stance as the outsider siding with the artists, the enemy of the record companies, would have had a lot more credence if he hadn't succeeded in negotiating excellent, many would say extortionate, terms when he parted company with his clients.

The Beatles' manager Brian Epstein might have built a financial empire, but it collapsed two years after he died in 1967. At that point, Allen Klein swooped in to pick it clean. By the time he met the Beatles, he was negotiating megadeals for the Rolling Stones. John Lennon admired his street smarts, and George and Ringo followed suit, but Paul never fell prey to his charms. In fact, he often had nightmares about Klein in which the manager surfaced as an evil dentist. Although Paul McCartney posed for photos with the others at the Dorchester Hotel in London, he never put pen to paper on a deal with Klein, preferring to rely on the advice of Lee and John Eastman, his wife Linda's father and brother, which created further tensions.

The moment Klein took control of the Beatles, he gutted the band's production company, firing those he deemed superfluous. He then negotiated lucrative publishing and recording deals for the band with excessive commissions. Eventually McCartney sued not only Klein, but also the three other Beatles in the High Court. The group eventually paid Klein an estimated $4 million when all litigation between Apple and ABKCO was finally settled in January 1977. After the manager's contract with Lennon, Harrison, and Starr expired in March 1973, they opted not to renew it. Klein was the subject of veiled references in the Harrison song 'Beware of Darkness' and the Lennon composition 'Steel and Glass.'

Throughout the years, Klein soured several relationships. In September 1967, Klein took over as sole manager of the Rolling Stones after buying out their current manager, Andrew Oldham. Klein oversaw the most tumultuous period in the group's history with the fallout from Jagger and Keith Richards' drug bust earlier that year and Brian Jones's death in July 1969. A year later, with their Decca contract at an end, the group decided to make a clean break and oust Klein, who had grown increasingly uncommunicative, and to start their own label with distribution from Ahmet

Ertegun's Atlantic Records. The Stones went on to launch various lawsuits against Klein and his companies. Klein had no fear of litigation reportedly declaring, 'Nobody sues a failure, they only sue a success,' (*Independent*, 2009). He seemed to relish his reputation as 'the biggest bastard in the valley,' used colourful, earthy language, and declared, 'Artists fuck groupies. According to my reputation, I fuck the artists' (*Independent*, 2009). There are too many examples to give them all here, and unfortunately such disputes continue, with Taylor Swift in conflict with her former manager Scooter Braun being one such recent example.

In addition to these well-publicised examples, it is not unusual for there to be tensions between managers and artists at all levels. The narrative of the non-instrument playing friend who is given a role of manager is common. Band members meet in school or university, initially coming together as a friendship group, who then find commonality in music. Those who can write or play music form a band and have the dilemma of what to do with their enthusiastic friend who does neither of these things. Often that friend will become indispensable as the carrier of instruments, the driver of the van, etc., graduating to booking venues, arranging accommodation, and generally and gradually taking on the role of manager, often with this not being formalised until much later when the money starts coming in. This may immediately cause disagreements about the percentage they will be entitled to. The question may be dodged because of strong friendship links and ideas, leading blindly to the manager being given the same cut as everyone else, or this may come about as a value led decision on the part of everyone involved. One such scenario is described in one of the case studies in Part Two.

As we can see the structure of the music industry and the close relational aspects make it rife with conflict.

4 Current Responses to Conflict in the Music Industry

Some conflicts can be prevented or quickly resolved through the use of coaching or by the disputants using a set of skills to enhance the way they listen to each other. Unfortunately, it is not often that the music world goes to or uses these preventative measures, instead disputes tend to quickly escalate and become increasingly hostile.

By the time the conflict gets to this hostile stage, it becomes quite difficult to resolve without some sort of intervention. This is because more people are now involved in the original unresolved conflict, and this additional complexity creates group dynamics that are tricky to manage. For many of those dragged into the conflict, the whole matter starts to become about saving face, 'winning,' making the other suffer or punishing them, rather than about actual problem-solving and conflict resolution.

Currently, the industry tends to look to 'old' ways of resolving conflict, relying on expensive litigation. It is interesting that an industry that relies on being creative and fresh fails to make effective use of newer and more appropriate methods of dispute resolution.

Even if the coaching and intensive listening has not happened or has failed to work, there is a different and more appropriate way forward which picks up on the creativity of the industry by offering a creative way forward which can prove more beneficial to artists, management, and labels – mediation.

Given that, on paper, mediation looks so much more attractive than litigation, why is it that it is still not the regular first port of call? Most disputes head to litigation because the disputants are unaware of the alternatives and the benefits they present. Above I have given a brief overview of the differences between litigation and mediation and the advantages mediation offers.

Unfortunately, many people still see mediation as a 'soft option,' which will require them to 'rollover' or 'compromise.' This does not seem too attractive when emotions are high, each side believes they are in the right,

DOI: 10.4324/9781003675938-6

Table 4.1 Comparison of Litigation and Mediation

Litigate	*Mediate*
Can take years	Can be completed in one day
Expensive • You pay to instruct lawyers • You pay for the time you lose whilst going through a long process	Inexpensive • The costs are usually equally divided amongst the parties • An average mediation is in the region of £1,750 (disputes involving potential large pay outs may cost more)
Very stressful, formal process	Less stressful, less formal process
Court cases are open to the public and to the press	Confidential
Competitive • Tends to focus on wants • Focuses on differences • Sets up each side as being enemies in competition with one another • Provides an opportunity for the lawyer to 'battle' a colleague with a view to beating them	Conciliatory • Tends to focus on needs • Focuses on commonalities • Aims to see the dispute as the joint enemy – not the different sides
Destructive • Encourages one party to destroy the other	Creative • Encourages critical, creative and collaborative thinking and processes

and the disputants want revenge, to humiliate the other, to be proved 'right,' and to have their 'day in court,' no matter what the cost. Many people are aware of the financial costs involved in litigation but are unaware of the emotional and psychological cost of a long drawn out adversarial process.

Given that many people are unclear about what mediation is and how it works, let us have a quick look at the process and the philosophy underlining the approach.

5 Alternatives to Litigation

What Can Mediation, Coaching, and Consultancy Offer to Those in the Music Industry?

There are several ways of resolving conflict and also ways to manage it and avoid it being destructive. My original motivation in writing this book was to show what mediation can offer to those in the music industries as I believe that it provides a more creative, collaborative, and constructive approach than litigation, which is where most people still turn due to their lack of knowledge of mediation or because they 'want their day in court' and to prove they are right and 'put the other person in their place.' That is, they want to win, and that, in their view, requires someone else to lose.

Mediation still remains the focus of this section and of the whole of Part Two. However, in Part Three, I introduce some strategies and approaches which may help prevent destructive conflict developing to the level at which it requires the intervention of a third party.

Mediation

Mediation is well suited to conflicts in the music industry as it offers flexibility and encourages authenticity and creative thinking. Most musicians are creative and respond well to an invitation to be part of the creative process which mediation offers. The approach values lateral thinking and the exploration of non-traditional modes of settlement. By encouraging the participants to bring their own new ideas and thoughts into the mediation space, it is more likely to facilitate a settlement which has real personal meaning to the individuals involved and so has a greater chance of being honoured in practice going forward. Those mediators who employ a psychologically informed approach are best suited to working with creative individuals and accommodating the high level of emotional expression which may be present.

Psychologically informed mediators start with the belief that every individual is unique and so intercommunication between individuals is rich but innately complex, multidimensional, and unpredictable. This will be

DOI: 10.4324/9781003675938-7

true in any conflict situation, just as it is in all our interactions with others whatever the context.

Often a dispute may seem relatively simple in the first instance, and the mediator may believe that they immediately know how the whole thing can easily be resolved. However, a mediator must stop and ask themselves, 'if that is the case, why has it not settled without my help?'. It is arrogant to think that if there is a simple solution the mediator is the only one who can see it. It is rarely the surface issues which keep people in conflict; it is often the more sedimented reasons, often hidden from the conscious awareness of the disputants, which are the cause of prolonged disagreement. Kenneth Cloke (2006: 208) sums this up when he states,

> each person's attitudes, intentions, intuitions, awareness, context, and capacity for empathetic and honest emotional communication has [sic] a significant impact on their experience of conflict and capacity for resolution. As a result, no one can know objectively or in advance how to resolve any particular conflict, as anything chaotic and rapidly changing cannot be successfully predicted or managed.

My own training as an existential psychotherapist influences my approach as a mediator. As humans, we are all unique, and yet we are all very similar. These similarities, which bind us together in our humanness, are referred to, as mentioned in the introduction, as 'existential givens.' One of these givens is our need to be heard. This is a gift to anyone in a conflict situation. A common cause of conflict stems from a person not feeling listened to. If we truly feel listened to, we also feel respected, and so we are in a position to trust the listener. A mediator aims to develop a trusting relationship with all involved in any mediation. It is this strong working alliance with respectful and reflective listening at its heart which can help to unlock the conflict.

Phenomenologists, drawing on the works of Edmund Husserl (1859–1938), base their understanding about how we exist in the world on the premise that objects exist through the meaning that we give them. This is known as 'intentionality,' which occurs unconsciously. Husserl saw every act of intentionality as containing two parts; the 'noema,' which is directional, 'the object (the *what*) that we direct our attention towards and focus upon,' and the 'noesis,' which is referential, the '*how*' through which we define an object. It is important in a dispute that we listen to both the noematic (content) and the noetic (the individual's unique emotional experience of that content).

It is very rare that a dispute is simply about *facts*; it is about the way an individual perceives those *facts* and the emotional responses that perception evokes. We can only begin to really understand if we are aware of both the *facts* and the emotions attached to how these are perceived. It is like listening to both the top line (treble) and base (bass) line in a piece of music. Both these aspects are interpreted by the individual through the veils of their familial, cultural, and individual experiences, including their value sets and emotional context.

There are a few basic skills which help to elicit both these aspects. These include the use of encouraging body language, silence, not interrupting, open questions, reflecting back, paraphrasing, summarising, and the identification of themes, which are tracked and deconstructed (rather than analysed). This allows the listener to feed back any contradictions between noema and noesis, values and actions, body language and verbal content, any shifts in approach or outlook, the assumptions which are being expressed, and to explore the emotional content of the statements. To do this effectively the mediator has to learn to set aside their preconceptions and judgements and listen in an open way.

Through using these skills, mediators develop greater understanding of the individual's response to the dispute (e.g. emotions, value and belief systems, coping strategies, and factors influencing self-esteem) thus helping to understand the individual's fundamental world view and facilitate a deeper and more authentic dialogue.

Emotions

If we listen to the noesis, then we are listening to emotions. People are never without emotions, but the emotional context of what people say is often overlooked by the listener or disturbs the listener to such an extent that they attempt to filter it out. This may be due to lack of skill or fear of emotional expression. In understanding a person's emotional stance, the mediator gains an entry to their inner psychological world and is helped to interact more thoroughly, effectively, and empathically. Having one's own emotions noted may be a rare luxury which allows an individual to feel heard, leading to a major shift in the dispute, with an individual being more willing to shift from a stuck position to a more fluid approach.

Values and Beliefs

By gaining insight into the emotional world of those embroiled in a dispute, we discover the centrality of an individual's value system. Emotions are always attached to something, whether the object is within the person's consciousness or not. We often feel at our most emotional if our beliefs or values are attacked in some way. The attack may come from others or from ourselves (when we find ourselves behaving in ways which go against our beliefs). By understanding this, we can identify emotional stressors. A too rigid adherence to a value may be problematic; for example, if an individual places 'loyalty' high in their value set, they may feel the need to follow the behaviours of their peers or institution even when they experience those behaviours as destructive or wrong. We see the development of 'group speak' when individuals in a band make statements on behalf of all members without checking that everyone is in agreement or choosing to ignore any solitary voice of discontent. It is a very lonely place to be when you hear others speaking for you and saying things which may not be in tune with your values and beliefs.

The mediator's task is not to challenge the values, making a value judgement of whether they seem right or wrong to the mediator, but to understand how these values and beliefs are being played out within the dispute and to then challenge tensions, ambiguities, or rigidity, working towards a settlement which takes account of the values of each individual involved. To ignore these beliefs risks coming to a 'logical' solution in what is, essentially, an emotional situation. If the mediator misses this 'emotional point' in any way, then the chance of any agreement being adhered to diminishes.

Coping Strategies

People develop coping strategies in response to life's challenges. Often these work well, and the individual automatically employs them without being conscious of doing so; they become an automatic response. A common strategy is to choose a position as a 'leader' or a 'follower.' For some, their successful coping strategy is to adopt a leadership position and to forge forward, hopefully taking others with them. Others may adopt a position as follower, preferring not to be in the front line. It does not mean that by taking a follower position, one cannot lead. Many good leaders seek out the opinions of others, empower others, and lead from the back.

Unfortunately, a coping strategy which works well in most circumstances can cause problems in others. In a mediation, the disputant can be facilitated to see different ways of coping without losing self-esteem.

Through the mediation process, the mediator needs to be both follower and a leader. The mediator has to 'tune in' to the unique world of the individuals and to follow their stories without any judgement. The mediator follows where the party takes them, respecting and working with the values, emotions, and coping strategies expressed in order to explore their perception of the dispute.

Challenging

People in conflict often feel powerless. It is important that disputants are reminded of their responsibilities and potential for choice. Although we are unable to change the incident which led to the dispute, we can change the attitude towards it.

Tuning in is not enough. The disputant has to learn to understand and be sensitive to the perceptions of the other without getting stuck in their newly found mutuality and ignoring what steps need to be taken to address the specific conflict and move towards a resolution. This can only occur when trust has been established and both parties are respectfully heard. People are more inclined to be open and creative if they feel they have been listened to with respect. They no longer need to fight their corner because there is no one to fight against – they have been heard and witnessed. Identifying when that moment has arrived is a skill which uses knowledge of human behaviour but also relies heavily on experience.

The mediator may help the individuals identify what might happen if they choose not to agree to a resolution (e.g. go to court, lose their job, their family, their pride, their self-esteem, etc.). It is equally creative and sometimes surprising to consider what would happen if they do get exactly what was asked for, as there may well be losses attached. Getting what they thought they wanted may achieve material gain but fail to bring the emotional state they were hoping for. This is often the case when the focus of a settlement is financial.

Self-esteem

People in conflict often have low self-esteem stemming from a sense of embarrassment that they have been unable to resolve the dispute. They may feel disempowered and have lost any sense that they have the power to choose how they respond to the dispute.

To maintain a good level of self-esteem, we need opportunities for self-expression and respectful listening. We need to understand the world views and responses to conflict of the disputants – do they provoke it, fear it, enjoy it, tolerate it, run from it or see it as an opportunity for creativity? The mediator works with the disputant to help them to clarify their own stance.

A psychologically informed mediator will seek to maintain or even increase the self-esteem of all those involved in the mediation. At the same time, they will haul in their own natural desire to increase their own self-esteem by appearing to know the answers and to hold the solution in their hands. The disputants are always responsible for the solution; the mediator's role is one of facilitation.

What Happens in a Mediation

On a very practical basis, a mediation follows a simple but flexible framework which the mediator can adapt to meet the needs of the parties and context. Indeed, I have mediated in lush corporate spaces, on the streets with gangs whilst sitting on walls, in the townships of Cape Town, South Africa, in the barracks of paramilitary organisations, and many other unconventional places. The process I use, although obviously adapted when used in some of the situations I have just outlined, is based on the Harvard model, sometimes referred to as shuttle mediation. It was developed originally in response to conflicts in the car industry in the US.

The Mediation Process

The mediator will have confidential, individual pre-mediation conversations with each person who will be attending the mediation day (including lawyers, union officials, friends, etc.). These may be in person or by phone or online. These sessions allow the mediator and the party to clarify what will happen, agree times, venue, fees, etc., but also for the mediator to hear what is important for that person and any worries they may have about mediation.

Everyone will then meet for a day of mediation, which ideally starts with everyone in the same room. The mediator will lay out the ground rules and remind everyone of the process, that everything is confidential and without prejudice, and that the mediator is there as a facilitator not a judge. Each person will then be invited to briefly say what has brought them to mediation, before splitting into individual sessions. The mediator will go between sessions with each of the parties, and when they consider that there is some commonality or movement, they will bring them together to see if an agreement can be reached which everyone is willing to sign and which the mediator will witness.

The Psychological Ebb and Flow within the Mediation Process

Unfortunately, it is often not quite that simple, as the mediation process is neither chronological nor linear. The trusting working alliance may be built and lost a number of times throughout the process. The 'tuning in' process (through active listening) is the central element in building that alliance, with the requirement to enter into the other's world view with its value sets, coping strategies, and emotional reactions.

Once the alliance is established and an understanding of the other's world view developed, the parties in the dispute need to 'tune out' and enter back into the 'world of the dispute' with its concrete and emotional implications. By moving into this phase, we begin to focus on possible solutions in order to facilitate a 'good enough' solution.

When mediating, I hold an internal image of a funnel with the early parts of the process being very open – the mediator following the party – whereas towards the end of the process, the focus needs to be closed down, becoming more focused towards identifying potential elements of the dispute and potential agreement.

In 'tuning in,' the emphasis lies in consciously listening for descriptors of the inner world of the speaker that show their values, emotions, and behaviour patterns. It is important to take everything that is said as being of equal importance and significance. Heraclitus found every 'unapparent' connection to be stronger than an 'apparent' one – everything is connected and meaningful. Freud and other psychoanalysts taught us to accept that all that is presented contains unconscious communications as well as conscious ones. The client may find it hard to tell the mediator things which can make them feel vulnerable, silly, or guilty or where they feel the mediator may potentially disagree with them. They may experience paradoxical responses to the dispute and/or the people involved.

The mediator may pick up on any theme, even if it seems very far removed from the actual dispute, and unpack it, controlling their own needs to offer a solution or make 'inspirational' links. At this stage, the client is the leader, and the mediator follows, slowly unwrapping the meaning of what is being presented through paraphrasing, reflecting back, and summarising without judgement. The mediator must trust in the process and believe that everything said in the early stage is relevant, giving indicators of the values, life strategies, and emotional stance of the speaker.

This intense listening, in itself, builds trust which can then be used to focus down / 'tune out,' allowing focus on the conflict and possible resolutions. The mediator can then challenge the client to think differently about their response to the dispute and to consider what they really want as an outcome.

Coaching

Mediation can be used as soon as people recognise that there is a dispute. Unfortunately, most people use it as 'the last chance saloon.' Before things get that far, there are other interventions which may help. Some psychologically minded people use a coach to work with them collectively and/or individually. Some individuals prefer being on their own and are challenged by working and often needing to live closely with others. This preference for being and working alone can eventually result in a talented and valued individual leaving the group.

A coach might help to sharpen and test out some dialogue and negotiation skills or prepare for unexpected turns or worst-case scenarios. With conflict coaching, a conflict resolution practitioner can work with an individual, mentoring in any of the particular skill areas required. They enable the person to prepare effectively to approach someone they have a problem with. The aim being to work through the issues together in a productive and positive manner.

A coach can work with individuals to identify what they find most difficult and help them to identify coping strategies and develop additional interpersonal skills. They can provide ongoing telephone, online, or email support, particularly during stressful times such as touring or when the group are away working and living closely together in the recording studio. They can also work with other members of the group to enable the group to better understand and work with the needs of a more introverted individual.

Another thing a coach can do is to look at the group dynamics and identify any negative recurring behaviours which are likely to increase tension within the group and potentially cause disputes. This often requires addressing internal competition, jealousy, and resentment. Group members are often very reluctant to expose what they see as their vulnerabilities, deciding instead to stay silent and risk the group disintegrating.

Coaches may also work with those working at the business end of the music industry. Often the different world views of the artists and the businessperson can result in both sides making it difficult for each to understand the other, leading to misunderstanding and conflict. A coach can work as a kind of 'translator,' helping develop that understanding. The coach may also be able to facilitate the development of a language (verbal, emotional, and psychological) which makes sense to both sides and allows them to communicate more effectively.

Coaches would seek to explore similar issues to those already described in introducing the potential for mediation, but they can focus on how these impact each individual and work with the person to quickly identify triggers and hot buttons and develop positive strategies to address them.

Consultancy

Consultancy can be particularly helpful to those at the business end of the music industry. It can form a bridge between the creative and the business manager or organisation. It can help each side better understand the other, identify common needs and potential cultural (values and beliefs) incompatibilities. If these differences are acknowledged they can be discussed and worked with.

In Part Two, I offer some semi-fictionalised examples of mediation in practice.

Part Two

Case Examples of Mediation in Action

Introduction to Part Two

I have worked a lot with creative people. This has often included working with bands. Bands, no matter the music genre, share important commonalities. They require people to work together towards a common goal and to make decisions which impact on all members. The structure for this decision making can be conscious or unconscious, formal or informal.

Most bands experience both external and internal conflict. As I have mentioned earlier, potential sources of this strife are common across the array of band styles. Disagreements often occur due to the differing aspirations of the members, the different level of time members contribute to the group, musical direction, egos – upstaging one another, substance use, relationship with management/record companies, the type of decision-making structure which is in place (or indeed, absent), competition among the participants, monetary issues – share of royalties/bills/money, workload, punctuality, career conflicts, who to hire/fire, relationships with families, girlfriends, boyfriends, partners, etc., what will be worn on stage/for photo shoots etc. The list is endless.

Often, at the core of all these conflicts, lie issues of self-esteem and a perceived lack of fairness, empathy, and/or acknowledgement. Some of these conflicts create more acrimony than others, but a band that wishes to survive must find ways to mediate these differences.

The dialogue, in the case studies which follow, is taken from individual meetings or phone conversations between the mediator and each of the parties in the dispute before they met together to mediate the dispute. In the actual cases, I spoke with all the people in the dispute. This often meant one person on one side and several on the other.

I have semi-fictionalised some of the mediations I have worked on, changing names, venues, gender, and occasionally running two separate but similar disputes into one in order to protect confidentiality. The conversations are of course shortened and presented through different

DOI: 10.4324/9781003675938-8

voices, as all these mediations involved several people and many telephone conversations, plus a day of face-to-face mediation. I believe that although they cannot show a true representation of a full day of mediation and several hours of pre-mediation meetings, they do give a realistic flavour of people's thoughts and dilemmas and show how mediation can help.

As mediator I used the tuning in and tuning out phases and the techniques of active listening referred to earlier – reflecting back, paraphrasing, and summarising. Each session was strictly confidential with nothing reported back to the other party unless I was specifically asked to do so.

6 Case Study 1 – The Producer: Creative Battles

Jamie He thinks he is fantastic, that's his problem. Who does he think he is? OK, he has produced a successful album for someone else, but that isn't the same as being a band member, working together, being creative together, having fun together. I think he wants that. He is jealous. I think that is what must be behind all of this. He doesn't like being a 'behind the scenes guy.' He wants his moment in the spotlight. None of the fans are interested in who produces the record.

Anyway, even when he was a success producing a hit album for X, they didn't ask him to produce their next album and that was an even bigger success without him. I'm not surprised they didn't want to work with him again. He is a pain in the arse.

He acts as if he leads this band. I … and the others … are treated as though we have no importance at all, as though we have nothing to offer and should just stand in the corner and play what he wants us to. He messes around with the songs we have written so they end up totally different to how we want them to sound.

Henry Look I am incredibly successful. If I say it myself, and I'm not the only one saying it, I am really brilliant at what I do. Lots of bands seek me out, wanting me to work with them. I don't have to go looking for work. They know that I am successful and that I can make them successful. I know what it takes to make something a commercial success. I work all over Europe. I have my own studios here and in Spain.

Jamie is just a pain in the arse. He hasn't a clue, and I am fed up of his moods and negativity. If he wants success he should listen to me and be grateful. He can learn a lot. I can help him. He just needs to get on with it, do what I suggest, and he will be part of something good and successful. He knows that deep down, so what is his problem?

DOI: 10.4324/9781003675938-9

Jamie Look, having a major input into how the end product sounds is really important to me. I love seeing how something which I have written can be added to by the other band members. We all offer each other ideas but respect whose work it is ... where it originated. I like performing, but I find the process of taking an idea through to the finish probably even more fulfilling. Seeing and hearing it out there ... sounding as I hoped it would sound ... you know ... it's quite a buzz.

In my previous band I wrote all the songs. In some ways I was the band. It couldn't have existed without me. I forged its identity. Despite that, what held us together was that we were all friends. We had known one another forever, from school. Our parents knew one another. They would take turns driving all our equipment to gigs. You get the picture?

I thought we were going to make it big. We did get interest from record companies, but I guess life and events took over. I was all for giving it a real go, not taking up my place at uni, and working full-time with the band. I think Phil and Joe were up for that too. Brian got a lot of pressure from his mum to go off and do a degree, but he stood up to her. Anyway, we all decided that we would give it a year and throw all our energy, time, and savings into making an album and see where we went from there.

We worked really hard and got some amazing demos together. I wrote all the lyrics, but we collaborated on the music. We sent the demos off to a few places. There was interest but basically the message was the same – we weren't commercial enough. The companies didn't think they would make enough money from us.

That was when we made our first mistake. Brian had been left some money from his grandfather, and we decide to use it to get in a producer who could make our stuff more commercial and so more attractive to the record companies. We reckoned that if we got some initial interest we could slowly, over time, revert to the less commercial, more innovative new stuff, the stuff we were really interested in. We just needed the break. Well, as you can probably guess, the nearest producer who seemed to be having success was Henry, and so we approached him to work on the album with us.

Henry I have known Jamie for years, and he has always been a pain. I came across him some years ago when he was with his previous band. They were doing well on the local circuit and had played a few small festivals, but they were a bit too arty-farty to be a commercial success. That was mainly due to Jamie's style and song writing. He wanted to be Tom Yorke ... There is only one of him ... thank God, in my opinion. It was the likes of One Direction that were making the money and the record companies wanted clones of them. People wanted simple and danceable, not something to make them think and feel like ending it all! It's the young girls who finance the music industry; they want pretty boys and upbeat music to make them feel good.

Anyway, Jamie financially realised that to get anywhere they needed to be more commercial, and so the band approached me to work with them on producing an album. I reckoned I could make a success of it ... give them that commercial edge they needed. Jamie is a good-looking guy, so they looked alright; they just needed something which appealed to a bigger market.

Jamie Henry came on board when we already had the songs together and knew what we wanted on the album. At first, he was very positive about the songs, full of praise for them, but gradually, he started imposing his ideas, radically changing what we sounded like. We were prepared to make some changes. After all, we were employing him so that we could get some recognition, and that does mean sounding more commercial. I know that, but we don't want to end up sounding like everyone else. We want our sound to be recognisable and different.

Brian was funding his employment and is desperate for the album to succeed so that he doesn't let his family down or be seen to have wasted his grandfather's inheritance money. I think he was a bit overawed by Henry because Henry has been involved in some major hits.

Henry is very manipulative and knows that Brian is the one with the money, so he is always incredibly nice with him ... invites him on his own round to his studio ... goes out drinking with Brian You get the picture?

Henry It was Brian who invited me to produce their album. He's a great guy. We get on really well.

I gather he is funding the album from money he inherited from his grandfather. He approached me because of the work I had done with X. They had a huge success with the album I produced for them and are still raking the money in as two of the tracks are being used on car commercials ... . That's where the money is these days. In fact, I am surprised that X haven't used me on their second album, perhaps they thought I would up my fees given what I did for them with the first ... .

Anyway, Brian sees things how they are; he knows what is needed to have a hit … . He is more realistic and commercial than the others, especially Jamie. Jamie sees himself as a creative genius … out there … blazing a new trail. Well, that's all well and good but that gets you nowhere financially.

Jamie Henry has Brian twisted round his little finger. Brian keeps saying we should do exactly what Henry says as he knows what he is doing, and we need his expertise. Now, I think it was a mistake bringing him on board in the first place. I have spoken to Jake, the songwriter for X, and he said he was about to lay one on him by the time they finished their album. Jake said they had to fight Henry all the way to avoid sounding like some X Factor boy band. He wouldn't work with Henry again no matter what.

I agree that this album has to be commercial, but it also has to be 'us,' our sound … show who we are … what we believe in. What's the point of becoming well known for work you are ashamed of? People will expect the same style in the second album. You will have attracted fans who like stuff you don't want to keep producing and then you are stuck.

As well as trying to change our sound … who we are … now he is insisting on playing in the band!!! He is fed up of being in the background, like some weird Wizard of Oz. Oh no, manipulating us like a puppet master isn't enough; now he wants to be out there too. OK, he starts just playing guitar, but I can see where it is all heading … . Next thing he will suggest that he sings a couple of his own songs and then he becomes lead singer, and I'm ousted! That's his real plan.

Henry I am excited by what they are doing … . Really … . Jamie has got an amazing voice and incredible stage presence. He makes a terrific frontman. He's got the looks, the attitude … one that works well with the crowd … but one that makes him a pain to work with. They just need a bit of commercial know-how, and that is where I come in. I appreciate that they don't want to sound like everyone else, but they have to be accessible, at least with the first album. Too weird, and they will frighten people off. They won't get the important airtime.

I was really surprised when Brian asked if I would like to play on one of the tracks. After all, I am a frustrated performer. There really is nothing better than being out there, on stage … feeling it. I enjoy the production work but it's not the same. The additional guitar really adds something. I think it would work with most of the tracks. I'm not sure what Jamie thinks … . He hasn't said anything. I'm hoping he will hear the power the extra guitar brings and invite me to join the band, but I think that's very unlikely … . He clearly doesn't like me. I know when we first started talking, I wasn't very complimentary about him. He is arrogant and doesn't want to listen to my suggestions. I can understand that really… . He has written all the songs, and I wouldn't like someone coming in and telling me what to do with something I had created. I guess in many ways, we are quite alike.

Ideally, I would like my own band. I tried it once, but it didn't work out. Once I have finished working on this project, I am going to give it another try. I have already got a few people together who are interested. I have learnt a lot through producing for others but now I want to get out there and let people hear my own stuff.

Jamie I can't tell you how shocked I was when Henry just sauntered into the rehearsal with his guitar and just joined in. Everyone has lost the plot. I have no idea what is going on … what Henry thinks he is doing … why the others aren't saying anything. I just about held it together and thought 'enough is enough' and rang you before I did anything I would live to regret. I need this sorted. I can see what his game is … edge me out … leaving him to lead the band.

Henry I don't really know why Jamie is hacked off with me and why he set up this mediation. I think he has mixed feelings about the need to change his work to make it more commercial … . He is a good songwriter. Personally, I admire his work a lot. Jamie is pushing the limits … . He is doing really new stuff. I wish more people would buy the sort of stuff he is producing. It has depth, but that means the listener really has to engage with it.

It's not really very stimulating for me to have to stick with a successful formula to try to get a commercial hit. It gets very boring. I would like to try different things but that is not why Brian brought me in. He needs to show his family he is not wasting his time or his inheritance. He needs a success.

Reflections on the mediation

Bands, no matter the music genre, share important commonalities. They require people to work together towards a common goal and to make decisions which impact on all members.

Jamie and Henry's experience is reminiscent of many I have mediated. Some of the toughest issues in bands have nothing to do with writing, recording, or performing music. They have to do with the other people in the band and how you perceive them and work with them.

It is quite common in a dispute, for characters who are, at least initially, negatively portrayed by each other to, at some level, admire each other. When this is expressed, however subtly, it is something the mediator will mentally note, as it is usually an indication that if things can be clarified, the two people would like to continue to work together.

Having listened to Jamie and Henry separately, I began to identify some of the themes of the conflict and some of the commonalities in the two characters. Both loved the world of music. Both were jealous of the other. Jamie envied Henry's fame and past commercial success, whilst Henry envied Jamie's charisma, innovation, connection with an audience, and creativity.

Both wanted a leadership role. Jamie literally took centre stage whilst Henry was behind the scenes. Both had a desire to be recognised as central and acknowledged for their talents. There was a lot they had in common. All of this may not have been apparent from what each of them were saying at the beginning but through a developing dialogue with the mediator it was possible for these things to be expressed.

When we are in a dispute with another person, it is often hard for us to accept that we have anything in common with the other person. That other person takes on an 'alien' presence. They are someone we cannot understand and, equally, a person who cannot understand us. Indeed, we don't want to accept that we are like them in any way, and there may be no desire at all to understand them; what we want is to be understood and validated by the other! A mediator will listen out for commonalities and, when the time is right, will try to bring these to the fore.

In the beginning, it is important for the mediator to focus entirely on the individual they are in dialogue with, to just listen and use the skills of reflecting back, paraphrasing, and summarising to clarify what is being said and to ensure that the speaker knows they are being heard. At this stage, the mediator does not challenge each individual's view of the situation. The task of the mediator at this stage is to build rapport and develop a trusting relationship. This is the tuning in phase.

Once this relationship has been established, the mediator can then start to tune out of the single perception of the dispute and begin to gently challenge, still using active listening skills. A mediator will reflect back any ambiguities and, as in this case, will look for misconceptions about the other person. Here, Henry expressed a lot of ambivalent feelings towards Jamie, starting out expressing the negatives, implying Jamie was naïve with regard to making music a commercial success but then going on to also acknowledge his strengths as a frontman and, much later, show real admiration for his songwriting.

It became clear that Henry was trying to work to the agenda of the person who had brought him into the project – Brian. It was Brian who really needed a commercial hit to justify his decision not to take up his university place and the way he was choosing to spend his inheritance. Indeed, Brian was a key player in the dispute, but he was absent from the mediation. The whole conflict was being presented as one between Jamie and Henry.

When Jamie and Henry met together for the mediation, I was able to reflect back to each of them, with their expressed permission, that there were skills and attributes each admired in the other and areas of commonality. During the mediation I was able to challenge and seek clarification about several assumptions:

- Was Jamie aware of how Brian was feeling and his need for commercial success and what was driving it?
- Did he know what Brian was asking of Henry?
- What made him believe that Henry wanted to take over the band?
- Had he talked to Henry about this?
- Was he aware that Henry intended to start his own band when he had finished work on their album?
- Did he know that Henry admired his work?
- Was Henry aware that Jamie believed he was trying to usurp him?

Once it was clarified that Henry was not interested in taking over from Jamie and was playing guitar in the band at the invitation of Brian as a temporary means to gain stage experience before starting up his own band, Jamie began to see that his fears weren't justified. Henry was not trying to take his place. For Henry, this band was not his future but a means of transition.

Jamie was also able to start questioning himself – did he really want the kind of commercial success that Henry's style might bring? He began to see that some of his anger was directed at himself. He knew deep down that he wanted to continue producing work he believed in and that commercial success was not his main priority. He had felt a kind of 'duty' to seek that success as reward for all that Brian and the others had put into the band, but he was deeply unhappy with what that would mean for his creative authenticity. Bravely, Jamie expressed all this in Henry's presence, allowing Henry to witness Jamie's internal struggle.

At this point, Henry and Jamie's relationship took a dramatic turn. Instead of being opponents, they became collaborators. Henry asked Jamie if he wanted him to continue to produce his album. After a long pause, Jamie responded that he wasn't sure it would still feel like 'his' album if he did. Henry clearly understood this and helpfully suggested a different producer more sympathetic to Jamie's needs. He added that this would enable Jamie to make an album that reflected his true style and creativity and that he wished him well with it. He also reminded Jamie that what would result would be more of an 'art-house album' and unlikely to be a commercial success. By now, Jamie was clear that he would be happy with that and that he could live without being well known as long as he was respected and enjoyed by those who understood his music.

This led them on to collaboratively discuss Brian's needs. It was clear Brian did want and need a commercial and financial success, and that Henry was well placed to help make this happen. At this point, they brought Brian into the mediation.

Brian felt the need for Jamie's stage presence and command of the audience and was not happy at the thought of Jamie leaving the band and 'going it alone'. Together, they came up with the idea that Jamie would make a 'solo' album, under his own name, and make a commercial album with the band, not focused on his own songs.

A band meeting was called, and the two album strategy was agreed. It seemed that two members of the original band had also written a number of songs, and these now became tracks on the album, together with one by Henry! The success of the more commercial album meant that Jamie has some finance to back his solo project.

7 Case Study 2 – The Stolen Equipment: Internal Rivalry

Josh I knew it was a mistake taking her on as our drummer. Yes, I guess it adds a bit of interest, a female drummer … not many of them around, so a bit of a USP for us. She is OK at what she does, not technically as good as Joe, our last drummer, but she thinks she is the bee's knees and should have special privileges 'cos she is a girl.

Nicole I feel very let down by all of them. They came to me. I didn't go begging to them to be a member of the band. I was already with an all-girl band. We were doing alright but weren't getting the opportunities that Josh's band were getting. There were good things about my previous band. We acted more as a collective. We wrote stuff together although most of the original ideas came from me. It was less competitive. I tended to lead on ideas about what we might wear and what the set list should be, and the others were happy with that … . I studied fashion at uni, so they knew I had an eye for design and that sort of thing.

I would say we all liked one another. They weren't too happy with me leaving though … . We aren't on speaking terms now. That hurts.

Josh She turned out to be really unreliable and quite a prima donna. I think she had seen herself as a bit of a leader in her previous band and wanted to impose her presence on us. That wasn't what we were looking for. We just wanted a replacement for Joe.

Joe and his girlfriend have a small child, and she was kicking off about all the late-night shows. I don't think she was finding it easy looking after a teething baby all night and then have Joe arrive home late on a high. It's a shame as Joe was really easy to get along with and an amazing drummer … high energy … you know … .

DOI: 10.4324/9781003675938-10

Nicole I was hopeful that things would really happen with this new band but as I got to know them all better, I realised that they don't really have much to offer creatively. They just play what Josh wants to play. He started the band, and I think they kind of feel they owe it to him to do what he wants as they have never played with anyone else.

Josh We were a great band of brothers, but now Nicole has ruined all that. She is very domineering, and as I said before, she is unreliable. She skips rehearsals and turns up for gigs at the very last minute. She relies on us to get her kit there and to set it up.

Nicole I offered some really helpful ideas about how the band could be more stylish. Wear more interesting gear and all that. But they weren't interested, said they wanted to be true to who they are.

I chose to be a drummer because there are a lot of female singers and guitarists around. I thought it would make me more marketable. It is still unusual for there to be a female drummer in an otherwise all-male band, and I suggested they could make more of that. I don't want to spend all my life in the background. I want people to notice me. I would stand out more as the only female in the band. I could be on a riser, so it was easier for the audience to see me. But oh no … 'We are all about equality … . No-one should stand out.' Well, of course, that is all bullshit. Of course Josh stands out … . It's all his music, and he positions himself centre stage. The others do offer some harmony vocals and have guitar solos, but it is still all about Josh.

Anyway, I have had enough. Who does he think he is? About a month ago, he took me out for coffee but only to have a go at me. He told me I was ungrateful for all they did for me … like them taking my kit to gigs, etc. Well, it wouldn't make sense not to! All the guitars and mics etc. go in the same van so why not my drums? Who does he think he is? He spoke to me as though he was my headmaster and I was a naughty schoolgirl.

Josh I tried to talk to her. I took her out for a coffee and explained that she couldn't just expect people to carry her. We are all responsible for getting our stuff to gigs and arriving in plenty of time. She just pops the keys of her garage, where she keeps her kit, through my door, and expects me to pick it up in the van. It probably sounds pretty stupid, of course it isn't a problem to take all the equipment together … . It is just that she *assumes* this is what will happen and never asks or thanks anyone.

She really hated me talking to her about it and stormed out of the café. That meant I didn't get the opportunity to talk to her about missing rehearsals and all the other things which are driving us all mad.

Nicole The way I was treated in that café was the final straw. How dare he! Anyway, after that meeting I began to get in touch with all my contacts as I intend to jump ship. I can't go until I have another band to go to. My old band replaced me, and we still aren't on speaking terms, so I can't go back to that. I got a couple of auditions recently, which meant I missed a few rehearsals, but that is no problem; I know my stuff and don't need to rehearse with the rest of them. Anyway, I think they see rehearsals as time for the lads to get together and have a few beers.

Josh Things didn't improve. They got worse and worse. She hardly came to any rehearsals and looked fairly sullen throughout gigs. She wasn't speaking to any of us. She would turn up late and leave immediately we left the stage … leaving us to sort the kit, of course.

Anyway, two weeks ago, she just failed to turn up to a gig. Well, by that I mean no keys were dropped through my door, and when we turned up at her garage anyway, it was locked and there was no one there. Fortunately, the drummer from the support band stood in and did an OK basic job, but it felt awful. We were letting our fans down and not doing ourselves justice.

Nicole Fortunately, about two weeks ago, I was asked to play with another girl band. I didn't hesitate. They had a gig that night, I already knew their set, and so I just decided to join them there and then. I didn't owe Josh and the others anything; they had made it clear they didn't value me, so it was their loss.

I have high hopes of this new band. They are quite young and inexperienced, and I think I can make my mark here. They have agreed to move the drums centre stage and to follow up on some design ideas I have, so we look different, and people will remember us.

Josh Not only did she just fail to show, but we heard afterwards that she had performed with another band that same evening! We talked about it and decided that we were better off without her, and we would just let it go, whilst making it known around the circuit what an unreliable bitch she is. We thought that would be more productive than trying to have it out with her.

We got a new drummer pretty quickly, and we already had drum tracks laid down. It was then we realised that she had walked off with the drum machine, which belonged to the band. This is just too much. We didn't make a fuss when she left as we were glad to see the back of her, but walking off with our equipment is just taking the piss and we want it back.

Nicole I heard they got a new drummer pretty quickly, which was fine with me. I didn't want any more to do with them.

Then I heard they were using backing tracks which I laid down and that isn't on. I had forgotten to return their drum machine ... . It's only a crappy little thing anyway ... but I thought that was playing dirty ... using my work and not acknowledging my work or paying me for it, so I have decided to hang on to the machine until they pay me for using those tracks without my permission.

Josh I really don't get her. She left us in the lurch. She has loads of kit, and I can't see why she wants to keep that thing. It ain't the greatest piece of kit, but it's important to us. It has programmes on it, which would be great for our new drummer.

Reflections on the Mediation

These are snippets of conversations I had with Nicole and Josh. From these individual conversations I was able to identify the key aspects of the conflict and why Nicole was acting in the way she was. Nicole had seen joining Josh's band as a great opportunity. Nicole is very ambitious. She believed that being the only female in the band meant she had the chance to stand out, something which wasn't possible in her previous all-female band. She wanted to be raised above the band so that the audience could see her, and she wanted to direct the look of the band, offering to act as stylist and choose what people wore on stage. In most bands the drummer is at the back of the stage and can feel invisible. Nicole was very clear that she wanted visibility and ultimately to be a celebrity. The music was of less interest to Nicole than style.

Unfortunately, that was not how the rest of the band wanted it. They were all about the sound and were only looking for a good replacement drummer not a superstar. They were not interested in focusing on Nicole, and they found her to be arrogant, irritating, and profoundly unprofessional with her casual attitude to rehearsals and timekeeping.

In many ways Josh considered this was 'water under the bridge.' The band and Nicole had not found what they wanted from working together. Nicole had wanted attention, and the band had wanted a reliable drummer who was a team player. Although Nicole's behaviour had irritated Josh and the guys, they felt that they just wanted to put that behind them and move on with their new drummer. The point that had brought them to mediation was Nicole holding on to the band's drum machine. Nicole was angry that the band was using tracks she had recorded, and they were angry that she was refusing to return the machine.

During the mediation, Josh and Nicole were able to express their anger and disappointment. Although Josh had considered this to be something which should just be forgotten, it was important that they had the opportunity to speak to each other about these feelings.

Nicole acknowledged that she had been thoughtless in expecting the band to sort her equipment for her and that now she was having to do it herself she understood that it wasn't just a small thing, and she should have shown that she appreciated what they did rather than take it as a given. She still did not acknowledge that her timekeeping was a problem, claiming that it took ages for the guitars to be tuned and mics sorted and that she did not need to be there for that. Josh tried to explain that being there was important because it showed commitment and developed trust and a feeling of 'all being in it together.' Being in it together was never part of what Nicole wanted as she wanted to be seen as different. Josh understood this and agreed this made it impossible for it to work with her in the band, as they saw themselves as a collective. Nicole did argue with this, claiming that everything centred around Josh, but Josh explained that if she had attended band meetings, she would know that the others were fine with how it was and offered that she could check that with them. Nicole shrugged her shoulders and said it didn't matter now anyway, the others were grown-ups, and if it was ok with them then so be it.

Both acknowledged that Nicole being in the band did not work for either of them. Nicole was not getting the individual exposure she wanted, and the band was not getting a reliable member.

Nicole expressed how angry she had been when she heard the band was using the tapes she played on. She felt that 'something had been stolen' from her. In turn, Josh expressed his anger that she had 'stolen something from the band' – the drum machine. By the mediation day, the band had rerecorded the tracks using the new drummer. Josh brought the original tracks in and gave them to Nicole, who handed over the drum machine. Both signed an agreement which stated that neither the band nor Nicole would use tracks which Nicole had played on.

By the end of the mediation both had what they had requested and were able to move on with their careers.

8 Case Study 3 – The Manager: Saying Goodbye to a Lifelong Friend

Tom I have known the guys most of my life. We met up when they first got the group together playing local pubs, colleges … that sort of thing. I knew them from the local music scene … as fellow music lovers and friends. We would often turn up at the same gigs and end up in the pub together afterwards.

I love their music. I was one of their first 'fans', almost a 'groupie,' I guess you could say. I went to all their gigs.

I'm passionate about music although I can't play any instrument well or sing … more's the pity. I felt part of the scene as I wrote articles for the local music paper and always made sure to cover what the band were doing, publicise their gigs, and give them positive reviews. We got along really well. I saw us as close friends and enjoyed being with them.

Gary We have all known Tom for ages. We became friends as we were always turning up at the same gigs. We were into the same kind of music. He was a great guy and used to write articles for the local music press. He made sure to feature the band a lot, and that got us quite a few of our early gigs. He was a very loyal follower. He had incredible local networks on the scene, knew where the best venues were, that sort of thing. He really helped us in the early days.

Tom When they started to get busy with gigs, they needed a hand organising things … organising themselves mainly. Si couldn't be trusted to turn up to the right place at the right time, Russell tended to forget things, extra guitar strings, change of shirts … that sort of thing. Gary was the most straightforward and Martin the most anxious. Anyway, they asked me to help them, and I was really pleased to be asked. It felt like being part of the band.

Over time I took over finding and booking venues. I drove the van to and from gigs. I made sure they knew where they

DOI: 10.4324/9781003675938-11

had to be, for what time, and what they had to do. It was an amazing time.

Gary Tom started suggesting venues for us to play. They were all great places he found. We wouldn't have known about them if it wasn't for him. He offered to drive the van and pack the stuff – he was sort of a roadie-cum-manager. He even started to negotiate what payment we could get. We weren't very good at negotiating money. In those days we were just grateful that people would let us play.

I think it was around that time we thought he should take a cut of the money we made as a way of thanking him. We liked to think of ourselves as equal, so we gave Tom a fifth of our earnings. Nothing was ever written down. There was nothing formal. It worked well. Tom was good at anticipating what we needed and just got on and did it.

Tom After a few months, the band was really busy. I had helped to find them many of the gigs, and they suggested that they would like to pay me something to show their appreciation of the help I was giving them. I was amazed.

To be honest, at that time, I just like hanging out with them. It gave me a buzz to be on stage getting their kit ready, really feeling part of making everything happen. I would have continued to do it for nothing, but in those days, they were good guys; they wanted to be fair. They gave me an equal share of what they earned, which in those days just about bought a pint or two!

It wasn't a formal relationship. We never agreed what my role was or what I was responsible for. I just did what needed doing to make things run smoothly … and it worked. They did well.

Gary Well, as you probably know, things really started to take off. People became really interested in us. We were being asked to play outside our hometown of Leeds and getting featured on radio. Things were happening and they happened very quickly. We were kids really, eighteen, nineteen … and without anyone making any kind of decision, people started to treat Tom as our manager, and he took to the part with gusto.

Tom Quite suddenly, things really kicked off. I was getting calls from radio stations and magazines asking for interviews and from venues trying to book the band. It was a bit overwhelming. I was working full-time in a bookshop and trying to deal with all the band stuff in the evenings and weekends. The guys all gave up their jobs and gave all their time to the band. I couldn't do that. I'm a few years older than them, and I was married by then and had a small child and needed the financial security of the nine to five. I worked incredibly hard holding it all together, and I did. They gigged all over the UK, and in year two, they were doing quite large festivals. It was difficult working out all the logistics, not just where they were playing but how to get them and all their equipment there and sometimes even sorting places for them to stay overnight.

They were always good at paying me a fifth of what they earned, so as they got more work, the money I got increased. Eventually I moved to working part-time in the shop to give more time to them.

Gary It was surreal how things just took off. One minute we were begging people to agree to let us play in their pub, then suddenly we were getting airplay on the radio and being asked for interviews. To this day, I don't quite know how it all happened. We were buzzing on all the attention. It was exciting but also scary. We were so young.

Tom moved to working three days a week at the bookshop where he had worked full-time for years, and he spent more time sorting stuff for us. By then it was just sort of assumed that he was our manager. Other 'professional' music managers approached us, but we were loyal to Tom, and we thought he was doing a good job, so at that time, we were happy to leave things as they were.

Things really started to go wrong when we started playing outside the UK.

Tom Suddenly, I wasn't just getting calls from people in small UK venues. It seemed everyone was interested in them. I got requests for them to play at festivals, including some in Europe. I really wasn't too sure how to handle this, but I did. I said yes to most things; they needed the exposure. I realise now that I probably should have said no to a few things. Some of the gigs were incredibly close together, and I remember one occasion when they were playing two festivals in one day … . Well, least said about that … .

Gary There were always things going wrong, even in the beginning. Tom would get the timings wrong, and we would arrive places with hardly any time to set up. Sometimes pieces of kit were left behind, but there were always other bands we could borrow things off. In those days, it still just seemed like fun, and no one bothered if little things went wrong.

But I as I said, I think it really started to go wrong when we started getting interest from big festivals and venues outside the UK. We were all fairly naïve, just soaking up the excitement and believing in Tom. I remember the first time that we really recognised that he was out of his depth. He had booked us to do two festivals in one day, miles apart. It was a disaster. First off, he sent all our kit to the wrong festival, and then we had a mad dash to go and get it and take it where it should have been.

After we played at the first festival, we had to pack everything up and head back to the place our kit had been first thing. Needless to say, he hadn't allowed enough time to cope with all the festival traffic, and we arrived late … no sound check … no nothing … it was a disaster.

Tom By then I was feeling pulled apart. I loved being part of what was happening with the band. I still went to all their gigs and supported them in everything they did but the pressure of managing them was enormous. I gave up working at the bookshop to focus on the band.

They began to tour. There was so much for me to sort out. They aren't the easiest. There would always be one of them who forgot his passport, wasn't there for the bus, or even missed the plane. It was all becoming a nightmare.

I didn't want to say I was finding things difficult. I wanted to be part of it all. I could tell they wanted more from me, but I had nothing to give. In Leeds, I really knew the music scene. I could call on favours, find them gigs, do good deals on kit … . Once they started travelling, first to France, but then eventually to Japan, I felt alone; there was no one I could call on.

I could tell they weren't happy with me. Things did go wrong. I admit that, but I was doing the best I could do … . I love those guys … . I think their music is amazing. I still buy everything they produce, and until recently, I went to all their shows even those overseas.

Gary Things got worse and worse. As we toured more abroad, more mistakes happened. Tom would tell one person the time of the plane but not others, so we had people missing flights. He got visas wrong. All the sort of things you look to your manager to have in hand.

We were really unhappy with how things were. We moaned about it a lot to one another, but none of us had the guts to talk to Tom. He was still our mate, and we didn't want to upset him. We couldn't understand why he came on tour with us and wasn't at home sorting out future bookings. We became quite angry with him but never said so.

On the way back from a tour of Japan, we decided we had had enough and contacted one of the professional managers who had approached us in the past and signed up with his company. We had never had a written contract with Tom, so we were within our rights to do that, but I do accept it would have been better if we had talked to him. It's played on my mind a lot since, but the others still just take the view he was screwing us and getting a fifth of what we earned whilst not delivering what we needed.

When we signed with new management, we just told him we were taking a rest after a gruelling tour when, actually, we had a new manager and were in the studio recording an album.

Tom I couldn't believe it at first. Things changed. They told me they couldn't afford for me to go with them on tour. Well, the main reason I was doing all that work was so I could be there at the gigs, enjoy their music. As I said, basically, I'm just a big fan. I really admire what they are doing … where they are taking things … . I was really hurt and very sad.

They went off to Japan without me. When they came back, they said they wanted a rest. I could understand that. They had been working non-stop for nearly three years. I needed a rest too. I thought we would still see a lot of one another socially, but no one got in touch. Nothing. Not a phone call. Nothing … .

I messaged them a few times but none of them replied. I didn't know what was going on. I asked if we could meet but they just ignored me.

Eventually I heard that they were busy in the studio … not the local one they had used before. I was shocked. Next thing I discovered was that they had signed with a music management company!

I don't know how they could treat me so badly … . I don't know why they are being like this. Financially I am in a mess. I stopped working at the bookshop, as I said, and I haven't had anything from them since the Japan tour, and that was months ago. I'm in a mess. I owe on the mortgage. I have accepted that they don't want me to work for them, and I have been talking to the bookshop to see if they will have me back and looking round to see what other work is around.

I am really sad … and depressed. I never thought they would treat me like this. We were friends. I feel very alone.

Gary Well eventually Tom found out we were recording and had a new manager. He had tried to talk to us. I wanted to meet up with him, but the others were dead against it. They have really turned against him, saying he has been making money off us for years and messing up. They say they are scared that if we did all meet up it would get nasty. I felt torn I didn't want to separate myself from the guys, be the odd one out, but I would have liked to talk with Tom.

Tom I am really angry about the way I have been treated. I have spoken to a few people, and they said we had a verbal contract even if it wasn't written down and this is proven by the regular payments I received from them. I need some money. People are saying I should sue them for loss of wages.

Gary I did think about meeting with Tom on my own. Just so he knows what happened and why, but now things have got even worse. We have had a formal letter saying he is going to sue us for breach of contract and loss of earnings.

I know we never had a written contract with him, but we don't understand the law, and someone suggested we try mediation before we get involved with costly lawyers.

Reflections on the mediation

Unfortunately, this is quite a common tale. Bands can often start out being 'managed' by family or friends. No one realises the full responsibility of the manager role, and as success grows, the work can become overwhelming for someone who is inexperienced and primarily doing it out of love for the performer/s.

In this case Tom, Gary, and the rest of the band had been very close friends for many years. The trouble started when the music stopped just being something they enjoyed doing and became their livelihoods.

We often find it hard to confront friends about things we are not happy with, and this is certainly the case here. Resentment grew, and through a misguided decision not to upset Tom, he was left not understanding what was going on. He only wanted the best for the band and felt he was doing the best he could.

Feelings in the band were mixed. Gary felt sorry for Tom and was not happy with the band decision not to communicate with him. He saw how quickly other band members were able to cut themselves off from Tom, and he feared he too might suffer if he did not go along with the majority. Other band members came to see Tom as someone who had exploited them and only wanted to 'be along for the ride.'

Initial contact with the mediator was through Gary. The rest of the band were not particularly in favour of mediation but were concerned that Tom would escalate things, and they would become involved in a legal battle they could not afford. They agreed that Gary would be their spokesperson in any mediation meetings as they feared 'they would lose it' if they were in the same room as Tom. They agreed to abide by any decisions which resulted from the mediation, although it was agreed that if there were any financial agreements, they would all be consulted before any agreement was drawn up. They decided against involving any lawyers at this stage and all wanted to be present at the mediation while leaving Gary to speak.

When Tom was first approached about mediation, he had mixed feelings. He desperately wanted to talk with the band, but he no longer trusted them and was very angry no one had contacted him for months, leaving him to hear about the new management and the new album from someone else. However, he felt he had no option but to try mediation as he was deeply unhappy and rapidly running out of money. His confidence was low, and this was making it difficult for him to get another job.

The band decided that it might be overwhelming if they all joined in the first joint session. So, the mediator met firstly with Gary and Tom, and the rest of the band stayed in an adjoining room. Tom made it clear that he was not happy with this and that he wanted all band members to hear about the impact their behaviour had had on him. To move things on, all band members agreed to be present.

Tom explained how upset he was. He did not understand what had happened, and now he found himself unemployed, in debt, and feeling abandoned and used. He spoke of how he did not feel he could go to their gigs in the future and how important that had been to him. He became very tearful, which shocked the band members who looked to Gary to respond.

Gary was clearly moved by Tom's state. He explained how the band had felt let down by some of Tom's decisions and mistakes and how these mistakes had caused problems for the band. They felt that although it had worked well enough in the beginning, Tom did not have the skills or experience to help them at this stage in their career when they needed a manager with international experience.

To the surprise of the band, Tom said he agreed with them. He explained that he wanted them to do well, and he knew that he was out of his depth. He had been thinking of talking to them about this but didn't want to let them down and didn't want to lose his close contact with the band, as he loved being part of it all. However, he still considered that he had been badly treated by their lack of communication and the hurt caused through hearing what they were doing from a third party. He explained that he was depressed and on antidepressants and was out of work.

The mediator moved to private sessions. In speaking with the band members, they all expressed how shocked they were at how thin and ill Tom looked. Si was still very angry and felt that Tom was trying to manipulate them, but Russell, Mark, and Gary all felt sorry for Tom. They did not believe he had purposely failed them or used them for monetary gain.

There was quite a heated discussion when Gary suggested that they offered to pay Tom some money as 'a goodwill gesture' to give him time to get well again and to find work. Eventually, Si agreed with the others that if they did this, they would all feel better about themselves. As he listened to the others, he had begun to question his own opinion and was willing to give the benefit of the doubt to Tom.

They decided that they would work out an average of what Tom had been paid monthly over the years they had worked together and offer him the equivalent of six months' pay on that rate. They were doing well financially, and the sum was very small in comparison with any legal fees which may have been charged if Tom sued them.

Tom agreed this settlement and wished the band future success, saying he would miss being alongside them and might go and see them when they were performing locally. They all signed a written agreement and left together for a pint at the local pub. Tom would never get that level of friendship back but at least they would not move forward as enemies.

9 Case Study 4 – Physical Needs: Never Mind about the Mind, What about the Body?

Stan I really can't see how they think it is fair. It blatantly isn't.

I have been in this band since the start. We all got together at school. I thought we were mates and would have each other's backs and that the whole thing was going to be great, fun and laughs all the way. Julius was like a big brother to me. He would stand up for me against the bullies. It feels like a betrayal now that he isn't supporting me over the massages.

Liam Stan is taking the piss. He is always in victim mode. He thinks he is treated worse than anybody else, but that simply isn't true. It's always 'poor me' with Stan. It's hard to put up with that attitude. He never stops to think what it is like for other people. He believes that no one has things as hard as him.

Stan Drumming is physically hard. It takes it out of you, and if I don't look after my body, I won't be able to drum. It's particularly hard when we are touring. We spend so much time squashed in the bus travelling that it is impossible to exercise. I get really stiff.

They would be the first to complain if I made mistakes because I was out of shape.

Liam We know Stan doesn't have it easy. He has a sick child who he worries about a lot, but we have tried our best to be supportive. We have tried to avoid long tours during school holidays. As you can imagine, this pisses George off no end. He doesn't have children but does have an enormous debt and so he wants us to take on all the work we can so we can make as much money as possible. When we turn down gigs because Stan can't make them, George gets furious. It has got so bad that George barely speaks to Stan, and when they're in the same room together, the atmosphere is awful. Imagine what it is like being cooped up with that atmosphere.

DOI: 10.4324/9781003675938-12

Stan It was me that designed the artwork for our first posters and album, but I'm never given any credit as I don't write the music. I have put more than my fair share into making this band a success, and now they are being petty, not letting me put the cost of my massages through the band accounts. I think they see me as less important than the rest of them.

George Look, I am just sick to the back teeth with Stan. It's Stan this, Stan that, no thought for anyone else. We have bent over backwards for him. At times, we have had to bring in and pay for a session drummer to cover for him when he needed to be at home, and he gives us stick about that, saying we don't value him. I know it has been tough for him, but has he ever thanked us for our support? No! There is always something else he needs, and now it is bloody massages. He is never pleased; he just moans on and on.

I don't have children, not because we didn't want them. We tried ... went through four cycles of IVF and did everything else we could possibly think of, but no success! I am still paying off the debt from all the money we borrowed for the fertility treatment. It's a huge amount. You can imagine what it is like; I have a depressed wife at home who wanted nothing more than to be a mother.

I need to take on as much work as possible to try to bring that debt down. It's hard when Stan says we can't work in school holidays; there are loads of summer outdoor gigs and festivals we have said no to because of Stan. Does he thank us? No! Can't he get family to help his wife while we are touring?

I told Julius and Liam about the IVF, but there was no way I would say anything to Stan. He goes on and on about how hard it is having a sick child, but at least he has got a child.

Julius I can see Stan's point. Drumming is physically tough. OK I have strained my shoulder once or twice as my Gibson is so heavy, but I am only carrying that weight for short times on stage, and I have a guitar roadie for the heavy lifting.

I see how important it is for Stan to keep fit. He goes to the gym a lot and will snatch time to do Pilates or go for a run whenever he can. He has never asked for any financial support towards any of that. I think it is fair enough that we should collectively pay him to get massages when we are away on tour. His body is his equipment and needs looking after.

I think this fallout about massages is really about something else. We just need to get on with things, play our music, and enjoy success and life as long as we can. We all need to be adults and cooperate so we can enjoy this special time … . It will be short-lived.

Stan I really think that if they don't pay for my massages, then that's it. I have had enough. It is clear that they don't care about me; they show no respect or consideration.

Julius I just want to get to a place where we can get along when we are on tour and to enjoy what should be quite a special time. We get to go to amazing places and see amazing things, although it's exhausting, and if we don't make the effort, all we see are hotel rooms, but this won't last forever, and we will regret not doing all we can to make it pleasurable.

Stan is a couple of years younger than us and didn't have an easy time growing up. I think we have always rather mothered him. That was ok when we were at school and just playing around with music and having fun … . we could deal with his neediness and his moods … but now, we are all so busy; it's stressful being successful and exhausting. We just don't have the time or energy. We need everyone to pull their weight and get on with it. We could all choose to moan about something.

I don't think Stan ever thinks about what might be going on for other people. It is obvious that it is really difficult having a sick child and he worries about him a lot, but others are going through things too. I wish George was able to share with Stan about his IVF and how awful that has been for him and his wife. Perhaps it would make Stan understand that we all have struggles not just him, but I can't see George doing that as he is so angry with Stan.

George I don't know. I still think he is being a prick and spoiling everything for everyone, but he says we don't treat him equally, and I guess, after I had told you that I had spoken with the others about the IVF and my debt and not him, he may have a point. However, I think he needs to think about why I haven't told him and be less focused on himself and less negative about everything.

Liam We all find Stan difficult, and at times, he drives me up the wall, but I have a soft spot for him. I have known him since school, and he didn't have a great childhood. His confidence isn't great, although I don't know why; everyone knows he is a great drummer, and the band would suffer if he left. We constantly tell him how good he is (although George has given up saying anything to him), but somehow that isn't enough. What does he need to know how important he is to us? Perhaps you can ask him.

It's strange, but until a few years ago, George and Stan got on really well. I guess it was about the time that George and his partner were going through IVF (he told me that he had mentioned it to you) that the relationship between the two of them became difficult. I know he didn't want to tell Stan about it, but it seems odd that the rest of us know and Stan doesn't.

Stan Well, you have spoken to everyone, so what are they all saying?

Mediator Well, just a reminder that everything in those sessions was confidential. Just as I haven't disclosed anything you have said to anyone, I can't tell you what has been said unless I am specifically asked to do so. I have been asked to ask you how the band can show you how important you are to them.

Stan Pay for the bloody massages!

Mediator I know the massages are important, and by paying for them, you would feel respected and acknowledged. We are still discussing the massages, but they are also wondering if there are other ways they can show you that you are important and needed.

Stan Instead of paying for the massages?

Mediator The question of what you needed was not tied into whether or not they would pay for the massages. They were interested to hear about what would make you feel more connected to them and better than you are feeling now?

Stan I am surprised that they are interested or care enough about what I need, and I doubt that they would listen if I told them, but I shall think about it.

Reflections on the Mediation

The mediator had a number of confidential sessions with each person in the band. These initial individual sessions confirmed that Julius was right in thinking that it wasn't really about the payment for massages. When she spoke separately to each person, it became clear that there were a number of different perspectives on the situation and several different things were causing tensions. Some were about Stan, but others were about more personal things which were impacting on the lives of the individuals in the band.

The mediator wondered if Stan may find it hard to again be in the position of having to put extra effort into looking after his son, as he had been forced to do for his siblings, and at the same time feeling that the care which the band members had afforded him in the past was being withdrawn, as symbolised through their refusal to pay for his massages. As a young boy, his own needs, and his feeling of loss and grief at the death of his mother, had needed to be put aside for the benefit of his younger siblings. It was not the mediator's role to explore these in any depth with Stan; this would have belonged to therapy. However, she needed to hold in mind the themes which these represented, including the need for reassurance, for others to show interest in him, and to be cared for.

George was struggling with the pain of not having a child and the debt which unsuccessful fertility treatment had left him with. He was jealous of Stan having a family and had at first been supportive agreeing that the band should try to accommodate school holidays etc., but as it became clear that he was not going to be able to become a father himself, he grew to resent his perception that the band made decisions based primarily on the needs of Stan's son. Yet it was the conversations with George which gave the mediator most hope of changing the dynamics within the band. In one session George had been adamant that although he had told all the others of his struggles, he did not want Stan to know. The mediator had left him with the question as to what he thought might happen if he chose to tell Stan. He had waved this away, but when he returned for another individual session, he said that had set him thinking. He was worried that if Stan found out that he had told the others but not him he may feel even more pushed out and bitter, and yet he also wondered whether it may be useful for Stan to know that others had hard times too. The mediator left him with those thoughts and confirmed that it was entirely up to him whether he said anything in the joint session.

Liam had less to say in the separate sessions but seemed to move more than the others. He moved from anger at Stan to posing the very important question: 'What does he (Stan) need to know how important he is to us?'. The mediator responded that this seemed an important question which could be addressed in the joint session, but Liam asked the mediator to ask Stan when she next spoke to him. A mediator holds everything confidential unless specifically asked and given permission to carry something across to another person.

Liam expressed loss for the ease of engagement they had all enjoyed when younger and was realistic in knowing that the life of a band is usually short-lived. He therefore was keen that they all got the most out of all their experiences. He valued the ability to visit different countries and experience new sights and cultures. Whenever he was in a new place, he would take himself off to explore. In the early days, Stan had joined him, and he missed the non-band related conversations they had as they walked. He wondered whether Stan was aware that he missed those walks. He talked of Stan's love of history and architecture and how much he had learnt from him on their travels. He felt that Stan's anger had shut him down to everyone's loss and again began to wonder whether Stan had known how much he admired Stan's knowledge.

The Mediation Day

When everyone came together on the mediation day, Liam and George took seats next to one another. Stan sat on the opposite side of the table and was joined by Julius who chose to sit next to him.

The mediator reminded everyone of how the mediation process would work and invited everyone to take the opportunity to say whatever they wished as an opener.

Julius started by expressing how sad it was that they needed to be in mediation and how he hoped that they could get back to the days when they were all enjoying making music and being together. He addressed Stan directly, telling him how much they admired his drumming skills and how the band would not wish to continue without him. He spoke about how he had found the previous year tough, with Stan complaining all the time and George being depressed so that it was no longer enjoyable to be together.

Liam followed agreeing with what Julius had said, adding that he had missed his walks with Stan and asking everyone to be honest and to say what they each needed to improve the situation. Liam also expressed the view that they probably should see Stan's massage sessions as a legitimate business expense and cover the cost, but that there may be things which other members hadn't mentioned that also fitted that criterion and needed to be discussed.

At this point Stan asked what George was depressed about and stated that he was very sorry that he hadn't noticed or known how he had been feeling. George became quite tearful and told Stan about the failed fertility treatment and how it had left him depressed and in debt. He apologised to Stan for not telling him but also stated that he hadn't done so because he was angry with Stan who he no longer trusted as he had seemed self-obsessed and not interested in what was going on for anyone else. He told Stan that he hadn't wanted to be in the same room as him, and that every time Stan spoke about his son, it reminded him that he would never be a father, and it was just too painful to hear.

This threw Stan, who then asked for a private session with the mediator. In this session, he was very emotional and said he hadn't realised how much he had disconnected with and stopped caring about the others, and it was not just them cutting him out. He couldn't remember when he had last given any positive feedback to any of them, feeling they were fine and didn't need anything.

He had been shocked to hear what had been going on for George for over 18 months and horrified that he had failed to pick up on any of it. He wanted to say this to the whole group and resumed the joint session by sharing this insight with them.

From there, everyone was honest about what they had found difficult and acknowledged that they all wanted the same thing, which was for the group to be successful for as long as possible and for them to find ways of making it more enjoyable again. They all expressed the need to hear that they were important and respected members of the band even if they did not overtly ask for that reassurance.

They spent some time giving each other reassurance but then returned to the issue that had first brought them to mediation. It was agreed that they all felt payment for the massages was reasonable and something they would take on. It would never have been an issue if they had not been feeling overwhelmed by what they saw as Stan's constant demands and so had said no to something rather than address a painful issue. Stan was very grateful and asked if others were having to pay for things they thought should be picked up by the band, but it was agreed that the physical demands of a drummer were different and required extra attention. Although there was a lot of joking, with people asking for payment for yoga, alcohol, anger management lessons, and other ways in which they had sought to deal with the stresses of the last few months!

Stan then asked if there was anything they could do to help George with his debt. Several things such as sponsored marathons were discussed, and although nothing was agreed on that day, George expressed his thanks for Stan raising it but also said that he did need the band to take on work so that he was earning and able to bring the debt down himself. Liam then came up with the idea that perhaps all their families could support Stan in some way with the demands on his wife during summer holidays. The families had known one another since school days, so it was likely that they would all pull together if needed.

The mediation changed the dynamics in the group and allowed them to start to rediscover and develop their friendship and to work in a more adult and collaborative one.

10 Case Study 5 – Repertoire: To Be or Not to Be… Classical

Nicola/Nic Clare and I have known one another from school, and I would have said we were the best of friends. We were in the school orchestra together, and as we played different instruments, there was no competition or jealousy. We were delighted when either of us did well.

We were very lucky to both get accepted into the Conservatoire and really excited when we found a beautiful house to share with Antonia who was also studying at the Conservatoire. It seemed natural for us to form a trio to play classical pieces together, and this has really taken off, and we are getting lots of bookings, ranging from concerts to festivals and weddings. We also have a contract to play in a large hotel when they are hosting special events. It is all very exciting, or was until Clare dropped her bombshell.

Clare I'm really upset with the way Nicola is behaving over my wish to broaden our repertoire and for me to explore new music for myself. I have become very bored with playing the same old (literally old) stuff over and over again. It doesn't challenge me and no longer excites me. Nic would be happy if we were still playing the kind of music we were playing at school … just with a bit more expertise and skill.

I know it's hard for her as we have been more like sisters since schooldays. We would stay at each other's houses in the holidays and do practically everything together. I don't think Nic likes change; she is very shy and introverted.

When we moved to London, I was excited to see what living in a city was all about and to get out, meet people, and see and do new things. Nicola just wanted to stay in and practise and do the gigs we had coming in. We do seem to work well together with Antonia, and the trio is

DOI: 10.4324/9781003675938-13

very popular, and we are getting a lot of work, but it just doesn't excite me. I don't want this to be my life .... I want something more stimulating.

I don't want to give up on the sort of thing I do with Nic .... I enjoy it, but I do get a bit bored and need to be doing other things as well. I understand that what Antonia and I are working on just isn't Nic's thing. I think that's OK; I can't see the problem with doing more than one thing with more than one person.

I shall always be Nic's friend whether we play music together or not (although I can't see that ending) we have shared history ... . We are more like sisters than friends, but it doesn't mean we have to be joined at the hip.

I wish Nic would be more confident and feel she can do some things on her own or make new friends. I shall always be her friend, but surely, we can also have new friends too. They are not a threat. It is an exciting time in a new place, and I don't think she is getting as much from all the opportunities we have now. I don't like seeing her miserable, but I am going to make most of my time in London.

Antonia/Ant Do call me Ant; Antonia sounds so ... I don't know ... posh ... all hockey sticks and ponies.

I'm a bit embarrassed by all this trouble which seems to have developed. It doesn't seem such a big thing to me.

I had lived in this house for a few months and was very pleased when Clare and Nicola moved in. They are great girls. Very different from one another. Nicola is very quiet, and so was Clare when they first moved in.

They are both fantastic musicians, and as we would often practise together, it seemed very natural for us to form a trio and begin performing together. It has gone really well, and we are getting lots of work.

To be honest, it's not really my kind of thing, a bit staid, but I enjoy performing, and it's great to be earning some money. I'm happy to continue doing it, but I also want to perform my own music, which is quite quirky and contemporary. Claire is quite interested in what I am doing, but Nicola hasn't even bothered to give it a listen.

Nicola I guess I feel abandoned. Clare has always been by my side; we have always done everything together, but now I spend less and less time with her. Usually, now, it's just when we are performing in the trio.

She seems to have developed a close friendship with Ant, and the two of them are often in the basement together where Ant has a studio full of unusual instruments, many electric. I have always preferred acoustic instruments and don't enjoy contemporary popular music. One of the worst things has been Clare and Ant going to clubs to listen to loud music and dance. I hate the idea, so I am often left here on my own.

It was a terrible shock when Clare told me that she and Ant had been recording music together and had linked up with a drummer and were going to do a gig at a nearby pub. She seemed to think I would be delighted and would be in the audience cheering them on. She seemed surprised when I couldn't stop myself bursting into tears.

Clare I couldn't understand what was happening when I told Nic about Ant and I getting a spot at the local pub to perform some of Ant's music. She burst into tears, ran from the room, and locked herself in her bedroom. She wouldn't come out until I had left the house and isn't really speaking to Ant or me. The trio has a big concert coming up in a month, and that is why I called you to arrange a mediation. We need to sort out what is going on for Nic. It isn't as though I am married to her (laugh), but she seems to think she owns me and that I have to be with her all the time. I do care about her and want her to be happy, but she smothers me. I do want the trio and the band to be successful. I enjoy doing both; the trio on its own isn't enough for me.

God knows what she would say if I told her I have started going out with Tim, the drummer in the band Ant and I have put together. I daren't have him round here because I don't know how she would behave; it would be so embarrassing if she started crying and ran from the room!

Antonia At first, I thought it was going to be a bit boring having them here, but Clare was keen to make up for lost time after living in such a quiet rural place and wanted to see everything that London has to offer.

Often, Nicola would stay home practising while Clare and I went clubbing or just shopping or visiting galleries. We always invited her, or at least at first, but Nicola seems to have no interest other than classical music.

Clare and I have got to know each other really well, and we 'get' one another. We love the music we do with the trio, but it isn't enough; we want to do innovative things and not be serious all the time. It is brilliant that Clare likes the music I have written, and we have had great fun recording it in my basement studio. We have even got a gig at the local pub with the band we have put together, which includes Tim, Clare's boyfriend. It is so much fun.

I understand from Clare that when she told Nicola about it, she ran from the room and hasn't wanted to speak to Clare or me since. I do hope we can sort all this out. As I say, it doesn't seem a big thing to me but the atmosphere in the house is horrid, and as a trio, we have a concert booked which we are really looking forward to ...or were ... . Now I don't even know if Nic is still wanting to do it. It is all such a mess!

Nicola My greatest fear is that they are fed up of me and of the trio ... . that we are just not exciting enough. I worry that they want me to leave and the trio to disband. I would be distraught. I don't know anyone else in London ... . Where would I live? What would I do? I love performing in the trio; we play brilliantly together, and we are getting a name for ourselves.

I realise things cannot stay the same as they were in school, but I am jealous of the friendship Clare now has with Ant. I feel left out and alone. They do invite me along to things, but what they do is of no interest to me, so they are inviting me less and less often. I don't want to be left on my own with no friends and no trio!

Reflections on the Mediation

In the initial conversation Nicola had with the mediator, she described the dispute as being about musical differences in the work being performed by a trio she was in with her colleagues Clare and Antonia. As is clear from the snippets of the confidential individual conversations above, which each person had with the mediator, the real issue was much more personal. This is often the case in disputes, particularly those between creatives. Although, it is always worth remembering that when anyone takes part in a mediation, they have an emotional investment, not just in the outcome but in how they come across in the mediation, in what everyone will think of them, particularly the mediator. Even when someone is at a mediation as a 'representative,' say of a legal firm, a trade union, a business, bank, or insurance company, and the dispute is not one they have personally been involved in, their self-esteem is still under threat. They will have to convey a 'successful' or 'unsuccessful' outcome back to the entity who they are representing and who, in all likelihood, is their employer. Everyone in a mediation, including the mediator, is vulnerable.

Existentially, we all share certain things, givens and needs, which make us vulnerable. We are concerned about our identity, both our self-concept and how we are seen by others – the extent to which we are accepted by others and have a sense of belonging, as opposed to feeling alone and isolated. This is part of the whole human challenge regarding the broader topic of 'relatedness.' We are all faced with the question of to what extent we can be content to be alone or to what degree we are dependent on others for our sense of self and acceptance in the world. Most people want to be liked.

As unique creatures, we are challenged to understand and welcome different perspectives, even when they challenge our beliefs or desires. This requires an open mind and a level of bravery to challenge one's assumptions and sedimented beliefs. This does not require us to agree with another's viewpoint but invites dialogue and discussion and an acceptance that it is OK if we don't agree and perhaps even that the existence of a variety of different views can make life more interesting.

When we create strong friendships or partnerships, as Nicola and Clare did at school, these questions are brought under the spotlight. Nicola had seen their friendship as special and destined to last a lifetime. As school pupils, they had developed a joint world view, deepened by their love and understanding of a particular music genre. The introduction of Antonia into their lives at first felt like welcoming a fellow spirit into their group. Nicola had expected Antonia to be 'like them' and for the three of them to have shared beliefs, values, likes, and ambitions. When it became apparent that this was not the case and that Antonia was introducing Clare to new ideas, music, and experiences, this became a threat to Nicola's security and self-concept. The dispute not only threatened her professional future but also her personal life and her self-confidence.

A mediator steeped in a more legal, rather than psychological, approach may have focused the mediation on a discussion about an agreement as to what type of music the trio would play or intellectual property issues should the trio disband. Although this undoubtedly needed to be part of the exploration in the mediation, it was not really the primary source of the conflict. That the issue was more one of Nicola's identity, fears, and sense of abandonment became clear early in the mediator's confidential discussions with all three before the mediation day. Although this may seem like a 'deep' issue and one more suited to therapy, the mediator heard enough in these initial discussions to be positive about the outcome of the mediation.

The mediation day itself was very emotional, with all three women crying at some point. The mediator did not try to stop this as it was important for all concerned to see how deeply the issue was affecting each of them in different ways and for the depth of disappointment, hurt, and anger to be acknowledged and respected. The pre-mediation sessions had already shown everyone that the issue was not merely about a musical repertoire but was concerned with deeper more existential issues such as loneliness, fear of abandonment, the desire for or fear of freedom, different levels of comfort with uncertainty. It came as no surprise that the mediation focused on their relationship.

Clare was able to reassure Nicola that their friendship was not under threat, but it was changing. She spoke of how she loved Nicola 'like a sister' and always would, but that did not mean they had to be 'joined at the hip,' and that there was a benefit in both of them doing 'their own thing and returning to tell their adventures to one another.' Nicola was able to understand this, but also share with both Clare and Antonia that this was not exciting for her, as it was for them, but instead felt very scary and isolating.

Both Clare and Antonia were able to confirm that they had no intention of leaving the trio and that they very much enjoyed working with Nicola. They could see that the idea of broadening out the repertoire of the trio probably wouldn't work as the music would appeal to different audiences and they agreed to stick with their current programme.

The three came to a signed agreement, which committed all of them to continuing working together as a trio for the next two years, by which time they would be leaving the Conservatoire anyway, and all three would be seeking work. This may necessitate them moving to pursue different things in different geographical areas. In the meantime, Antonia would also continue trying to develop the band she had set up but would prioritise trio commitments if there were any diary clashes. Their future direction would depend on the success or otherwise of both the trio and the band. They foresaw that this may lead to further difficult conversations in two years' time and asked for a clause to be included in the mediation agreement that if they were unable to resolve such future difficulties they would contact their mediator and set up a new mediation.

Two years after the mediation, Clare phoned the mediator to say that the trio had really taken off and was very successful with a diary full of bookings. The band, however, had lasted a year and been good fun but had now split up, with Tim joining another band which was doing well. She was now married to Tim and had just discovered that they were expecting their first baby. She was phoning to ask if the mediator could set up a proactive facilitated meeting between herself, Nicola, and Antonia to plan how the trio would deal with her pregnancy and maternity leave and potential future childcare needs. She was aware there were practical decisions to be made soon about work schedules, but she was also concerned how Nicola may take the news of her pregnancy. She told the mediator that everything had seemed fine since the first mediation, Nicola liked Tim and had been bridesmaid at their wedding, and she did not want anything to go wrong this time.

Before any mediation could be set up, Clare contacted the mediator to say that she had spoken to Nicola and Antonia and told them about the baby. Both were very excited and positive; they had discussed together what they may need to do to keep the trio functioning and had jointly come up with a shortlist of names of people who might 'understudy' for Clare. They were in the process of auditioning them.

This shows the transformative nature of mediation, with all three women now able to discuss together a potentially challenging situation without the need for a neutral facilitator.

11 Case Study 6 – Cultural and Gender Differences: So, We See Things Differently, No Surprise There

Hao We were very lucky; we won a competition in China, and the prize was for all our fees and costs to be paid to do this course in the UK. We were so excited. The course is great; we don't just get mentoring on performance, but we learn about production and the music industry in general.

Yize had been out of China before, but Runchu and I hadn't, so it was exciting on many levels. It felt like getting freedom and being given the opportunity to explore. It is very exciting but also bewildering at times.

I don't really understand what is happening with Carol, but I feel really upset and confused.

Yize It is such an honour to win this fantastic opportunity. I do hope that what is going on with Carol won't ruin everything.

I have toured in South Korea and spent some time with K-pop bands there. The training they get is amazing, but it's really tough. You have to be prepared to give yourself heart and soul to the process and lose a bit of your own identity. A bit like being in the army (laughs). Very regimented and strict … really hard work. I think I expected it to be the same here, but it is much more laid-back, and you have the opportunity to find your own style rather than being given one.

Han, Runchu, and I were already a band, but we were looking for something which would set us apart, and I thought we had found that in Carol.

Runchu Carol is amazing, something special. She is so different from all the girls I know at home. She is independent and knows what she wants, and I think that's brilliant. I think Yize thinks that too but definitely wants to be the leader, and in some ways, she threatens that.

DOI: 10.4324/9781003675938-14

I'm not sure what Hao thinks. He is a little naïve and a year younger than Yize and I. He isn't used to any disagreements, or strong women … or women in general!

Carol I have worked mainly as a solo artist, and I want to continue to develop that part of my career. I write my own stuff, I design my own stage sets, which are totally cool, quite wild. I make all my own outfits, and a fashion group have contacted me saying they are really impressed with my designs and wondering if there is a way I can work with them. Everything is going well. I feel the whole world is opening up to me.

I thought it was really great to be invited by Yize to join the band. I thought it would be a lot of fun and really cool. I didn't have any intention of *joining* the band, just jamming and having fun with them. They are very different to me, and I like the way that challenges me. They are very tight musically and in the way they live. I'm the opposite. I like taking risks, shocking people, pushing the boundaries a little. They are very choreographed; they do the same movements when they perform. Each of them knows the next step the other will make and will freak out if anyone does even the slightest unexpected thing.

I thought it would be fun to become a robotic anime style figure for them … a sort of visual extra to what they did. It was fun; I could play a part and see if I could be as disciplined as they wanted me to be. I found I could, but only for a short time.

I think we were all surprised that we sounded so amazing together. They had a gig booked and asked if I would like to come along and feature live on a couple of songs, which I did. It was really successful, and now the band want me as a permanent member. The guys seem determined that I only work with them and abandon my own projects.

I really don't mind doing the odd thing with them, but that's it, and we are beginning to get into arguments when we are in the studio or rehearsing. I have some great ideas to make them a bit more fun, but Yize is having none of it. He clearly sees himself as the boss and has started ordering me about. Well, he can eff off. They don't own me.

Yize It's really confusing. The first gig we played with Carol was amazing; the audience went wild. It was a real surprise as our audience is made up predominantly of young girls. The second gig, we noticed there were more guys there, so having her in the band is broadening our appeal. We have quite a few gigs lined up, and she should be really pleased, but now she is saying she doesn't want to do them.

She is a very strong character. I am the group leader, but she just talks over me, and now she is suggesting changes to how we perform. I think that's out of order and arrogant. I'm worried that she is disturbing the group and making Runchu and Hao question what we are doing.

I do think she adds something … but it's not her ideas we want … . She is good to look at … a bit of individuality, which has its good points if kept in check but also definitely has its bad points. I don't think she understands about responsibility to others; she just wants to do what she wants.

She has a different work ethic to the rest of us. Our music is everything, and we aren't going to risk success by drinking, partying, and doing drugs … and Carol does all three. I also think her morals aren't great, and she can be sexually promiscuous. She invited us all to go to a party with her recently, and I was shocked when Runchu said he wanted to go. I told him quite firmly that he wasn't going! He is young and could be easily led.

Runchu I think Carol has been quite a challenge to Yize. He is used to getting his own way … people doing what he says without question. Carol just isn't like that. She stands up for what she thinks, and I like that. We are young and in the UK; it is an amazing opportunity to see and try new things, but Yize wants us to rehearse all the time.

Hao I want everyone to sort this out. We only have a year here, and I want us to establish ourselves in that time; it means hard work and commitment. Yize and I understand that and will put in the hard work. Runchu was like that when we arrived, but Carol has been a bit of a disruptive influence on him. We aren't about 'I, I, I' like Carol; we are about 'we.' That's how we were brought up; that's what we believe in. We are in it for each other.

It doesn't make sense for Carol to be a core member of the group, but having her appear as a guest works really well. Yize is determined that it should be total commitment from her or nothing. We have to accept she isn't going to come back to China with us, and there are her own projects she wants to get on with.

Reflections on the Mediation

This case highlights a number of the existential issues, such as uncertainty, freedom and responsibility, authenticity, and time and temporality, which

I introduced earlier in the book. In addition, there are strong cultural differences in play, including how gender is seen culturally.

China is considered to be an example of a collectivist culture. Such cultures value maintaining harmony and avoiding conflict, and Carol's questioning manner, self-knowledge, and independence were very different from what the group were used to. Her manner was both refreshing and attractive, but also threatening and unknown. The guys were literally in foreign territory and facing uncertainty. Carol did not behave how they expected women to behave, and this was confusing for them.

In China, the family is considered to be of utmost importance, and as I have stated before, being in a group is very like being in a family with all the expectations which accompany that. The respect of elders and leaders is part of that, as is prioritising group goals and striving for consensus. Yize was the eldest and most travelled and saw himself as the leader of the group and so expected his decisions to be respected and acted upon. Carol would often disagree with him and had no difficulty making her views known. This was beginning to influence Runchu who was more open to embracing different cultural ways of being. This was causing the first sign of some friction within the group as, being the youngest and most inexperienced, no one had previously listened to him.

Individual people's relationship with uncertainty is another of the key differences here. Carol welcomed uncertainty and the freedom it gave her to explore what was possible. The guys wanted to build a detailed five-year plan, believing, perhaps rightly, that their style had a limited life. Each one had a personal alternative plan which would provide for a different career. Carol didn't look beyond the end of the week and was not willing to commit to gigs six months in the future wanting to 'keep all her options open.'

She wanted to pursue a solo career in which she held control of her own image and music. She wanted to remain as authentic as the industry would allow, seeing music as an avenue for self-expression. The guys were used to collective decisions, based on tried and tested formulas, with Yize holding the final decision. They were skilled and disciplined musicians and wanted to follow a formula which promised financial success and fame. All the free time they had was given over to practice and a desire to hone their skills. It was frustrating that Carol was rarely available, being busy designing her stage costumes, working on her own music, or just partying or hanging out with friends.

Even the relationships with time and temporality differed. The guys had one year to make their mark whereas there was no such timetable for Carol.

The pre-mediation work was able to highlight some of these essential differences, and so by the time it came to the mediation day, everyone was more aware of what was causing the tensions. Not unexpectedly, Carol spoke first. She explained that she enjoyed working with the band and taking on the persona of the doll-like girl they needed for their performance, but that wasn't her. She explained that for her it was like an actress taking on a part just for the period she was on stage. Musically, she had little to do, and so she saw no reason to go to 'endless rehearsals and practices,' but she now understood that her unwillingness to commit to dates was difficult for them.

The guys reminded her they were only in the UK for the year, and they would really have liked her to be a permanent band member and tour with them after that, but they now realised that her true commitment was to her solo career and that she had a right to pursue that.

Carol said she would make a commitment to perform at all the gigs they got in the UK during the year. She was still designing her own stage act and so not committing to any solo live performances in that period. She also agreed to prioritise any recording they may do, with the understanding that she would only 'come in to add her bits and not hang around.'

These were very different values from the guys', but they understood and accepted that if they wanted to work with Carol those were the conditions.

Runchu confessed that he had been making some solo recordings but had decided to give his full attention to the band for their UK stay, although he suggested that they could all benefit from being a bit 'less uptight' and perhaps attending a few gigs for the fun of it while they could, adding, 'We may enjoy ourselves and learn something too.' He suggested that they should have one day a week which they left free for each of them to do what they wanted, arguing that this would keep them fresh and bring in new experiences and ideas.

Yize was quiet in session, merely expressing that everything that was agreed 'made sense … but wasn't how I would do it.' He expressed his concern that the guys should not be too influenced by Carol, as he now accepted that she was only going to be involved for a short time, and they should remain true to their 'work ethic and professionalism.' Hao and Runchu reassured him that they remained committed to their original plan. It was agreed they would schedule in one 'rest day' a week, which Yize said he would use for writing new stuff for the band, but recognised that the others were free to do what they wanted.

They all came to understand that they would meet several strong-willed people like Carol in the industry, and many would openly disagree with them, and so the whole experience, though unsettling, had 'provided a valuable lesson.' Carol said she was 'even more sure that being in a band is not for me, long-term, but it's great to get the opportunity … and what's more, it is great fun, when you lay off me and we just create together.'

12 Case Study 7 – Name: Who Do You Think You Are?

Ross I can't believe it. Why now? What is this all about? I mean … it really doesn't make any sense.

I mean, we haven't heard from Ged for nearly two years, and then out of the blue, we get a solicitor's letter saying he thought up the band name and we must stop using it!

It's a lie! But what does it mean for us? We have been told we should stop everything – not tour, not bring out the album we have been working on. It feels as though everything is dead in the water … the end … . That's it. Where do we go from here? It is a disaster.

We all feel so powerless, and if I'm honest, we are scared. We don't want to be dealing with lawyers. That's a very costly game we don't want anything to do with. We have no idea what this is about. He didn't come up with the name; I did.

Ged You know that I was in the band from the beginning, don't you? I answered an ad in a music journal for a bassist, and we all got together, and the band was formed. You can't understand what it is like to see them out there, making music, touring, all that, without me. I have been written out. It is as though I never existed, never contributed anything. They haven't even kept in touch since they moved to London.

Ross I thought Ged was a good guy. We all came together from an ad in a music magazine. He is a great bass player. I thought we were all good together.

What happened in the end was nothing to do with me or the rest of the guys; it was management. It was their decision to replace Ged with Sasha. We were all a bit dubious, given she is George's girlfriend, but she is an amazing bass player, incredible energy and stage presence, so it has worked out really well.

I'm sure Ged wasn't happy. I know he wasn't … . He was furious. I met him for a drink when it was all going on, and

DOI: 10.4324/9781003675938-15

although he didn't say anything, I could see he was really upset and angry ... but that was two years ago, and we haven't heard anything from him since. We did send him tickets for the first gig Sasha played at, but he never replied and didn't turn up.

Ged I can't believe how heartless and cruel they all are. We were good ... . It worked. It worked so well, in fact, that we got noticed and were signed up by George, a music manager. He was good at getting us loads of publicity and lots of work, and we were all very excited.

I could hardly believe it when he told us that we would be playing one of the smaller stages at a really big festival. I had gone there in my early teens, as a punter, and loved it. I remember looking up at the bands on the stage and thinking, one day that will be me, that is what I want. Well, I got so near.

I will never forget the day Ross suggested just he and I met up for a drink. I wondered what was going on. I knew Ross was writing some songs on his own ... not the sort of thing that fitted with what the band plays, and I thought, perhaps he was going to ask me to work with him on them ... lay down some demo tracks ... or something like that. I know the others weren't interested in his music, but I thought it was good, and I would like to have been part of it.

How wrong I was. It seemed he had been 'delegated' to speak to me by George and the others as he and I got on well together. He wasn't wanting to talk about his work but to tell me I was sacked! Nothing wrong with my playing or attitude, of course ... . They all loved me and thought I was amazing ... loads of crap like that, but the bottom line was I was being replaced by George's girlfriend! I couldn't believe it. Was it a joke? But why play such a cruel joke on anyone?

No, it wasn't a joke. Apparently, George thought, visually, we all looked too similar and didn't have much stage presence. He thought it would 'spice things up a bit' to have a girl in the band. Lo and behold, he knew just the person, his girlfriend Sasha.

I have to admit, she is quite a looker, and if I am really honest ... a good bassist, but it's not right. I was committed to the band, excited by what we were doing, and had been in there from the start. Things were just starting to take off and that was it for me ... . The end. End of the dream. End of everything I had always wanted.

Ross I know what I told you sounds harsh ... replacing Ged with Sasha. As I said, it wasn't our idea, but George was right. We did look a bit boring, and Sasha adds some visual interest. She is great on stage. She moves around, flirts with the audience, and the kind of things we are useless at. She is really spontaneous. If things go wrong, she can make a joke of it … entertain the audience whilst things get fixed, that sort of thing. Ged was like the rest of us, so interested in the music that we lost sight that there was an audience, and as George keeps telling us, they are the ones that pay the bills; they are the ones that allow us to play our music and make a living from it. I don't think we would have got to where we are if Ged was still in the band. We just wouldn't have been noticed. We weren't different enough.

Someone had to go to bring in a bit of glamour; it could have been any of us. Ged was great. He hadn't done anything wrong. If Sasha had been a drummer and not a bassist then George would have got rid of Seb, our drummer, not Ged. It was just bad luck for Ged that Sasha played bass. I know it came as an awful shock to him.

I remember the others asking me to tell him. George wouldn't do it because Sasha is his girlfriend, and he thought that looked bad. So, I met up with Ged to tell him. I will never forget that meeting. He was stunned. I thought he would be disappointed but understand that this was needed for the band's future. When I told him he didn't shout or anything. He didn't say a word. He just got up and walked out of the pub.

I tried messaging him, but since then he hasn't been in touch with any of us. When we moved to London, we invited him to a party, but we have never heard anything from him until now, two years on. I know it would have been good if we had stayed in touch with him, but things have been hectic. We have been touring most of the time and hardly had time to even speak to our families never mind anyone else. The time has flown by. We have been working hard and enjoying ourselves.

Ged I do get it that the band needed something to make it stand out, but why did that mean getting rid of me? I haven't stopped asking myself that question since it happened. I thought we got on well. I thought they liked me. No one ever complained about my playing or my commitment. If anyone's commitment was a bit dodgy it was Seb's. Why didn't they replace him? I'm sure there are glamorous girl drummers out there.

I wonder if they talked about me behind my back. Maybe they always disliked me but were nice to my face whilst slagging me off to one another. Since it happened, I can't trust anyone. I have become more and more depressed. I'm on medication from the doctor. I can't play music; it makes me feel worse. I can't listen to the radio in case 'they' are on. It doesn't feel as though life is worth living. I am not who I thought I was. I have lost friends, purpose, and my identity. I don't know who I am anymore and that is scary.

Even my relationship broke up. Sal said I just became miserable and horrible to be with. She couldn't take it after a while and left me a few months ago. I thought that's it … . Those guys have destroyed me, and they need to pay for it.

I was there at the beginning. I helped make them who they are. I thought up the band name, and I won't let them continue using it and acting as though I don't exist. I need to be acknowledged, and they need to feel some pain for what they have done instead of enjoying the life that I should have been part of.

Ross It must feel hard for Ged, knowing he did nothing wrong and yet feeling pushed out … watching us doing well and not being part of it. I get that and I am sorry it happened in the way it did, but this stuff about him coming up with the name … well, it's just a lie. It isn't true.

We all spent ages coming up with possible names. I can see us now, with everyone scribbling ideas on paper and us all trying them out seeing what they sounded like. I came up with the name we have now. I know because I have always kept a journal of what we have done as a band. I can be a bit obsessive. I still have the journal, and one page is littered with possible band names, mainly crap, but there it is, our name … in my journal. I thought of it.

Reflections on the Mediation

It was clear very early on that this was not really about the band name. Ged had been unable to get over the feelings of abandonment, rejection, and hurt he had experienced when he was replaced by Sasha. He was looking for a way to show his old band members how hurt he was and to 'punish' them for their actions. He saw the dispute over the name as a way of damaging them and stopping them playing, of bringing them to the place he found himself to be in.

Ged had come to believe that his old 'friends' had wanted him out and that they had been dishonest with him during his time in the band. He now found he could trust no one and that this affected his mental health. He could no longer play music. He had lost his identity, his relationship, his purpose, and his joy in life. He needed the others to know the impact on him of what had happened. He needed to be acknowledged and not forgotten.

It was very apparent that the guys in the band had really liked Ged and had initially been upset and embarrassed by George's action in replacing Ged with Sasha. However, they craved success and could see that from a business perspective it made sense and so had gone along with it. Their embarrassment at what happened had kept them from really discussing it with Ged, and then the busyness of their lives had meant that they had quickly moved on. As Ged had not contacted them, they assumed he was OK and that life would have moved on for Ged too.

When they all arrived in the same room for the mediation the band were shocked when they saw Ged. He was extremely thin, pale, and bent. He looked like a defeated old man. This visual shock had a huge impact on them. They had entered the room ready for a fight over the name but seeing the sorry state he was in, all the fight went from them.

In that first joint session Ged was angry and focused on the issue of the name. He had no evidence that he had thought of the name but continued to claim it was his idea. The band were upset by his appearance and merely stated their belief that Ross had thought of the name. We quickly moved into private sessions.

In their first session without Ged, everyone in the band was very upset and worried about Ged and could clearly see that he was unwell and depressed. They no longer wanted to fight him about the name and wanted to find a quick resolution.

In Ged's first private session, he was in tears and acknowledged how much he still wanted to be part of the band and for them all to be friends again. Yet, he understood that too much had happened and too long a time had passed for him to return to the band. 'After all, all their success has been with Sasha in the band. We weren't known when I was part of it. It was beginning, but I guess most of the fans they have today will never have heard of me. They certainly wouldn't think of me as part of the band they love today.'

He didn't really hold a strong belief that he had thought up the name. He remembered hazy smoke-filled evenings of them all trying to think of something. He felt it would be impossible for any of them to prove who had finally come up with the chosen name. Taking legal action against them was his way of reminding them of his part in their success and to 'punish' them for the 'dreadful way' they had treated him. He did not want to be written out of history, to be a nobody. He had been told by others that he could make money out of the claim but that was of little interest to him. In his depressed state, he would not even know what to spend the money on. It could not buy him the self-respect he needed to rebuild his life. He regretted getting a solicitor involved but remained angry and depressed about what had happened. The solicitor had suggested that he made a claim against George too, but there had never been any emotional attachment to George, and so Ged was not interested.

He presented as a broken man, and after that first joint session, he said he hadn't the heart or energy to go ahead and pursue the claim. He wanted to 'slope off and just go home and hide.'

The band requested that he stayed, and we moved into a very emotional joint session. Instead of sitting facing one another, Ross and Seb moved their chairs to be either side of Ged. Ross started by putting his arm around Ged and apologising for what happened two years ago.

Through sobs, Ged described his life, his loss of confidence, his depression, the breakdown of his relationship, and his feelings of rejection, disrespect, and abandonment. He found it impossible to look any of the band members in the eye as he spoke. He seemed happy to have Ross's arm around him and at one point reached out for Seb's arm. Seb responded by covering Ged's hand with his own.

Seb told Ged in detail how they had not wanted him replaced. They had valued what he had brought to the band – thought he was a great bassist – but had been too young, naïve, and powerless to go against George when he was offering success. They explained that they had thought Ged would be picked up by another band as soon as he was free, and they were shocked to hear what life had been like him.

They asked what Ged wanted and how they could help. They were doing well, and if he wanted some financial compensation, they were willing to discuss it. Ged explained that finance would not make much difference at the moment. He wasn't short of money. His parents had died a year ago, and he had inherited their house and a considerable amount of money.

The band members were very upset by Ged's emotional and physical state. They discussed with him what might help. They wanted to resume a friendship but could not offer him a place in the band. Ged understood this was impossible and wasn't looking for that, but the offer of resuming the friendship was welcome. Ross who had always been the closest to Ged suggested that he may want to take some time to recover and wondered if he would like to stay with him in his London flat for a while.

Ged was overcome by this offer and accepted, agreeing to spend two weeks at Ross's place with them all meeting up daily to talk through the impact of what had happened two years ago and to see if there were ways they could help Ged to start making music again and to change his life.

I heard later that the stay had been a great success. Whilst staying at the flat, Ross had played Ged some of his own compositions, which would never fit with the style of the band and which Ross did not know what to do with. Ged picked up his guitar for the first time in many months and worked with Ross to develop these tracks. Eventually, over a year later, Ged started his own band, with Ross writing the music for his new band. Everyone has worked hard to stay in touch and support each other.

13 Case Study 8 – Hot Wheels: What Kind of Object Do You See?

Marni I am sick of all of them. Not a thought for me!

They think it's very PC to have a lead singer in a wheelchair. It's even got us press coverage, which we wouldn't have had otherwise. You know the kind of thing … me dressed in amazing gear, draped over my chair! Do they ever think what it is like, I mean really like, on a day-to-day basis? It ain't glamourous, I can tell you that!

Sharing a tour bus with the other four in the band and the crew, all male of course, is no fun. I asked endless times for them to sort out a ramp or a lift to get me and the chair into the bus, and to sort out some privacy for me … not just as a woman … but also someone living with a disability. Taking a shower, getting dressed, or going to the loo are major operations!

In the end I gave up. I used all my savings and a mobility grant to buy an adapted van and so I now drive myself to gigs and studio sessions.

Tony With Shaun, I was one of the founder members of the band and couldn't believe what an amazing singer Marni is. Shaun, Gaz, Will, and I were in the studio recording one day, and we heard this fantastic voice in one of the other rooms and so wandered in to listen, and there was Marni, a mind-blowing talent.

We immediately asked whether she would consider joining us. We were beginning to take off at the time, and she seemed really pleased and excited at the possibility. To be honest I don't think any of us noticed her disability that day. She was sitting down … . I'm not sure where her wheelchair was, but I didn't notice it. It was when she joined us for our first rehearsal session that we realised that she struggled to walk and could only stand for very short periods.

It worried us, but she brushed off any concerns, and we sort of took her lead and never mentioned it. I guess over the

DOI: 10.4324/9781003675938-16

months we have been working together she has been struggling more and more, but it has been such a slow change, and we have been very focused on our music so well … .

Shaun I feel really bad that Marni is so unhappy. She has always seemed so cool about everything. Very independent. Whenever I have asked if I can help her with anything, she has always refused and said she could manage it herself. I didn't think she wanted us to acknowledge that she was in any way different to us.

It can be difficult with women; you can get shouted at if you open the door for them. It's hard to get it right.

Gaz I was so pleased when Marni bought her van. It's an amazing piece of kit. It's got this ramp thing which she moves herself and her chair onto, and it lifts up so that she can easily get in and out. It's got an amazing sound system in it too. It must have cost a bomb now I think about it.

Before that, when she travelled with us in the bus it was difficult. We would all lift the chair in and out, and there really wasn't much room for it once we got it in there.

I keep thinking about how I would kit a van like that out with all my gear.

Will Marni did mention that she found travelling in the bus difficult … . If I'm honest, we didn't take much notice as she always seemed to manage. She never missed a gig, and she would always tell us not to fuss around her … so we didn't.

I was concerned when I realized how much she struggled with walking and standing, and I did talk to management and the others about whether it was such a good idea to have her in the band when we were touring. I thought it may be better if she was just involved in recording … . Her voice is amazing, and it does add a lot to our sound, making it really different and interesting. I thought it would be a good solution; we could record her and play it through the computer on tour. I sounded out all of them, but they did not want to talk to Marni about it, so it never went any further.

Marni I think they were all relieved when I bought the van, but no one has asked how much it cost, how I can afford it, or whether they could help with the cost. I don't suppose they have given any thought to what it feels like to travel on my own. It wasn't easy in the bus, but I did enjoy the camaraderie and now I feel like a spare part that is just rolled onto the stage when needed and rolled off again at the end and left to make my own way home in my van. I'm not enjoying things as I did at the beginning.

I suppose I'm most angry with Bluey our manager. It is his job to look after us.

Bluey I was worried when they told me Marni was joining the band. They are a naïve and idealistic lot. It was only Gaz who seemed to give any thought to what it meant to have Marni on board. I thought his idea that she shouldn't tour but would do all the studio recordings was a good one, but it seemed that Toni was worried about raising it with Marni, in case she took offence and walked out … well not walked … but left … . You know what I mean! After all, everyone does what Toni wants in the end. So that was the end of that.

I could see there are some advantages for the band. Marni stands out, she is very beautiful, has a great voice, and the wheelchair sets her out as different, and with all this focus on diversity and equality and that stuff, it has brought press attention which has been positive and increased the profile of the band. She has really punked up the chair too, so it looks quite funky, lots of colour, glitter, and sometimes even lights on it.

However, they didn't think about the complications involved when I have to organise tours and everything. It was hard enough adding a woman into the mix, I had to make sure there were separate showers and loos etc. To add to that, checking that every venue offers wheelchair access and has accessible toilets is an added complication. Some venues say of course they have access, they need to in order to operate legally, but they often think about the audience and forget about the stage. Getting Marni in her chair on and off the stage can be complicated, and with all the guitar racks and the drum kit, some places have very little space to accommodate a wheelchair. Marni has complained that once she is wheeled into place, it is impossible for her to move and that she worries what would happen if there was some kind of emergency, like a fire, and everyone had to evacuate quickly. I'm sure we would cope somehow.

Reflections on the Mediation

The desire to get things right and be politically correct can often lead to tension and conflict, even when the intentions are good. Sometimes the desire to show an openness to diversity and difference can mean that people end up feeling abused, merely a tick on some checklist. Marni spoke of believing she was being exhibited as an attractive woman, given centre stage on photoshoots, and that her disability was used in some way to buy the band praise for inclusivity. In one confidential session, she also spoke of her worries about such publicity attracting the attention of people with abasiophilia, who show a psychosexual desire towards those with impaired mobility, especially those who need to use orthopaedic appliances such as leg braces, casts, or wheelchairs. She had already needed to block some individuals from her social media because of the sharing of unwanted fantasies of that nature. She had felt unable to share this fear with other band members as she was concerned that it may introduce or further promote the idea of her as a sexual object, and she even worried that some of the band may turn to Google to find out more about the condition and come across sexual fantasies about women with disabilities. This concern speaks to the existential dimension of the unterwelt and the degree to which we may, or definitely may not, want admittance to this very private domain of our work colleagues and concerns about the inevitable change that would bring to a relationship.

In this mediation, we see five men with different motivations for having a lead singer who is also a wheelchair user, some more positive than others. We also have a woman who has struggled to form a career in a male dominated industry when her embodied self is very much on show and often sexualised. Her social (mitwelt) and physical (umwelt) domains were sometimes in opposition to each other. She valued her independence and did not wish to be pitied or seen as less able. This has both advantages and disadvantages. The obvious advantage is that she is seen as her true authentic self and treated with respect as an equal peer and fellow professional. A disadvantage is that she has learnt to reject offers of physical help even when she was aware that they would have made life easier.

In our discussions Shaun showed sensitivity to Marni's needs but held back from offering assistance or talking to her about them because he did not wish to draw attention to her disability, be disrespectful, or to imply that she was in any way needy. He got himself tied up in knots over what to do. He seemed to find it hard to know how to treat women (whether they had a disability or not) as equal colleagues, fearing that whatever he did may be misinterpreted. In our discussions, it was clear that he had chosen not to share his concerns and confusions with other members of the band or seek to open up any discussion with Marni about her thoughts and feelings.

Gaz seemed very impressed with Marni's van without ever spending much time wondering why she had felt the need to buy it. He assumed that lifting her chair in and out of places was enough. His interests in the world centred round physical things, equipment, and the technical aspects of music-making rather than the other people involved with him.

Although Will did seem to show understanding of how difficult it could be for Marni, his solution was to relegate her to the recording studio rather than exploring what needed to happen for Marni to be a full member of the band including tours. He took a logical rather than emotional approach to what he saw as fixing the problem, without any thought about what Marni might want or what it may do to her own sense of self as a full member of the band and her desire for equal respect.

Bluey had a very commercial stance. He saw his role as bringing success to the band. He foresaw lots of practical problems as soon as he knew they were considering bringing Marni on board. He saw the commercial benefits Marni brought and was the one who most reflected Marni's fears that she was seen objectively, with the band using her good looks to attract attention. This was clearly the case with Bluey who openly stated, 'Marni stands out, she is very beautiful, has a great voice and the wheelchair sets her out as different and with all this focus on diversity and equality and that stuff it has brought press attention which has been positive and increased the profile of the band.'

The Mediation Day

Marni was very honest with the mediator about her concerns and the degree of hurt and anger that she was carrying. In those private pre-mediation sessions, she spoke about whether she could find the courage to voice these in the joint meeting with all the band members. She rehearsed how she might phrase it.

She was keen to start by telling the band how much she loved the music they played and her part in creating it, that she enjoyed the buzz of performing live, and that she wanted to continue as a full member of the band. She then hoped to articulate what was blocking her from currently enjoying the experience, explaining that she was proud of what she had achieved as a wheelchair user but that like everyone she needed help and consideration at times. She felt very vulnerable about her concerns about the sexualisation of disability and did not wish to raise this in the mediation. She was hopeful that if the mediation was successful, she would have a growing trust in her colleagues and there may be a time when it would be safe enough to discuss it.

When the mediation day began, Marni was able to talk about this. As soon as she had finished speaking Shaun said that all the guys had met together since their individual sessions with the mediator and wanted to tell Marni how sorry they were for their lack of consideration. He invited her to tell them more about her experiences and to let them know how they could improve things.

Marni thanked Shaun but said she wished to hear from all the others as she believed that he may not be speaking for everyone.

A very emotional Tony spoke in reply, again stating how sorry he was that they had placed her in a position which was so awful for her, declaring that they were all 'selfish bastards, a bit lost in the excitement of making music and beginning to have success.' He spoke of his early attempts to try to offer help and to speak to Marni and what he described as her 'Fuck off, I am OK, don't be patronising' response. He felt this had left him confused about how to be around her. A tearful Marni acknowledged that she had been giving confusing messages for which she apologised and that she could see how that was difficult for them. She told them that she did need help at times and promised that she would clearly signal when this was the case, but the rest of the time she wanted to be independent and 'just get on with being a professional musician' like the rest of them.

Will thanked Marni for being so honest and reported that he now felt in a more comfortable position to talk with her about things rather than fearing that she may be offended. He said he hadn't really given much thought to how it would feel if he had suggested to her that she only did the studio work and began to speak about how important her voice and strong presence was to the image of the band on stage. At this point he began stuttering and looked very upset, eventually asking if that was an awful sexist thing to say and if so he apologised.

At this point Marni burst out laughing and said it was fine, she was always up for compliments, and would now feel she could tell them if any such comments were out of line or uncomfortable.

Clearly there had been a huge shift in the atmosphere, but at this stage, neither Bluey nor Gaz had said anything. It was suggested that everyone take a lunch break, and the afternoon would start with individual sessions, firstly with Bluey, then Gaz, then Tony, then Shaun, then Will, and finally with Marni, before bringing everyone back together.

The session with Bluey was quite long. He had been quite uncomfortable with the emotions which had been expressed in the opening part of the mediation. He also expressed a bit of resentment that Tony seemed to be taking a leading role in the discussions, echoing some degree of jealousy which he had expressed in the earlier private session. Within the time frame of the mediation, there was not time to unpack this. He still had concerns about the practicalities presented by Marni's wheelchair but also expressed how much Marni brought something unique to the band and without her they would have less chance of success. He was clear he did not want Marni to leave, but he wanted the others 'not to be all sentimental and realise that making things Marni-friendly will cost money' and that they all had to be willing to equally cover those costs.

In Gaz's session, he expressed surprise about everything that had been said earlier reporting that 'all that kind of stuff regularly goes over my head; I am a very practical guy.' He went on to say that over lunch, he had been researching the different kinds of wheelchairs there were out there and had found some 'real cool stuff' which was lightweight and foldable.

He said he couldn't wait to talk to Marni about what would work best for her and that he had some great ideas of his own for developing a few things which might make life easier for her.

The individual sessions with Tony, Shaun, and Will were all short and focused on their desire to move on and make things better. In her final individual session, Marni expressed the same feelings, saying she was so relieved to have heard what Tony, Shaun, and Will had said but was still concerned about Bluey's views, saying she was less worried about Gaz as he was 'never really there in discussions as he was a bit of a geek and was usually thinking up new instruments or engineering projects.'

In the final joint session, Marni started by asking Bluey where he was with things. He spoke of how important Marni was to the success of the band and said he wasn't sure it would survive if she left. He expressed some of his practical and financial concerns and asked that everyone engage with these and not leave him to be 'the wet blanket, spoiling everyone's parade.' At this point, Gaz very excitedly said he would really like to work with Bluey and Marni on exploring some of the practical things they could do to make things easier, as he already had some fun cool ideas he wanted to share. At this point the band began to work collaboratively and creatively to identify practical obstacles. It was clear this was going to take time, and they all agreed to have a meeting in the studio the following week to really work through all these. Bluey said he would research some of the venues they currently used and those they might want to play in the future and see what they offered to wheelchair using musicians, pointing out that they must have legal requirements they had to meet.

At this point everyone was excited, and creative juices were flowing, but the mediator reminded them that Bluey had mentioned that there may well be financial implications. They agreed on principle that the band would cover these collectively and did not see them as something Marni had to shoulder alone. Bluey pointed out that financially they were so much better off since Marni joined, as her presence had attracted attention which had resulted in a lot more bookings and so they could afford to spend money ensuring she stayed a 'full and respected member of the band who we can't do without.'

Part Three

Ways to Prevent or Deescalate Conflict

14 Proactive Measures to Reduce or Deal with Conflict

Although I earn part of my living by mediating conflicts, it is always better if conflicts are prevented or resolved without the need to bring in a third party. However, I do believe that mediation, in addition to potentially enabling disputants to solve a specific conflict, can also bring about long-term change. Participants can develop a greater understanding of self, including an increased ability to recognise early what their triggers are, and can therefore respond in a more positive way. It also provides an opportunity, to experience, in a safe place, other people's world views and to develop awareness that there are different perspectives on each situation – perspectives that have equal validity and are in need of exploring, rather than rejecting, in order to better understand the underlying issues, which are often emotional and psychological, that are in play and need to be addressed to find a meaningful solution for all parties.

Most disputes do not need to get as far as litigation or mediation, and it is not necessary to go through a mediation process to develop the type of insight I have just referred to. Indeed, using insight, reflection, and communication skills to avoid the dispute in the first place is the ideal way forward. Failing that, recognising when a disagreement is brewing and taking active measures to resolve it early is a good response. This may include bringing in others, such as coaches and consultants, or could be achieved through band members and those in the music business further developing their own communication skills and knowing themselves better, including what triggers them.

Disagreement, as well as the anger associated with any dispute, is natural and can be harnessed positively. It is healthier to acknowledge early any disappointment, anger, and frustration, both to yourself and to the person perceived as causing those emotions. Some people are good at identifying and expressing their emotions; they are in touch with their body as well as with their thoughts. Indeed, they may notice bodily tension and stress such as increased heart rate, shallow breathing, tensions in

DOI: 10.4324/9781003675938-18

the muscles, etc., before they are aware of it cerebrally, slowly becoming aware of feelings of fear, sadness, loneliness, and hurt as well as anger. Repressing such emotions can lead to depression, whereas acknowledging them and working with them, although not easy and at times uncomfortable, can motivate positive change.

The benefits of developing deeper self-insight and resilience are not just for those in a group; a solo artist will still need to find ways to understand themselves and others better, as no one truly works in isolation. There are skills we can develop and practice which can build our resilience so we are better able to quickly identify and address a developing conflict.

Unfortunately, most people try to avoid any discussion about conflict, widely regarding it as ineffectual as a general approach and potentially very damaging (De Dreu & Van Vianen, 2001; Friedman et al., 2006; Liu et al., 2009; Lovelace et al., 2001; Ohbuchi & Atsumi, 2010). If we choose to thrust our heads into the sand, and there is no discussion or even acknowledgement of any disagreement, then there is unlikely to be any commitment to make positive moves to become skilled in managing conflict.

Conflicts seldom disappear by themselves and often fester and grow without direct discussion and action (Bacon & Blyton, 2007; Eisenhardt et al., 1997). The first step in preventing destructive conflict is to be realistic and accept that it is natural for us to not always like the people we are working with, be they our peers, authority figures, or even fans, and acknowledge that disagreements will happen and can be used creatively.

Working in the music industry requires an intimate understanding of the creative process, and such understanding usually involves fostering specific cognitive and emotional qualities including open-mindedness, resilience in the face of failure, curiosity, and intrinsic motivation to explore. All these elements are foundational to the development of creativity, and they are also the very qualities needed to resolve conflict.

However, we cannot assume that all those working in the industry will have developed these attributes to the same level. Earlier, we saw that cultural and environmental factors, which each individual consciously or unconsciously brings into their experiences within the industry, will mean that such qualities will be demonstrated in very different ways. Although difference is often linked in people's minds to conflict, it is our very difference from each other which makes it possible to create something new, as only I can fully experience my own life.

For most music professionals, the choice to enter the industry shows a certain level of ability to cope with uncertainty and a call to innovation, or perhaps a degree of naivety and optimism. Of course, as already noted, there are some who are 'just in it for the money.' There have been many approaches developed to solve problems and deal with disagreements that require a creative approach. Most creatives will have the tools to use these very effectively and perhaps prevent conflict getting to the stage where mediation or litigation is required.

For members of a band or orchestra, it is important to develop a collective culture which allows emotions to be expressed honestly, clearly, and quickly and in a way which is not judgemental or aggressive. It is the behaviour associated with emotions which builds the conflict, not the emotions themselves. Behaviours such as raised voices, name calling, invading another's space, refusing to speak, sarcasm, attempts at belittling the other, laughing, walking away when someone is speaking can all inflame the situation as much as physical violence.

Those listening to shared feelings need to develop an attitude of curiosity, patience, and respect, with a genuine desire to understand why the person is upset, angry, overwhelmed, or sad. This is hard to do when all you want is to get on with the creative process. It can be frustrating and annoying, but if all parties are committed to 'staying with the process,' not storming out or sulking, time will be saved and relationships strengthened, making it more likely that the creative juices will flow and the individuals can remember what brought them together in the first place and get back to enjoying being together. However, before we can engage with others effectively, we must first know and understand ourselves.

The Individual and One-to-One

Know Yourself

If we are going to deal successfully with conflict, we must first know ourselves. There are many well-known sayings which remind us that we cannot change others – we can only change ourselves, and that internal change may generate change in others.

We need to be aware of our own ways of being, our own triggers, tendencies, and desires. These aspects are key authentic parts of who we are but may not always serve us well in every context. We must stay in touch with our purpose and emotional energy. The main task, whether we like it or not, is to understand the other person, and only then can we work on getting them to understand us. Only by understanding the other and the difference in the way they are perceiving things will we understand why there is a conflict at all. But remember, firstly, we must understand ourselves.

We all have a tendency to hang on to grievances. We hold feelings such as resentment, misery, or anger. Eventually, the reservoir holding these feelings overflows, and we explode, vomiting unreflected feelings everywhere. If this happens, it is hard for the other person to hear or respond in any positive way; they are too busy getting out of range or fighting back. It is just overwhelming for both people, and the danger is that our genuine concerns become lost and we are merely experienced as being out of control. We can avoid this by refusing to let resentments build up by expressing feelings, both good and bad, in the moment.

Another thing which gets in the way of successfully negotiating a difficult conversation is our human need for love and affirmation. It is natural to want to be liked. However, if this need dominates, it causes trouble for you and others. If we let our need to be liked take over, we will find ourselves:

- Saying 'yes' when we want to say 'no'
- Doing things we don't want to do, just to keep the other person happy
- Avoiding making decisions that we fear will be unpopular
- Becoming resentful
- Being seen as 'a doormat'

As well as holding on to resentment, we may hold onto sedimented beliefs which we can think of as 'Head Tapes.' These are beliefs (often unconscious) that we hold about how we should behave. Some of these are useful and serve us well, but others can make life difficult. These beliefs are often picked up in childhood from parents and teachers, for example:

- It is terrible if someone is angry with me.
- Putting myself first makes me a bad person.
- I must never disappoint anyone.
- Trying to get what you want is selfish.

When we are feeling uncomfortable about our relationship with someone, we need to try to identify which head tape is playing and replace it with a more helpful one, as shown in Table 14.1.

This 'reframing' can help bring us back in touch with the severity or otherwise of what has happened. It provides a way of preventing us setting ourselves up to fail or to be continually disappointed in or frustrated by others because they are not acting according to our world view.

Identify Triggers

Having identified stuck beliefs and outmoded coping strategies, we also need to know what 'triggers' us. Different things upset and worry different people. Sometimes it is hard to see why someone is anxious or upset about something which, to others, seems insignificant. We all react differently to emotional stimulus. We are generally upset by something which is not in

Table 14.1 Negative and Positive Head Tapes

Old Unhelpful Head Tape	*New Helpful Head Tape*
It is terrible if someone is angry with me.	*I might be uncomfortable but it's not the end of the world. Their anger is their problem.*
Putting myself first makes me a bad person.	*I need to look after myself, so I am able to look after others.*
I must never disappoint anyone.	*People are going to be disappointed sometimes. It is unavoidable.*
Trying to get what you want is selfish.	*It's OK to meet my needs, so long as I don't trample on other people.*

line with our values, beliefs, hopes, and ambitions or which is perceived as a threat to our self-concept and self-esteem. If we want to avoid getting into an unhealthy conflict situation, we need to be able to identify what our personal triggers are.

Common 'hot buttons' or conflict 'triggers' are based on our perceptions of what is happening and include:

Being told off
Being touched
Being tired
Being ignored
Being misunderstood
Being disrespected
Being hurt or in pain
Being scared
Being bullied
Being interrupted or things not going as planned
Being told what to do
Being stressed
Being judged
Being treated unfairly
Being physically uncomfortable – waiting, hunger, tiredness, subjected to loud noise
Being the subject of rumours or gossip
Being misunderstood or misunderstanding others

A key trigger is often linked to our values. We may be with a group of people who we feel safe with because we believe that we share the same main values, beliefs, and goals. If it becomes apparent that this is not the case and that our values and desires differ, this can not only be unsettling but the cause of major conflict. We move from a sphere of safety – I know these people; we are alike; we all share the same goals – to a place of uncertainty and loneliness.

Unfortunately, even while we consciously choose to avoid our triggers, it doesn't necessarily mean that the other person(s) in the conflict won't be using them. The other person may know our triggers and seek to use them against us when they start to feel nervous or uncomfortable. When this happens, we need to avoid taking the bait. Rise above it.

Don't rise to the bait of any 'You' statements such as 'You always do this … . You never do that.' It never helps to retaliate; it just deepens resentment. We can help the other person in a disagreement reduce or eliminate their use of triggers by modelling how it's done. Try to avoid judgmental words or unhelpful communication methods, such as exaggerating, minimising, or criticising. Not everyone has the necessary conflict resolution skills, so we need to take the lead.

Try to avoid conflict in the first place by giving time to recognising when someone is unhappy and to acknowledging that and seeing if there are ways it can easily be addressed. Sometimes, for a person to receive this acknowledgment whilst being uncritically listened to is enough to restore their self-esteem and well-being.

However, this may not be enough to address the conflict, and it may be necessary to have 'a difficult conversation.'

How to Prepare for a Difficult Conversation

Many of us can be disabled by conflict. If we develop our skills, conflict can be creative rather than destructive. Many of the skills needed to manage difficult conversations and behaviour are often referred to, in a rather derogatory tone, as 'soft' skills. But there's nothing soft about dealing with an emotional or confrontational individual who may appear to be trying to unsettle or undermine us. There are skills to help understand not only what is being said but also what is *not* being said and what the people involved are thinking and feeling but not saying. These include:

- Tuning in (building rapport, understanding the problem from the other person's viewpoint, understanding its personal significance to them)
- Tuning out (at the appropriate time, moving the attention from understanding them to jointly addressing the problem)
- Checking we understand one another and agreeing a way forward

But the best way to start is by asking oneself:

1. What is the purpose in having the conversation?
   - What do we hope to accomplish?
   - What would be an ideal outcome?
   - Watch for hidden purposes. We may think we have honourable goals, only to notice that our language is excessively critical or condescending. We think we want to support but end up punishing. Some purposes are more useful than others. Work to enter the conversation with a supportive purpose.
2. What assumptions are we making about this person's intentions?
   - We may feel intimidated, belittled, ignored, disrespected, or marginalised, but be cautious about assuming that this was the speaker's intention.
   - Impact does not necessarily equal intent.
3. What 'buttons' are being pushed?
   - Are you more emotional than the situation warrants?
   - Take a look at your own 'backstory,' as they say in the movies.
     - What personal history is being triggered?

   We may still have the conversation, but we will be going into it knowing that some of the heightened emotional state has to do with us.
4. How is our attitude toward the conversation influencing our perception of it?
   - If we think this is going to be horribly difficult, it probably will be.
   - If we truly believe that whatever happens, some good will come of it, that is likely to be the case.
   - Try to adjust our attitude for maximum effectiveness.
5. Who is the person we are in conflict with?
   - What might they be thinking about this situation?
   - Are they aware of the problem?
     - If so, how do we think they perceive it?
     - What are their needs and fears?
     - What solution do we think they would suggest?
6. What are our needs and fears?
   - Are there any common concerns?
   - Could there be?
7. How have we contributed to the problem?
   - How has the other person?

We often get into disputes because something personal feels under threat. We feel that it is not just our views or work which are not being respected or valued but that our value as a person is being undermined. Our self-esteem is under threat. This is often linked to a perception that our values and beliefs are being challenged and when this happens our self-concept is challenged. Although it may not feel like it, the likelihood is that the other person or persons in the dispute are also feeling vulnerable in the same way. People show their vulnerability in different ways, so we need to understand our own instinctive reaction to conflict as well as understanding how other people may react. Without us knowing it, our actions can be so 'loud' that it will prevent the other person from listening to us.

In what has become known as first-generation thinking, we are governed by the fight, flight, or freeze response. This response is governed by the amygdala, a small almond-shaped part of the brain inside the cerebral hemisphere, which reacts to our emotions and when our being is perceived as under threat reacts intuitively and without any analysis or reflection. The perceived threat may be physical or psychological. We may fear physical harm or loss of life, or we may fear the loss of our self-worth and self-image. The brain tries to equip us to deal with the threat by cutting off the electrical messages to the logical part of our brain, thus allowing us to make a quick response. The response is a primordial one. When we were hunter-gatherers, we might often have been faced with a fierce animal. To take time to consider whether to jump to the left, jump to the right, run away or stand and fight may well have literally been the death of us. There was no time to think. The amygdala closes down the pathways to reflective thought, which would have taken time we did not have.

The nature of the instinctive response is governed by who you are, your values, and the personal assessment of the implications of the action. In the same situation one person will freeze, another will run, and a third will fight.

Features of the flight response may include:

- Not making eye contact with the other person
- Not saying much
- Fidgeting
- Flushing
- Speaking quietly or stuttering
- Adopting a submissive pose – head down, shoulders hunched

Features of the fight response may include:

- Strong eye contact
- Moving closer to the other person
- More animation
- Speaking over the other person
- Jabbing gestures (e.g. finger pointing)
- Talking more loudly

In the freeze response a person may appear to be unable to do anything:

- Unable to think
- Unable to speak
- Unable to move
- Numbness
- Feeling cold

The first step in controlling our response is noticing it is happening. We can then remind ourselves that what we are experiencing is OK, merely a normal human response. We then have the freedom to choose our behaviour, for example: I don't have to express my anger through physical actions; I can tell the other person how I am feeling. The trick is to be self-aware and to avoid responding too soon to perceived threats and criticism.

It also helps to know that the person you are in conflict with is also subject to their amygdala. They are not responding in a reflective way. They may say forceful things they don't mean or say them in a way intended to hurt as a way of defending themselves from a perceived threat.

'Second-generation' thinking moved on from 'flight or fight' to focus consideration on the concept of 'command and control.' In this, individuals respond to a threat of conflict by using a cleverly disguised veneer of interpersonal skills, aimed at achieving a short-term win/lose result through manipulation. These manipulative skills can be taught, but they will only result in eroding trust and increasing scepticism and resistance if they are not practised authentically.

More up-to-date, or so called 'third-generation', thinking involves a new level of consciousness based on a higher level of psychological understanding in which interactions are seen as 'mutual understanding conversations.' It is an approach no longer motivated by a binary mindset of win/lose or right/wrong. It is guided by underlying principles – the four 'C's' – compassion, courage, curiosity, and collaboration. This approach allows for there being a fighting chance of staying resourceful, looking after the relationship and finding a productive way forward.

Unfortunately, this approach is not easy and can seem counter-intuitive. Sartre did warn us that 'hell is other people.' Certainly, the response of others, their power to make us change how we think and feel about ourselves or threaten us in some way, can feel hellish. However, where would we be without others? People can block our creativity, or they can enable us to truly express and work with it. If you can always start with a curiosity towards others, it can help in a conflict situation. It is always worth asking oneself: What is it the other person is finding difficult here? What are our differences? Why do those differences exist? Can those differences coexist? What are our commonalities, etc.?

So, when having or preparing for a difficult conversation, try to cultivate an attitude of discovery and curiosity rather than one of defence and attack. Pretend you don't know anything about the other person, try to 'bracket' or put aside all assumptions about what they might be thinking, and try to learn as much as possible about the other person and their point of view by giving them time to express themselves.

When we are in conflict with someone, they can feel very alien to us, so why not try to use this creatively? Perhaps pretend you're entertaining a visitor from another planet and find out how things look on that planet, how certain events affect the other person, and what their values and priorities are.

Your most useful tool in avoiding conflict in the first place, and dealing effectively with it quickly should it arise, is through the use of effective listening. Active listening is at the heart of all good communication and relationship skills, but it sounds much easier than it is. Adults spend an average of 70 per cent of their time engaged in some sort of communication; of this, an average of 45 per cent is spent listening compared to 30 per cent speaking, 16 per cent reading and 9 per cent writing (Adler et al. 2001). Studies also tell us that 70 per cent of mistakes in the workplace are a direct result of poor communication.

If you ask a child 'what do you listen with?', they will point to their ears. But listening is not the same as hearing, and in order to listen effectively, you need to use more than just your ears. Effective listening requires concentration and the use of your other senses – not just hearing the words spoken. Listening engages all of our body. We pick up feelings from the other person; we feel our emotional reaction to what we hear; we see how the other person is expressing themselves through their body language.

To listen well, patience is called for. Let the other person talk until they are finished. Don't interrupt except to acknowledge and feed back what you believe you have heard. Whatever you hear, don't get hijacked and take it personally. This will only cause you to interrupt and feel the need to stop listening and start defending yourself. Even if the person seems to be talking 'off the point' or indeed 'talking rubbish,' let them continue, at least for a while. They will be telling you something if you listen carefully enough, even if it is just that they are nervous or they are so afraid of listening to you that they don't want to give you space. Just try to learn as much as you can in this phase of the conversation. They will stop eventually, and you will get your turn; just don't rush things. This phase is the 'tuning in' which I referred to earlier.

The other person needs to *know* that they have been heard by you, so acknowledgement and showing that you've heard and understood is vital. Try to understand the other person so well you can make their argument for them. Explain back to them what you are understanding their needs and wants to be. Guess at their hopes and respect their position, e.g., 'So for you, this is how things appear … . It seems to me that you are angry/upset because you believe … .' A person will not begin to reflect and change unless they first see that you understand where they are coming from and are not trying to ridicule their position but are open to trying to understand why they hold the view they do even if you don't share it. If you are wrong in your understanding then feeding back, paraphrasing, and summarising what you *believe* you have heard gives the other person a chance to clarify any misunderstanding. Getting it wrong can be the first step to getting it right and approaching understanding. As Foulkes (2018) pointed out, a good deal can be learned from mistakes, as long as one is not in too much of a hurry to correct them.

If the manner of the other person, or indeed your own manner, is getting in the way, then be brave enough to acknowledge that, e.g., 'I notice I'm becoming defensive, and I think it's because your voice just got louder and sounded angry. I would like us to try to stay calm. I just want to talk about this topic so we can get a better understanding of each other. I'm not trying to persuade you to agree with me.' Acknowledgement isn't agreement. It can help to calm the other person and take away their perceived need to defend their position, moving them from a 'fight' position where they are unable to hear or reflect, into a place where they can listen and engage. Saying, 'This sounds really important to you,' shows respect, and when a person feels respected, heard, and seen they no longer need to shout or be aggressive.

Once you feel you have an understanding of the other person's thinking and you have reflected back to them your understanding, you can start to 'tune out.' What you are tuning out from is the gathering of information to understand the other's world view; you have enough of that to move the dispute forward and can focus back onto the dispute. Having felt heard, the other person should be in a better position to listen to you. You can contextualise what you want to say around what you have learnt, e.g., 'From what you've told me, I can see how you came to the conclusion that I'm not a team player. I think I am; let me explain. When I introduce problems with a project, I'm thinking about its long-term success and what that will mean for all of us. I don't mean to be a critic, though perhaps I sound like one. Maybe we can talk about how to collectively address these issues so that my intention is clear and we can move forward.'

By this point you will hopefully both be able to move on to collaboratively exploring the issues which are in dispute. Brainstorming and continued clarifying and exploring are useful here. Ask the other person what they think might work. Whatever they say, find something you relate to and build on it. If the conversation becomes adversarial, go back to exploring commonalities. Asking for the other's point of view usually creates safety and encourages engagement.

All of this can feel very difficult and, for some people, counter-intuitive. People can worry that they may look soft or weak if they focus on the other person's views first. However, this is a necessary stage to get to the point when both people can listen to each other. To listen to the other person first shows strength. You are not playing a game of domination but are genuinely trying to find a solution to a problem, which is a problem for both of you.

It can help if you prepare for a potentially difficult conversation by thinking about how you will start it. This will set the tone and make a successful resolution more likely.

You could start with openings such as:

- I have something I'd like to discuss with you that I think will help us work together more effectively.
- I'd like to talk about X with you, but first I'd like to hear your point of view.
- I need your help with what just happened. Do you have a few minutes to talk?
- I think we have different perceptions about X; it would be good to hear each other's thoughts.
- I'd like to talk about X. I think we may have different ideas about how to resolve the situation.
- I'd like to see if we might reach a better understanding about X. I really want to hear and understand your feelings about this and to share my perspective as well.

Once you are engaged in the conversation you need to be an excellent listener. We have all experienced someone as a 'good listener' or a 'bad listener.' Ask yourself, when did you last feel really listened to? What was it that made it feel that the listener was truly interested and engaged rather than going through the polite motions? The ability to communicate to the person who is talking that you are genuinely interested in what they are telling you and that you really do want to understand their particular point of view is an essential part of the listening process.

Most of the time, the person 'listening' is having their own little conversation in their head, thinking about what they are going to say next and waiting for a moment to jump in and give their opinion. This isn't listening; it's just verbal tennis, and it leaves both people feeling dissatisfied. You need to try something different. Get into the habit of pausing when the other person finishes speaking. Give it three to five seconds, or even longer if you can see the speaker is mulling things over silently.

This isn't easy particularly if you do not agree with what they are saying. However, if you can manage it, the speaker will become aware that you are actually taking the time to consider what they have just said. In itself, this tells them that you are taking them seriously and that you value their words, opinions, and most importantly, them as a person.

Giving space for the speaker to pause for breath or gather their thoughts shows respect and that you were not just waiting for the earliest opportunity to contradict or challenge them. There are few things more irritating than being interrupted just as you are reflecting or seeking to get your point across, even when it is to share a similar experience of your own. It is their space and leave them to fill it. By giving a brief gap to absorb what the speaker has said you are actually hearing them at a deeper level. You understand what it is they are trying to get across, and you are more likely to glean valuable information from them.

One of the many things you are listening for are emotions. We are all emotional. Emotions are always present, but there is often a desire to conceal them. Some individuals and some cultures are more comfortable expressing emotion than others. Emotions play such a big role in our lives that there are more than 600 words in English to describe them verbally, not to mention 43 facial muscles to express them physically.

Our emotions often express what really matters to us and touch on our values and self-esteem. Emotions are a gift to the listener; they provide a shortcut to what is really important and are often more eloquent than words. They are not something to be afraid of or to try to shut down. They will help you to understand what is important for the other person.

Emotions are always intentional; they are about something: I am happy/angry/sad because … . They are normally associated with specific events or occurrences and are intense enough to disrupt thought processes, so trying to speak logically to someone who is emotional is not productive. Emotions not only reveal an individual's world view but also disclose the diversity of each individual.

Try not to sidestep expressed emotions. If someone is upset or angry, stay with the upset or angry person. Try to find out what is making them upset or angry. Don't guess and never assume you know. There is never a need to dig for emotions or to suggest to someone how they are feeling; you just work with what you hear, see, and sense.

To listen well, we use a number of non-verbal skills, which we employ daily without thinking, as many of them are very subtle, e.g., eye contact, facial expression, nodding, posture, and not interrupting. Added to these, we can verbally show that we have listened and encourage the other person to tell us more by using open hands, arms, and body language.

One skill is termed 'reflecting back.' This means simply giving back what you have heard using the words of the other person. However, if you employ this as a technique without any sense of connectedness or empathy with the other person, it can be irritating and annoy them. If you hear a powerful word, e.g., anger, despair etc., you may choose to show that you have heard its power by simply echoing what you have heard and importantly matching the tone in which it was said. By following this with a silence, you will encourage the person to say more and also to think about whether the word they used really conveys the level of their feeling. You may choose to paraphrase what you have heard. This means rephrasing what you have heard in your own words, but remember to always be tentative to allow for correction. Using summaries is also helpful, particularly after quite a lot has been said or you feel at a loss as to what to say next. Remember that we cannot change what has happened – the so-called 'facts' – but we can change perceptions, so it is important when summarising to include the mood and emotions that you have noticed.

I am not a great fan of asking questions, as it often feels to the other person that they are being interrogated. It is better to explore, rather than question, by inviting people to say more, e.g., 'Can you tell me a little more about that?' If you do choose to ask questions, then closed questions which require a yes or no answer will not move the process forward, so try asking open questions. Such questions often start with 'what': 'What was that like?'; or 'how': 'How did that leave you?', 'How did you experience that?' Try to avoid asking 'how did that make you feel?' as I can almost guarantee that they will have expressed clearly in verbal tone, pace, word choice, and body language how they felt about something and to ask that question will make them wonder whether they have been seen or heard.

Through both non-verbal and verbal communication, you are seeking to show empathy. Empathy is not about being sympathetic or caring; it is showing in a concrete way that you are able to see the speaker's point of view, to 'get' what that person has experienced. This is further evidenced through matching their mood, energy, and pace. Once again, by doing this you are not agreeing or colluding with their perception.

Through using these skills reflectively and appropriately, you create rapport and trust, show that you are really trying to understand, demonstrate respect and interest, reveal what really matters to the speaker, and enable the speaker to hear themselves. However, there are many factors that can get in the way. We might be distracted for any number of reasons:

- Being tense, nervous, anxious, and feeling insecure
- Trying to remember everything that is being said
- Worrying about our 'performance'
- Working out what to say next or what to do
- Wanting to rush to a solution
- Bombarding someone with fact finding questions
- Assuming to understand too quickly and from our own point of view

Once you are aware of this, you can try to put aside your impatience or need to rush the person. You need to park any judgemental feelings, boredom, or feeling the need to contradict what they are saying or defend your own position. They will only listen to what you have to say when they trust you. This tuning in part of the process should allow you to step into the other's world and see the dispute through their eyes. Tuning in and actively demonstrating that you have heard will create rapport and enable the speaker to open up more and more. Indeed, tuning in is 'empathy in action' – you are getting alongside the other person. This creates safety for the other person, allowing them to be more open to listening to your view.

When the time comes to share your perceptions, stay calm. The other person may not have developed their conflict resolution skills so may interrupt and contradict you. They may get angry and try to talk over you. Explain why you see things in a different way, how being in disagreement makes you feel, and your commitment to finding a way forward together. If you have heard common interests in what they have said, build your response around those. In the case of most music disputes, there is more to be gained from reconciliation and a lot to be lost if differences cannot be accepted.

The Collective

Most conflicts in groups could be avoided or at least prevented from building up and becoming a crisis. However, in my experience, it is rare for musicians to be proactive in this way. Perhaps it feels too businesslike or it feels dangerous to think that there may be trouble ahead when a band is in the early excitement of getting together and creating new sounds.

Other parts of the creative industries seem more advanced. It is not unusual for touring theatre companies to get together for a week's preparation retreat where they will talk about any issues they may foresee and may even roleplay them.

Before embarking on any proactive conflict avoidance work, it is worth asking 'do we all speak the same language?' By this, I am not speaking of national languages, English, French, etc., but what personal language does each band member use? What are the different ways people in the group express themselves? Does one person use a lot of narrative and metaphor whilst another uses straightforward transactional language? What pace is used – slow, thoughtful with silences, or fast, quick-thinking, innovative, with no space for interruption to clarify or challenge? Each person is likely to have a combination of all of these, but there will be an identifiable preferred communication style. If we ignore these differences, it is not very dissimilar to one person speaking English to someone whose first language is German and who has only a smattering of English words. The result is, we will not fully understand one another. If we can try to meet the style of the person we are speaking with somewhere in the middle it shows respect and a desire for understanding rather than a desire to override them.

Let me offer an example from a recent mediation. Two middle-aged, white, professional men, overtly very similar in experience, political views, and education had to work together and could not understand why they did not get on and were finding it impossible to collaborate. After speaking with them both separately, I was struck with how their language conveyed very different world views. One of them was very dynamic, spoke very quickly with few pauses, and used superhero metaphors – 'Together we can save the world,' 'Let us don our cloaks and soar above.' His leadership style was mainly charismatic but also direct and quite transactional. He believed he was very inspirational and could not understand why the other person had not responded positively to the image of them soaring together above everything and everyone else. The other man spoke to me of wanting to place his staff centre stage so that they could take credit for how well the company was doing. His pace was much slower; he would stop, reflect, and reclarify what he wanted me to understand. His leadership style was that of servant leader. During the mediation they were able to reflect on these different styles and how their use of language was not having the desired impact as it failed to speak to the way the other saw the world. Once they were aware of this, they could effectively collaborate as their goals were aligned.

The regularity of tensions in bands has made it the subject of a number of studies and Kramer & Yahm (2010) sensibly suggest that a lot of conflict in bands could be avoided if certain questions were discussed at the outset, for example:

- What do we want to accomplish together?
- What are my partners' expectations of me in this relationship?
- What will we each contribute to the effort?
- How will we handle conflicts or differences of opinion when they do arise?
- Will we be comfortable with total and complete openness?
- How can we discuss potentially uncomfortable subjects?
- How do you respond to issues that evoke strong emotions?
- If I disagree with your point of view, will I lose your respect?
- Can we agree to disagree without thinking less of each other?
- Do you feel judged by me when you do not agree with me?
- If you are disappointed with something said or done by someone else in the group, will you tell them? How will you let them know?

- How can we talk about problems in a way that will be constructive instead of leading to an argument?
- Is there such a thing as being too honest?
- How do we handle critical issues we prioritise differently?
- Which decisions need to be made together, and which can be left to each individual?
- What kind of behaviour makes you feel disrespected? Do I ever make you feel that way?
- If I could do one thing to improve our relationship, what would it be?
- How do I handle manipulative statements or leading questions?
- How do you respond to stress and conflict?
- How do you feel about your own anger?
- When is it acceptable to feel angry?
- When is it not acceptable?
- How do you feel when you are the target of someone else's anger?
- How do you respond?
- How do you handle money?
- What are your theories about handling debts and expenses?
- How will the group income, expenses, and savings be handled?
- How do you intend to integrate your family and career?
- How do you integrate your day job (if you have one) with your music career?
- What are your experiences and expectations in relation to alcohol and drug use?
- Do we all share the same cultural, religious, and political views?
- If not, do those differences cause any problems?
- Are you uncomfortable discussing any of these with each other?
- Where do you see your professional life in five years? Ten years?

Unfortunately, it is very rare that a band will ask these questions until something is going wrong. This is understandable as their main aim is to work together to create something amazing, which can then be released and hopefully in turn bring financial rewards. Asking these questions when a band is forming may feel a bit like making a prenuptial agreement and so taking the excitement and romance out of a new creative relationship.

Using Creative Conflict Approaches

If a group can get beyond healthy scepticism, there are exercises which may be helpful. Some, such as brainstorming, focal object method, etc., are quite traditional and have been joined by relatively new ones birthed from creative conflict thinking, such as virtual brainstorming, the method of mental pockets, design thinking, purposeful validation, dynamic and facilitated conversation, etc.

In the realm of creativity and innovation, conflict can be a powerful catalyst for growth, change, and the generation of new ideas. Creative conflict is not about hostility or discord but rather about the clash of differing perspectives and ideas that can lead to innovative solutions and breakthroughs through engaging in a constructive dialogue. It involves a respectful exchange of ideas where conflicting opinions are explored and debated rather than ignored or suppressed. This kind of conflict is essential because it challenges the status quo, stimulates critical thinking, and encourages participants to consider alternative approaches. For creatives, the benefit of such creative conflict is often clear but that doesn't always make it any easier for them to engage with.

I want to give a brief overview of how some of these approaches work.

Design Thinking

This is a problem-solving methodology that prioritises human-centred, creative, and iterative approaches. When applied to conflict resolution, design thinking helps address disputes not just by resolving surface issues but by uncovering the root causes and designing mutually beneficial solutions. It follows a process with five steps:

1. **Empathise:** The aim here is to understand the perspectives, needs, and emotions of everyone involved. Within the conflict context it requires deep listening without judgement, practising active empathy, and identifying the underlying values and interests of those in conflict.
2. **Define:** The group needs to clearly articulate the core problem based on insights gained through empathy and frame the conflict as shared and not focused on any one individual.
3. **Ideate:** At this stage, the group brainstorms multiple creative solutions without immediate judgement or criticism, encouraging collaborative thinking to generate win–win outcomes and allowing all sides to contribute ideas for resolution.
4. **Prototype:** From there, the work is to develop and agree to test versions of potential solutions, asking what could go wrong as well as exploring the positive potential outcomes.
5. **Test:** The final stage is to try it out, get feedback, and refine.

Dynamic Facilitation

Dynamic facilitation (DF) is a group process designed to help people address complex, emotionally charged issues creatively and collaboratively.

Jim Rough (1997) who is credited with developing DF in the 1980s refers to it as 'choice-creating' and describes the facilitator as 'an empathic listener.' Zubizarreta (2014) describes the process as an invitation to step into the fire of our passionately held beliefs and notice the larger possibilities taking shape among us, thus allowing us to get underneath ineffective expressions – shouting, whining, and bullying – to the deeper longings buried in the angst.

DF is particularly effective in situations where traditional decision-making or facilitation methods fail due to polarisation, complexity, or deep uncertainty. Zubizarreta (2014: 89) explains that it is an approach which

> values being able to meet people where they are, instead of asking them to behave differently or to censor themselves. Therefore, instead of using ground rules in an attempt to create safety, the approach emphasizes facilitation and modelling. As the saying goes, 'attitudes are caught not taught.'

Having said that, it doesn't encourage interpersonal confrontation, and facilitators may intervene to prevent that.

The aim of DF is not to explore interpersonal relationships but to help to generate a much deeper understanding of the different perspectives and considerations. It aims to facilitate group members to co-create a mindset for this context and purpose and so to develop new ways forward. Zubizarreta (2006) eloquently describes this process as welcoming whatever shows up – likening it to aikido – through which one harnesses the other's energy and reflects it back to the group. The facilitator needs the skills not just to listen to the individual speaking but also to the spoken and unspoken communication from the group as a whole, refraining from pushing for agreement or convergence but instead aiming to hold the space open for creative ideas to emerge. In following the 'emergent group process,' DF has much in common with other small group facilitation methods such as Bohmian Dialogue and T-groups, which are valuable in their own right but are not designed for addressing specific practical issues, which remains the aim of DF.

The process does not use structured agendas or step-by-step plans, it allows the group to follow the natural flow of conversation, emotions, and ideas and to express authentic concerns and emotions without filters. Most facilitators will use flip charts or a whiteboard to jot down all proposed solutions (no matter how feasible), any emotional or logical objections or concerns, factual information, etc. which any group member raises. The facilitator has to guard against pushing for consensus, instead giving equal respect to all suggestions by following the energy of the group and listening deeply. They can then help to reframe or clarify contributions without showing any bias or judgement.

The approach aims to open new doors of possibility within a group though establishing a field of 'choice-creating' in which:

- Everyone's wisdom and creative perspectives are evoked.
- Everyone's contributions are valued and held safe from judgement.
- Issues are explored and dealt with in their full complexity.
- The group seeks answers that work for everyone.
- Answers are co-discovered leading to 'co-sensus.'

Through this process it looks to achieve:

- Better solutions to difficult issues, faster with more consensus
- Clarity and empowerment: people determining and resolving what's *really* on their minds
- Trust, respect, and the spirit of community
- Increased knowledge and skills
- Everyone being engaged, enthused, and committed to the results
- Opening new doors of possibility for transforming large systems

Focal Objects

The method of focal objects (C. Whiting 2007; E. de Bono 2016,) gives properties of random objects to the object that is the subject of the problem being solved and can be very effective if properly mastered.

One example is The Robinson Method which was designed to:

- Unlock creative potential
- Encourage open mindedness
- Model that we all have different, possibly opposite, but equal and valid ways of thinking
- Promote collaboration
- Challenge assumptions about how objects 'should' be used
- Encourage unconventional thinking
- Promote discussion, imagination, and problem-solving

This can be used as a good warm-up exercise for creative discussion before moving on to discussion of more contentious issues. The format has five steps:

1. Firstly, choose an ordinary object e.g. shoe, spoon.
2. Then, list its conventional uses.

3. Begin to generate potential unusual uses, brainstorming as many non-traditional uses as possible. No idea is too wild.
4. Ensure everyone in the group is encouraged to offer new ideas, elaborate or build on ones already offered.
5. Reflect and apply: Finally, discuss which ideas could be useful or spark innovation in another context (e.g., songwriting, storytelling, problem-solving).

If you are wanting to try this approach, a handy acronym is **SCAMPER** – **S**ubstitute, **C**ombine, **A**dapt, **M**odify, **P**ut to other use, **E**liminate, **R**everse:

Substitute part of the product/process with something else.
Some useful prompt questions:
What else can be used instead?
Can we substitute materials, people, rules?

Combine by merging two or more elements
Some useful prompt questions:
What ideas can be combined?
Can we blend features or functions?

Adapt to serve another purpose
Some useful prompt questions:
What else is this like?
What could we adapt or copy from elsewhere?

Modify to serve another purpose
Some useful prompt questions:
What can we enlarge, exaggerate, minimise, or simplify?

Put to other use
Some useful prompt questions:
What other uses could this have?
Who else might benefit?

Eliminate by removing the unnecessary
Some useful prompt questions:
What can we get rid of?
What isn't really essential?

Reverse or rearrange – flip the order, process, or structure
Some useful prompt questions:
What if we turn the whole thing on its head?

Lateral Thinking

Edward de Bono (1992; 2016) is the person best known for the concept of lateral thinking, which developed in the 1960s as a way to solve problems through an indirect and creative approach, contrasting with traditional vertical (logical or step-by-step) thinking. It looks at a problem from new and changing angles, aiming to generate new and innovative solutions. It aims to challenge assumptions, generate alternatives, break out of logic traps and be provocative.

To do this it uses a number of techniques which include:

- **Random Entry:** Introduce a random word or stimulus to spark new ideas.
- **Concept Extraction:** Identify the underlying concept and apply it elsewhere.
- **Reversal Technique:** Reverse a common idea to uncover hidden alternatives.
- **Fractionation:** Break down the problem into smaller parts to see overlooked connections.

Mental Pockets

Although the term isn't widely defined or standardised, it can provide a useful metaphor for those who like to think visually. It is used in several ways, often by therapists and coaches, as a journaling tool, or in creative writing and by individuals and groups.

Cognitive Storage Spaces

The idea is to visualise *mental pockets* as compartments in your mind in which you can store thoughts, memories, emotions, or even coping strategies. This can be helpful when things are feeling overwhelming, and you can return to open individual pockets when the time feels right.

Mindfulness and Emotional Regulation

The pockets can represent emotional reserves or calming techniques you keep 'in your back pocket,' ready to draw on when you need to manage stress, anxiety, or difficult situations.

Task-Oriented Thinking

Some people use the idea in their work, using 'pockets' for work, creativity, relationships, with each pocket containing reminders of the mindset, knowledge, and behaviours which people have recommended to them or they have found best suited to that domain.

Cognitive Load Management

Visualising a capacity limit on each pocket may alert you to having too many tasks or thoughts, which can lead to overwhelm. This can relate to productivity or mental health.

Trauma and Repression

Used in a psychological context, with support, mental pockets can symbolise places where painful memories or unresolved experiences are stored until they are addressed.

Purposeful Validation

We all need validation, yet the word itself means different things to different people. Although we all need it, we may have been warned never to seek it, as we may be disappointed or thought needy.

Even those who seem supremely confident, even arrogant, or who are, usually incorrectly, labelled 'narcissistic,' a word which seems to be bandied about a lot at the moment, require validation. In saying this, I want to stress that validation does need to be authentic and not be used as a manipulative tool to disarm people. Fleck (2025) defines validation as communication that is mindful and understands and empathises with the other person's experience, thereby accepting it as valid. She indicates five categories of positive change which validation can bring about:

- Improved relationships
- Decreased conflict
- Increased influence
- Increased ability to drive behaviour change
- Increased self-compassion

It is an approach which is used in dialectical behaviour therapy (DBT) and coaching. DBT's creator, Marsha Linehan, defined validation as a way of communicating to someone that their emotions, responses, and experiences make sense. It is the key to building trust and fostering healthy relationships. She reminds us that it 'has nothing to do with social desirability and is not synonymous with praise' (1997: 357).

Linehan identifies six levels of validation, ranging from basic attention to deeply understanding and relating to another person's experience.

You will see that these mirror what I have already introduced in slightly different terms.

1. **Being present:** Actively listening and showing attentiveness to the other person, both verbally and nonverbally.
2. **Accurate reflection:** Summarising and paraphrasing what the person has said to demonstrate understanding.
3. **Reading the unspoken:** Going beyond what is explicitly stated and attempting to understand the underlying emotions or thoughts.
4. **Validating based on history and biology:** Acknowledging how past experiences or biological factors might influence current emotions or behaviours.
5. **Normalising:** Recognising that a person's emotional reaction is a common and understandable response to a situation.
6. **Radical genuineness:** Expressing a deep and authentic understanding of the other person's experience, including acknowledging one's own limitations.

The key skills involved are:

- Reflecting someone's input back to them to show they were heard
- Acknowledging emotional responses to foster psychological safety
- Affirming the relevance or impact of an idea within the group process

There are some helpful and encouraging phrases which can be used such as:

- That's an important and powerful insight.
- It sounds like that's something really important to you.
- You are raising a point that could help us all reshape how we see this issue.

It is important to remember that when we validate people, we are not agreeing (nor disagreeing) with them. Nor are we trying to please or manipulate them. We are showing our respect for their existence and their right to have their own perspective on things. It is only when people feel this acceptance that they are likely to feel understood, accepted, and supported and can believe that you will provide a safe space for open communication.

The use of validation in resolving conflict is acknowledged and used in many contexts to build trust and encourage honest responses. Researchers Laurence and Emily Alison (2017) from the University of Liverpool explored and disproved the popular notion that torture is an effective method of obtaining credible information from detainees, and showed that torture (including sarcasm, intimidation, and being judgemental) actually impaired communication and recall, increased resistance, damaged the reliability of information, and resulted in disengagement, withdrawal, and psychological trauma. Instead, rapport-oriented approaches gave better results. Rapport is more or less synonymous with validation and seeks to find common ground, using and encouraging self-disclosure and displaying understanding via empathy. When we have our views challenged, our first response is to defend our view; the more it is challenged, the more adamant we will become that we are right. If our views are listened to and accepted as a valid personal response to our experience, then we calm down and are more prepared to engage in dialogue and even be interested in hearing another person's view. If we are met with some validation, there is no need to defend or attack, it causes a physical response decreasing people's heart rate and sweating and removing the instinctive need to fight or flee, which increases the ability to reason and engage in perspective-taking.

Virtual Brainstorming

Most of you will be very familiar with brainstorming. I am aware that, for some, this is not an acceptable term as it was thought to be offensive to people suffering with epilepsy, and alternative terms are idea generation, mind mapping, or thought showers. Unpublished research by the Epilespsy Society (https://epilepsysociety.org.uk/) has shown that epilepsy suffers do not consider the word brainstorming offensive, so I shall use it here, as all the other terms are also used for other techniques.

The term *Virtual* brainstorming is used to describe a collaborative idea generation process which is conducted online, using digital tools rather than in-person. Since the Covid pandemic, we have seen its increased use as it allows individuals or groups, often working remotely, to contribute, discuss, and build on ideas in real time or asynchronously. It can be used effectively in disputes to explore the different perceptions of those involved.

Virtual brainstorming uses digital platforms such as MURAL, Google Docs, Jamboard, FigJam, and Zoom to enable visual collaboration and communication. It can be used synchronously, with participants brainstorming live during a video call, or asynchronously which makes it ideal for when people are in different time zones. Many platforms allow for anonymous submissions, encouraging honest participation and sharing of opposing views. It is automatically recorded and so can be revisited and analysed at a later date.

Although digital, it uses common techniques, such as digital 'sticky notes' or 'Post-its'; 'mind mapping' to visually organise ideas and map the places of connection; 'dot voting,' by which the group prioritises ideas and votes on what they would like to action; and the use of virtual breakout rooms to discuss ideas in smaller groups.

While less spontaneous and personal than its in-person counterpart, it may appeal to quieter personalities and those in remote locations. It is very scalable. For example, it can start with a small group of band members and extend out to include managers, promoters, etc., and its virtual and time flexible nature makes it easier for everyone to be involved regardless of location or diary commitments. Of course, it brings with it some technical challenges which not everyone may be comfortable with, and it needs very clear and skilled facilitation to keep everyone focused and engaged.

The Two Main Requirements for Successfully Dealing with Conflict

All the above approaches require two things: developing our natural curiosity and effectively using our skills in active listening.

The Importance of Curiosity

It is worth developing the art of being curious, as curiosity is the driver to know more, to hold a deep desire to explore and understand. This is essential in life, not just in resolving conflict. It is a mindset, a skill, and ultimately, a way of living. It requires us to be brave and embrace not knowing, reminding ourselves that we don't know – and that's exciting. It speaks directly to the existential concern of being with uncertainty, by welcoming uncertainty and seeing ignorance not as failure, but as a starting point. It is transformative, broadens empathy, fuels creativity, and deepens wisdom. When you live curiously, you're constantly evolving.

Albert Einstein once claimed that he had no special talents but was passionately curious! It is curiosity which brings about creativity, the very lifeblood of the music industry. It is a fundamental requirement in the art of being human, playing an important role in personal growth, innovation, and social development. It:

- **Drives learning and discovery** – motivating us to seek new information and explore the unfamiliar.
- **Fosters creativity and innovation** – through asking a curious question: 'What if?' or 'Why not?' Something small children are excellent at doing.
- **Improves mental health and resilience** – Curious individuals tend to experience greater life satisfaction. Curiosity is linked to traits like openness and adaptability, helping people handle uncertainty better and remain engaged even in difficult circumstances.

- **Enhances relationships** – through promoting empathy, active listening, and deeper connections, through being genuinely interested in the other.
- **Supports lifelong growth** – keeping the mind agile and receptive to new things.

Sometimes curiosity about the world, or the focused curiosity about the words we use in songs or the notes we choose to form music, means we have less time to be curious about each other.

Leslie (2014) offers us 'seven ways to stay curious.' I must confess that I have a little difficulty in differentiating some of these from each other, but the underlying message is that creativity requires curiosity.

Stay foolish

By this, I understand that he is speaking about nurturing the kind of inquisitive curiosity we have as children. As we become adults, we feel we should 'know things' and fear that to ask questions and seek clarity makes us look foolish. Those who create, innovate, and succeed are always willing to look foolish and accept that there is always more to learn.

There are many videos of bands and solo artists 'fooling around,' and this playfulness, with its distance from pursuing a goal, allows the freedom of creativity to blossom, resulting in a huge hit.

Build the database

In this section of his book, he asks us to embrace 'the inevitability of defeat' and introduces us to James Webb Young's book, *A Technique for Producing Ideas*, (1960), in which he proposed five steps towards being creative.

Gather Raw Material

Young (1960, 32) writes

> every really creative person … has two noticeable characteristics. Firstly, there is no subject under the sun in which he could not easily get interested .... Every facet of life has interest to him. Second, he is an extensive browser of all sorts of fields of information … an idea results from a new combination of specific knowledge.

Applying this to the music industry, we must ask ourselves to what extent the interest in the product – song, gig, etc. – gets in the way of a wider curiosity which cultivates an authentic interest about what others in the band and other sectors of the industry are experiencing in their professional and personal lives. Such interest brings a sense of worth to those who are invited to speak about their hopes, dreams, and worries, which develops a trust in the relationship making it easier to share joy and express differences.

Forage Like a Foxhog

Leslie references Paola Antonelli, a senior curator in the department of architecture and design at the Museum of Modern Art in New York and a self-declared generalist and 'curious octopus!' She speaks of two kinds of people: conservers and hunter-gathers, placing herself firmly in the latter category. She speaks of the need for those working in groups to be open to ideas from others and to quickly adapt to them, focusing on experiences and interactions rather than product outcome. Leslie (2014: 219) uses the narrative of the fox and the hedgehog to illustrate this, 'the fox evades his attackers in a variety of inventive but exhausting ways, while the hedgehog adopts one tried and trusted strategy – hunkering down and letting its spikes do the work.' He goes on to declare, 'the thinkers best positioned to thrive today and in the future will be a hybrid of these two animals.'

If we are lucky enough to be in a group, we don't have to individually be each of these animals. By recognising the strength in the differences each person brings, we are greater than the sum of the group's parts. By being afraid of difference instead of celebrating it we lose creative opportunities. Our fear of otherness and of not holding universal truths accepted by all around us means that we are operating on reduced power.

Ask the Big Why

We often make assumptions about things and people and then use those assumptions as a starting point to develop an internal narrative to make sense of a person's actions. The likelihood is that our assumption is wrong and that any action stemming from that will be doomed. Instead, we need to ask the right question: 'Why do you believe that/Why do you think that would be the best way forward?', or: 'I don't really get your point of view. Can you explain to me why you see it that way, so I can understand why you think/feel/believe that?' Any 'why' question needs to be asked tentatively, or it can sound judgemental, i.e. 'Why do you believe (such a foolish thing)?'

Be a Thinkerer

Think about your thoughts! Ask yourself why you are thinking a particular thing.

- Is it because to think the opposite would feel threatening in some way?
- Is it because you have insufficient information to think differently?
- What has brought you to that thought?
    - What others have said?
    - What you personally have experienced?
    - Things you have read or seen?

Question your teaspoons

This is a variation on the focal object method introduced earlier. Leslie (2014) writes about attending the Boring Conference set up by James Ward, an admirer of the French writer Georges Perec who was interested in the 'infra-ordinary.' Ward speaks of the transformative power of attention to all objects (Leslie, 2014). At these conferences, individuals talk about their fascination with things which may at first seem boring – the history of self-service supermarket check-out machines, hand dryers, paint catalogues, sneezes, cash registers, double yellow lines, and even teaspoons! Ward is not the first person to draw our attention to this. Warhol declared, on an exhibition poster he produced for Moderna Museet, Stockholm in 1968, 'I like boring things,' and he spent a long time studying and painting tin cans, and John Cage stated, 'if something is boring after two minutes, try it for four, if still boring, then eight, then sixteen, then thirty-two, eventually one discovers that it is not boring at all.' (1961: 25)

In relation to preventing conflict, it is again a call to remain curious. Your colleague may be boring the pants off you, but continue to listen; you may learn something, and at the very least, you will have enhanced the self-esteem of the person you are listening to, building trust which sets a better ground for dealing with conflict if it occurs.

Turn puzzles into mysteries

Leslie (2014) believes that a puzzle is something which commands our curiosity until we solve it. Whereas a mystery never stops inviting enquiry. He wrote,

> when we first meet a new problem, our instinct is to treat it as a puzzle ... then after gathering the knowledge we need to solve it, we sometimes

> start to think of the same puzzle as a mystery. One which will sustain our curiosity forever. A passing interest can be transformed into a life-long passion.
>
> (2014: 262)

I am sometimes surprised at the hours artists will give to review one line of a song, working hard to release its mystery, whilst showing little patience with their fellows. Each person's existence contains their own rich history and mystery.

I am never sure when reading Leslie that I am taking from it what he intended. The above is definitely my interpretation. I'm fine with that, as I see anything we read or hear as a jumping off point for our own thoughts, not a 'truth' which I must accept; instead, it is the embryo of a creative journey towards finding my own meaning. Obviously, the same is true of this book. Its intention is to promote thought about conflict, for individuals to reflect on their own stance to conflict and how they wish to address it, and wherever possible, for that to be shared with those they are closest to, as unfortunately they are the ones we are most likely to get into conflict with.

The Importance of Active Listening

I hope it has been clear throughout that the key skill in dealing with conflict is listening. Although we believe that we listen most of the time, this is unlikely to be the case. We usually half listen or even pretend to listen, because we believe we already know what is being said or because we lack the curiosity to hear other people's views.

Really listening requires a great deal of attention and presence. We cannot be fully listening to a person and thinking about the next gig, or where to get lunch. It requires our full attention not just to the words being spoken, but equally to those that are only shown through the body. It requires such intense concentration that it is impossible to fully listen all of the time. However, when we are in a disagreement, the need to fully listen is essential. Eugene Gendlin (2003), who founded Focusing, describes it as interhuman attention or, as Nelle Morton (1986: 32) wrote, we are required 'to hear one another into being.' It is only when we feel fully heard that we can open ourselves to fully listen to another person, to notice our differences and yet stay connected.

The above just highlights a number of ways in which we can improve our skills to avoid, manage, and resolve conflict. The purpose of this book has not been to give a comprehensive course on these skills, merely to indicate what they are and how important they are in dealing with conflict. There are many books out there which offer strategies and exercises for those who want them.

Conclusion

To all intents and purposes, the music industry is very like a family. Like all families, it has its villains and its angels. It forms alliances, and there are inevitably many ruptures, mostly small, but sometimes ones which threaten ongoing communication.

When people are in conflict, they believe it is the other person's fault, falsely believing it possible that one side could be solely responsible for the issue. They stew over it, clinging to any evidence that they are right and the other party is wrong, replaying the scenario in their heads, holding on to resentment and a sense of justice like badges of honour in their righteous fight. The truth is that in a dispute, both sides usually believe they are absolutely right. I hope I have shown that to work with conflict, we have to first know ourselves and be willing to reflect and critically analyse what we believe to be truths whilst remaining open to truly listening to the other side of the argument.

Those within the music industry have the creative skills to deal with conflict, but there is often a reluctance to admit such conflict exists and so no real push to be proactive in further developing the skills to manage conflict situations. This means that conflict is usually embedded by the time it is acknowledged and may need outside intervention such as mediation.

However, most disputes do not need to get as far as litigation or mediation. Indeed, using insight, reflection, and communication skills to avoid the dispute in the first place is the ideal way forward. Failing that, recognising when a disagreement is brewing and taking active measures to resolve it early is a good response. This may include bringing in others, such as coaches and consultants, or band members and those in the music business further developing their own communication skills and trying to know themselves and their colleagues better.

To help prevent conflict, people need to get better at identifying and expressing emotions, being in touch with their bodies as well as with

DOI: 10.4324/9781003675938-19

their thoughts. Indeed, we often notice bodily tension and stress, such as increased heart rate, shallow breathing, tensions in the muscles, etc., before becoming aware of it cerebrally, slowly becoming aware of feelings of fear, sadness, loneliness, and hurt, as well as anger. Repressing such emotions can lead to depression, whereas acknowledging them and working with them can motivate positive change.

The benefits of developing deeper self-insight and resilience are not just for those in a group; a solo artist will still need to find ways to understand themselves and others better, as no one truly works in isolation. There are skills we can develop and practise which can build our resilience so we are better able to quickly identify and address a developing conflict.

In this book, I have aimed to offer some proactive approaches, but as a mediator, I have focused on how mediation can assist when people have been unable to resolve matters between themselves. I believe that mediation, in addition to potentially enabling disputants to solve a specific conflict, can also bring about increased insight and long-term change. Participants can develop a greater understanding of self, including an increased ability to recognise early what their triggers are and therefore respond in a more positive way. It also provides an opportunity, to experience, in a safe place, other people's world views and to develop awareness that there are different perspectives on each situation, which hold equal validity and are in need of exploring, rather than rejecting, in order to better understand the underlying issues – often emotional and psychological – which are in play and which need to be addressed first in order to find a meaningful solution for all parties.

I hope I have shown that disagreement and the anger associated with any dispute is natural and can be harnessed positively. It is healthier to acknowledge early any disappointment, anger, and frustration, both to yourself and to the person perceived as causing those emotions.

For members of a band or orchestra, it is important to develop a collective culture which allows emotions to be expressed honestly, clearly, and quickly and in a way which is not judgemental or aggressive. It is the behaviour associated with emotions which builds the conflict, not the emotions themselves. Behaviours such as raised voices, name calling, invading another's space, refusing to speak, sarcasm, attempts at belittling the other, laughing, walking away when someone is speaking can all inflame the situation as much as physical violence.

Those listening to shared feelings need to develop an attitude of curiosity, patience, and respect, with a genuine desire to understand why the person is upset, angry, overwhelmed, or sad. This is hard to do when all you want to do is get on with the creative process. It can be frustrating and annoying but if all parties are committed to 'staying with the process,' not storming out or sulking, time will be saved and relationships strengthened, making it more likely that the creative juices will flow and the individuals can remember what brought them together in the first place and get back to enjoying being together.

Bibliography

Adler, A. (1937). Position in Family Constellation Influences Lifestyle. *International Journal of Individual Differences*, *3*, 211–227.

Adler, A. (1964). *The Individual Psychology of Alfred Adler* (Eds. H. L. Ansbacher and R. R. Ansbacher). New York: Harper Torchbooks.

Adler, R., Rosenfeld, L., and Proctor, R. (2001). *Interplay: The Process of Interpersonal Communicating* (8th edition). Fort Worth, TX: Harcourt.

Alison, L. and Alison, E. (2017). Revenge versus Rapport, Interrogation, Terrorism, and Torture. *American Psychologist*, *72*(3), 266–277.

Arts, H. and Ashdown, K., (2015). *Conflict Resolution for Musicians (and Other Cool People)*. Vancouver: Conflict Resolution for Creatives Press.

Attali, J. (2014). *Noise: The Political Economy of Music* (Trans. Brian Massumi). Minneapolis, MN: University of Minnesota Press.

Avila, D. (2025). Anitta Reveals Struggle with Identity Crisis over Her Pop-Star Persona as She Says It's Hard to 'Turn Off the Character.' *People*, 11th March. https://people.com/anitta-reveals-struggle-with-identity-crisis-over-pop-star-persona-hard-to-turn-off-character-11694426.

Avila, D. and Hansen, L. (2023). Pop Star Anitta 'Used to Struggle' with Sexy and Shy Sides: 'Now They Communicate'. *People*, 15th September. https://people.com/anitta-used-to-struggle-with-sexy-and-shy-sides-exclusive-7970156

Bacon N. and Blyton P. (2007). Conflict for Mutual Gains? *Journal of Management Studies*, *44*(5), 814–834.

Bassett, J. (2015). New Order and Peter Hook – How to Rip a Band Apart in 11 Easy Steps. *NME*, 2nd December. https://www.nme.com/blogs/nme-blogs/new-order-and-peter-hook-how-to-rip-a-band-apart-in-11-easy-steps-4754

Bauer, L. (2023). *Musicians and Hearing Health*. Pennsylvania: Pennsylvania State University.

Bazerman, M. H. and Neale, M. A. (1994). *Negotiating Rationally*. New York: Free Press.

Beaumont-Thomas, B. (2017). Liam Gallagher Attacks Brother Noel for Absence at One Love Manchester Concert. *The Guardian*, 5th June. https://www.theguardian.com/music/2017/jun/05/liam-gallagher-attacks-brother-noel-for-absence-at-one-love-manchester-concert-twitter.

Bennett, S., Robb, K. A., Zortea, T. C., Dickson, A., Richardson, C., and O'Connor R. C. (2023). Male Suicide Risk and Recovery Factors: A Systematic Review and

Qualitative Meta-Synthesis of Two Decades of Research. *Psychological Bulletin, 149*(7–8): 371–417.

Berlin J., Cantelmo P., and Wainer J. (Directors) (2025). *Larissa- The Other Side of Anitta,* https://www.imdb.com/title/tt35630679/.

Berninger, T. (Director). (2013). *Mistaken for Strangers.* https://www.imdb.com/title/tt2737310/.

Binswanger, L. (1946). The Existential Analysis School of Thought. In R. May E. Angel, and H. F. Ellenberger (Eds.), *Existence.* New York: Basic Books.

Black Lives in Music. (2021). *Being Black in the UK Music Industry: Music Creators – Part 1.* https://s3.us-east-1.amazonaws.com/nadworks.streaming/BLiM/BLiM-report-musiccreators_2109v01.pdf.

Bletchly, R. (2015). Adele: 'Fame is Toxic and Touring is Lonely ... People Have Paid to See Me but What if They Don't Like Me', *Daily Mirror*, 23rd October. https://www.mirror.co.uk/3am/celebrity-news/adele-fame-toxic-touring-lonelypeople-6693239.

Boehm, M. (1999). Life's a Breach. *Los Angeles Times*, 12 May. https://www.latimes.com/archives/la-xpm-1999-may-12-ca-36290-story.html.

Brett, J. M. (2000). Culture and Negotiation. *International Journal of Psychology, 35*(2), 97–104.

Brett, J. M., Shapiro, D. L., and Lytle, A. L. (1998). Breaking the Bonds of Reciprocity in Negotiations. *Academy of Management Journal, 41*(4), 410–424.

Bryant, T. (2012). Keith Richards Mocks Size of Mick Jagger's Penis. *Daily Mirror*, 16th October. https://www.mirror.co.uk/3am/celebrity-news/keith-richards-mocks-size-of-mick-254482.

Burgess, H. and Spangler, B. (2003). Conflicts and Disputes. In G. Burgess and H. Burgess (Eds.), *Beyond Intractability.* Boulder: Conflict Research Consortium, University of Colorado.

Burton, J. (1990). *Conflict: Resolution and Prevention.* London: St Martin's Press.

Bush, R., Baruch, A., and Folger, J. P. (1994). *The Promise of Mediation: The Transformative Approach to Conflict.* San Francisco: Jossey-Bass.

Cage, J. (1961). *Silence: Lectures and Writing.* Connecticut: Wesleyan Press.

Canetto, S. S. and Sakinofsky, I. (1988). *The Gender Paradox in Suicide. Suicide Life Threat Behaviour.* Wiley Online Library.

Chapman, D. P. (2021). *The Colour of Racism: The Criminalisation of Black Music Culture in Postwar Britain,* Hull: University of Hull, Department of Criminology and Sociology.

Citron, A. and Cerone, D. (1991). There Are No Limits in Michael Jackson's World. *Los Angeles Times*, 14th November. https://www.latimes.com/archives/la-xpm-1991-11-14-ca-1971-story.html

Cloke, K. (2006). *The Crossroads of Conflict: A Journey into the Heart of Dispute Resolution.* Alberta, Canada: Janis Publications.

Coser, L. (1964). *The Functions of Social Conflict.* New York: Free Press.

Costintino, C. A. and Merchant, C. S. (1966). *Designing Conflict Management Systems: A Guide to Creating Productive and Healthy Organizations.* San Francisco: Jossey-Bass.

Craig, Y. J. (1998). *Advocacy, Counselling and Mediation in Casework.* London: Jessica Kingsley Publishers.

Crossley, N. (2023). *The Importance of Hearing Damage Prevention in Musicians' Work*. Musicians' Union. https://musiciansunion.org.uk/news/the-importance-of-hearing-damage-prevention-in-musicians-work.

Daily Express. (2014). Barry Gibb Regrets Not Getting Along Better with His Late Brothers. 30th May. https://www.express.co.uk/celebrity-news/479188/Barry-Gibb-regrets-not-getting-along-better-with-his-late-brothers.

Dalla-Camina, M. (2025). This Is Such a Powerful Reflection from Taylor Swift on What It Means to Be a Woman Constantly Navigating Criticism [Video]. Facebook, 24th July. https://www.facebook.com/megandallacamina/videos/this-is-such-a-powerful-reflection-from-taylor-swift-on-what-it-means-to-be-a-wo/1915611762614574/ (accessed 13th November 2025).

Damasio, A. (2010). *Self Comes to Mind: Constructing the Conscious Brain*. New York: Pantheon.

Dearing, J. (1989). *Making Money Making Music*. London: Omnibus Press.

De Bono, E. (1992). *Serious Creativity: Using the Power of Lateral Thinking to Create New Ideas*. New York: Harper Business.

De Bono, E. (2016). *Lateral Thinking: A Textbook of Creativity*. London: Penguin.

De Dreu, C. K. and Gelfand, M. J. (Eds.) (2008). *The Psychology of Conflict and Conflict Management in Organizations*. New York: Erlbaum.

De Dreu, C. K. and Weingart, L. R. (2003). Task versus Relationship Conflict, Team Performance, and Team Member Satisfaction: A Meta-Analysis. *Journal of Applied Psychology*, *88*(4), 741–749.

De Dreu, C. K. W. and Van Vianen, A. E. M. (2001). Managing Relationship Conflict and the Effectiveness of Organizational Teams. *Journal of Organizational Behavior*, *22*(3), 309–328.

Degraff, J. and Degraff, S. (2017). *The Innovation Code: The Creative Power of Constructive Conflict*. Oakland, CA: Berrett-Koehler.

Deutsch, M. (1948). *The Effects of Cooperation and Competition upon Group Process*. PhD Thesis, MIT, Cambridge, MA.

Deutsch, M. (1973). *The Resolution of Conflict: Constructive and Destructive Processes*. New Haven, CT: Yale University Press.

Deutsch, M. (1985). *Distributive Justice: A Social Psychological Perspective*. New Haven, CT: Yale University Press.

Deutsch, M. and Coleman, P. T. (2012). *Psychological Components of Sustainable Peace*. New York, NY: Springer.

Deutsch, M. and Coleman, P. T. (2000). *The Handbook of Conflict Resolution: Theory and Practice*. San Francisco, CA: Jossey-Bass.

Donaldson, L. (2023). What David Gilmour and Polly Samson Have Said About Roger Waters. *Newsweek*, 7th February. https://www.newsweek.com/david-gilmour-roger-waters-pink-floyd-polly-samson-what-said-feud-twitter-tweets-1779392

Duffy, L. (2023). *Personal Witness Statement*. http://www.dafts.co.uk/louieduffystatement.pdf.

Edwards, G. (2015). Brothers in Arms: Rock's 12 Most Tempestuous Sibling Rivalries. *Rolling Stone*, 1st June. https://www.rollingstone.com/music/music-lists/brothers-in-arms-rocks-12-most-tempestuous-sibling-rivalries-20377/.

Embleton, T. (2023) *Touring and Mental Health: The Music Industry Manual.* London: Omnibus Press.
Eisenhardt, K. M., Kahwajy, J. L., and Bourgeois, L. K. (1997). Conflict and Strategic Choice: How Top Management Teams Disagree. *California Management Review*, *39*(2), 42.
Fisher, J. G., Frederickson, J. R., and Peffer, S. A. (2006). Budget Negotiations in Multi-Period Settings. *Accounting Organizations and Society*, *31*(6), 511–528.
Fisher, R. & Ury, W. R. (1981). *Getting to Yes*. Boston: Houghton-Mifflin.
Fleck, C. (2025). *Validation: The New Psychology of Influence*. London: Orion Spring.
Foulkes, S. H. (2018). *Selected Papers of S. H. Foulkes: Psychoanalysis and Group Analysis*. Abingdon: Routledge.
Frankl, V. (2006). *Man's Search for Meaning*. Boston, MA: Beacon Press.
Freud, S. (1930). *Civilisation and Its Discontents* (Translated by J. Riviere). London: Hogarth Press.
Fricke, D. (2010). Keith Richard and Brian Jones on Mick Jagger and the New Memoir. *Rolling Stone*, 19th October. https://www.rollingstone.com/music/music-news/keith-richards-on-brian-jones-mick-jagger-and-the-new-memoir-life-52581/
Friedman G. and Himmelstein, J. (2006). Resolving Conflict Together. *Journal of Dispute Resolution*, *2006*(2), 523–553.
Frith, S. and Marshall, L. (2004). *Music and Copyright*. New York: Routledge.
Gallagher, L. (2025). 11th June. X. Available at: https://x.com/liamgallagher/status/1932656755135164726 (accessed 9th November, 2025).
Gendlin, E. (2003). *Focusing: How to Gain Direct Access to Your Body's Knowledge*. London: Rider.
Gilmore, M. (2013), Love and War inside the Rolling Stones. *Rolling Stone*, 7th May. https://www.rollingstone.com/music/music-news/love-and-war-inside-the-rolling-stones-94552/.
Glasl, F. (1999). *Confronting Conflict*. Bristol: Hawthorn Press.
Green, A. (2018) Nick Mason on the State of Pink Floyd: It's Silly to Still Be Fighting. *Rolling Stone*, 10th December. https://www.rollingstone.com/music/music-news/pink-floyd-nick-mason-talks-roger-waters-david-gilmour-763670/.
Gross, S. A. and Musgrave, G. (2020). *Can Music Make You Sick: Measuring the Price of Musical Ambition*. London: University of Westminster Press.
Hackworth, F. (1996). Morrissey Fights to Keep Smiths Millions. *Manchester Evening News*, 2nd December. Available at: http://www.cemetrygates.com › vault › news › court (accessed 10th November 2025).
Hanaway, M. (2014). *Tales of Conflict and the Role of Mediation*. Henley-on-Thames: The CH Group.
Hanaway, M. (2021). *Psychologically Informed Mediation*. London: Routledge.
Hanaway, M. (2025). *Exploring the Role of Culture in Mediation: An Existential Approach for Mediators, Coaches, Psychologists and Organisations*. London: Routledge.

Hann, M. (2025). 'I Tried to Be Nice. Sometimes I Would Explode': John Fogerty on Creedence, Contracts and Control. *The Guardian*, 15th August. https://www.theguardian.com/music/2025/aug/15/john-fogerty-creedence-clearwater-revival-contracts-controlling-catalogue.

Harrison, A. (2014). *Music the Business* (8th edition). London: Virgin Books.

Haynes, J. and Marshall, L. (2018). Reluctant Entrepreneurs: Musicians and Entrepreneurship in the 'New' Music Industry. *British Journal of Sociology*, *69*(2), 459–482.

Help Musicians, Attitude is Everything, and Musicians' Union. (2024). *Musicians' Census: Disabled Musicians Insight Report*. https://mcusercontent.com/f8a7f535676e150d1ccb6a790/files/26eda189-360f-69ef-5ad6-8becbb7fadbf/Disabled_Musicians_Insight_Report_Sml.5cs.pdf.

Help Musicians, Musicians' Union, and Women in CTRL. (2024). *Women Musicians Insight Report*. https://static1.squarespace.com/static/6398a2cf26f9de4e45e94dd7/t/6603e1657146410e882a30b2/1711530351239/MC23+Womens+Insight+Report+0224+FA.pdf.

Hicks, T. (2000). *Seven Steps for Effective Problem-Solving*. https://connexusconflictmanagement.com/wp-content/uploads/2019/11/Seven-Steps-for-Effective-Problem-Solving-3.pdf.

House of Commons. (2024). *Misogyny in Music*. London: House of Commons. https://committees.parliament.uk/work/6736/misogyny-in-music/.

Hume, D. and McCormack, T. J. (2004). *Treatise of Human Nature* (Book 2). New York: Dover Publications.

Independent. (2009). Allan Klien: Notorious Business Manager for the Beatles and Rolling Stones. 6th July. https://www.independent.co.uk/news/obituaries/allen-klein-notorious-business-manager-for-the-beatles-and-the-rolling-stones-1732780.html.

Jae-heun, K. (2024). K Pop Idols Are under Intense Ethical Scrutiny. *The Korea Herald*, 16th August. https://www.koreaherald.com/article/3455012.

Jehn, K. A. (1995). A Multimethod Examination of the Benefits and Detriments of Intragroup Conflict. *Administrative Science Quarterly*, *40*, 256–282.

Jehn, K. A. (1997). A Qualitative Analysis of Conflict Types and Dimensions in Organizational Groups. *Administrative Science Quarterly*, *42*, 530–557.

Jensen-Campbell, L. A., Graziano, W. G., and Hair, E. C. (1996). Personality and Relationships as Moderators of Interpersonal Conflict in Adolescence. *Merrill-Palmer Quarterly*, *42*(1) 148–164.

Jepson, R. (2019). *Mental Health in The Music Industry: A Guide*. Stevenage: Neilson Book Services.

Johnson, D. W., Johnson, R.T., & Tjosvold, D. (2014). Constructive Controversy: The Value of Intellectual Opposition. In M. Deutsch and P. T. Coleman (Eds.), *The Handbook of Conflict Resolution Theory*, pp. 76–103 San Francisco, CA: Jossey-Bass.

Jolkovski, M. (2007). *How Bands Die*. Working Through: Thinking about/with Creative People and Groups [blog], 29th July. https://workingthrough.com/blog/40-how-bands-die.

Jones, C. and Manoussaki, K. (2022). *Bullying and Harassment in the Music Industry: 'Completely Entangled in Its Fabric.'* Winchester: University of Winchester.

Juslin, P. N. and Sloboda, J. (2011). *Handbook of Music and Emotion*. Oxford: Oxford University Press.

Kenny, D. and Asher, A. (2017). Gender Differences in Mortality and Morbidity Patterns in Popular Musicians across the Lifespan. *Medical Problems of Performing Artists*, *32*, 13–19.

Khomani, N. (2022). Ed Sheeran Wins Court Case Battle over Shape of You Plagiarism Accusation. *The Guardian*, 6th April. https://www.theguardian.com/music/2022/apr/06/ed-sheeran-wins-court-battle-over-shape-of-you-plagiarism-accusation.

Klein, M. (2017). *The Collected Works of Melanie Klein*. London: Routledge.

Kovel, J., (1995). On Racism and Psychoanalysis. In A. Elliot & S. Frosch (Eds.), *Psychoanalysis in Contexts*. London: Routledge.

Kramer, S. and Yahm, S. (2010). *And the Band Broke Up*, Kindle.

Kriesberg, L. (1998). *Constructive Conflicts: From Escalation to Resolution*. Lanham, MA: Rowman & Littlefield.

Kunze, M. (2015). The Troubles with Identity: The Role of Identity & Its Impact on Conflict Resolution in Northern Ireland. *Liberated Arts: A Journal for Undergraduate Research*, *1*(1), Article 7.

Kunze, R. A. (2015). *The Unpredictability of Conflict: A Reconceptualization of Political Instability and Its Potential for Forecasting Conflict*. Malmo, Sweden: Malmo University.

Lamont, T. (2016). Laura Mvula: 'My Body Spasms. I Think I'm Going to Collapse.' *The Guardian*, 20th March. https://www.theguardian.com/global/2016/mar/20/laura-mvula-interview-panic-attacks-music-anxiety-tom-lamont.

Leslie, I. (2014). *Curious: The DESIRE to Know and Why your FUTURE Depends on It*. London: Quercus.

Let It Rock. (2024). Interview with Dave Davies. https://dmme.net/interviews/interview-with-dave-davies.

Levy, D. M. (2010). *Studies in Sibling Rivalry*. Whitefish MT: Kessinger Publishing.

Lewis, R. (2014). Half of Rock Vocal Duo the Everly Brothers. *Los Angeles Times*, 4th January. https://www.latimes.com/archives/la-xpm-2014-jan-03-la-me-phil-everly-20140104-story.html.

Liebmann, M. (Ed.). (2000). *Mediation in Context*. London: Jessica Kingsley.

Linehan, M. M. (1997). Validation and Psychotherapy. In A. C. Bohart, and L. S. Greenberg (Eds.), *Empathy Reconsidered: New Directions in Psychotherapy* (pp. 353–392). American Psychological Association.

Liu, J., Fu, P., and Lui S. (2009). Conflict in Top Management Teams and Team/Firm Outcomes; The Moderating Effects of Conflict-Handling Approaches. *International Journal of Conflict Management*, *20*(3).

Lorey, I. (2011). Virtuosos of Freedom: On the Implosion of Political Virtuosity and Productive Labour. In W. Ulf, R. Gerald, and R. Gene (Eds.), *Critique of Creativity: Precarity, Subjectivity and Resistance in the 'Creative Industries'*. London: Mayfly.

Lovelace, K., Shapiro, D. L., and Weingart, L. R. (2001). Maximizing Cross-Functional New Product Teams' Innovativeness and Constraint Adherence: A Conflict Communications Perspective. *Academy of Management Journal*, *44*(4). 779–793.

Lowe, Z. (2025). Lady Gaga/Zane Lowe Interview [Video], 5th March. Available at: reddit.com/r/popheads/comments/1j49cby/lady_gaga_zane_lowe_interview_apple_music/.

McLaren, B. (2023). *Megan Thee Stallion: Rapper Settles Legal Dispute with Former Label*. BBC News. https://www.bbc.co.uk/news/newsbeat-67163267.

Mardon, A. and Schabert R. (2021). *Mental Health in the Music Industry*. Edmonton, AB: Golden Meteorite Press.

Marr, J. (2017). *Set the Boy Free*. London: Arrow Press.

Marsbar. (2017). *Bill Wyman Slams Jagger and Richards*. Marsden Global, 22 July. https://www.marsdenglobal.com/forum/viewtopic.php?f=4&t=1782.

Michaels, S. (2011). Dr Dre Wins Legal Battle over The Chronic. *The Guardian*, 21st April. https://www.theguardian.com/music/2011/apr/21/dr-dre-legal-battle-chronic.

Mier, T. (2022). Megan Thee Stallion Says She's 'Gotta Take a Break' after Her Home Is Broken Into: 'I'm So Tired.' *Rolling Stone*, 14th October. https://www.rollingstone.com/music/music-news/megan-thee-stallion-says-she-needs-break-after-home-burglary-1234611861/.

Mindell, A. (1995). *Sitting in the Fire: Large Group Transformation Using Conflict and Diversity*. San Francisco: Harper Collins.

Mitchell, S. C. (Director). (2011). *Talihina Sky*. https://www.imdb.com/title/tt1884431/.

Morrissey. (2013). *Autobiography*. London: Penguin Classics.

Morrison, C. (2003). Foreword. In Music Mangers' Forum (Eds.), *The Music Management Bible*. London: SMT.

Morton, N. (1986). *The Journey Is Home*. Boston, MA: Beacon Press.

Musgrave, G. and Lamis, D. A. (2025). Musicians, the Music Industry, and Suicide: Epidemiology, Risk Factors, and Suggested Prevention Approaches, *Frontiers in Public Health*, 13. https://www.frontiersin.org/journals/publichealth/articles/10.3389/fpubh.2025.1507772/full.

Musicians' Union. (2020). *For the Love of Music: Ending Sexual Harassment in the Music Industry*. London: Musicians' Union.

Music Managers' Forum. (2007). *The Music Management Bible*, London: SMT.

MusicWeek. (2017). Paul McCartney Settles with Sony/ ATV over Business Rights. https://www.musicweek.com/publishing/read/paul-mccartney-settles-with-sony-atv-over-beatles-rights/068984

Nemeth C. and Owens P. (1996). Making Work Groups More Effective: The Value of Minority Dissent. In *Handbook of Work Group Psvchology* (pp. 125–138). Hoboken, NJ: Wiley.

NME. (2000). 'Cause We Need Each Other. 18th July. https://www.nme.com/news/music/oasis-974-1397407

Ohbuchi, K.-I. and Atsumi, E. (2010). Avoidance Brings Japanese Employees What They Care about in Conflict Management: Its Functionality and 'Good Member' Image. *Negotiation and Conflict Management*, *3*(2), 117–129.

Onafuye, N. (2021). *Little Mix's Leigh-Ann Pinnock: 'I Felt So Overlooked and It Was Down to My Colour.'* BBC, 12 May. https://www.bbc.co.uk/bbcthree/article/51baf91b-c41f-496a-8c76-d3bdc345b1e4.

Parsons, T. (2012). The World's Greatest Rock Band Deserves a Better Epitaph than Playground Snickering. *Daily Mirror*, 24th March. https://www.mirror.co.uk/news/uk-news/the-worlds-greatest-rock-band-deserves-770430.

Passman, D. S. (2023). *All You Need to Know about the Music Business* (11th edition). New York: Simon and Schuster.

Paul, A. (2014). *One Way Out: The Inside History of the Allman Brothers*. London: St Martin's Press.

Petrova, I., Leonova, I., and Isidori E. (Eds.). (2023). *Creative Person and the Development of Creativity: A Challenge for Contemporary Society*. Rome; Nizhny Novgorod: Quapeg Editions.

Pruitt, D. G. (1983). Strategic Choice in Negotiation. *American Behavioral Scientist*, *27*(2):167–194.

Raeburn, S. D. (1987a). Occupational Stress and Coping in a Sample of Professional Rock Musicians (Second of Two Parts). *Medical Problems of Performing Artists*, *2*(3), 77–82.

Raeburn, S. D. (1987b) *Well-Being and Creative Careers: Interview*. Deuzestack. https://markdeuze.substack.com/p/well-being-and-creative-careers-interview-c02.

Raeburn, S. D. (1999). Psychological Issues and Treatment Strategies in Popular Musicians: A Review, Part 1. *Medical Problems of Performing Artists*, *14*(4), 171–179.

Rahim, M. A. (1983). A Measure of Styles of Handling Interpersonal Conflict. *Academy of Management Journal*, *26*, 368–376.

Reich, W. (1967). *Reich Speaks of Freud*. London: Condor.

Reid, W. and Reid, J. (2024). *Never Understood: The Jesus and Mary Chain*. London: Hachette.

Renshaw, D. (2015). Liam Gallagher Compares Noel Gallagher to Katie Hopkins in Twitter Insult. *NME*, 6th May. https://www.nme.com/news/music/oasis-54-1222219.

Richards K. (2011). *Life*. New York: Little Brown and Company.

Riches, N. (2012). *The Music Management Bible*. London: SMT Music Sales.

Robinson, M. L. (2009). *Just Conflict: Transformation through Resolution*, New York: Epigraph Books.

Rogan, J. (2012). *Morrissey & Marr: The Severed Alliance*. London: Omnibus Press.

Rough, J. (1997). Dynamic Facilitation and the magic of self-organizing change. *The Journal for Quality and Participation*, *20*(3).

Rough, J. and Martin, D. (2007). Dynamic Facilitation. In P. Holman, T. Devane, and S. Cady (Eds.), *The Change Handbook*. Oakland, CA: Berret-Koehler.

Rolling Stone. (2011). Rock's Greatest Feuds: Kings of Leon, the Rolling Stones, Aerosmith, and More. 13th October. https://www.rollingstone.com/music/music-lists/rocks-greatest-feuds-kings-of-leon-the-rolling-stones-aerosmith-and-more-18557/.

Sacks, J. (2002). *The Dignity of Difference*. London: Continuum.

Sacks, O. (2006). The Power of Music. *Brain*, *129*(10), 2528–2532.

Sacks, O. (2008). *Musicophilia: Tales of Music and the Brain*. New York: Picador Press.

Samuels, A. (1993). *The Political Psyche*. London: Routledge.

Sartre J.-P. (1989). *No Exit and Three Other Plays*. London: Vintage Books.

Scheff, T. and Retzinger, S. (1991). *Emotions* and *Violence*. Lexington, MA: Lexington Books.

Scorsese, M. (Director). (2005) *No Direction Home*. Paramount.

Sgubini, A. (2006). *Mediation and Culture: How Different Cultural Backgrounds Can Affect the Way People Negotiate and Resolve Disputes*. Mediate, 28th March. https://mediate.com/mediation-and-culture-how-different-cultural-backgrounds-can-affect-the-way-people-negotiate-and-resolve-disputes/.

Shantz, C. U. (1987). Conflicts between Students. *Child Development*, *58*, 283–305.

Snapes, L. (2022). Taylor Swift Files in Shake It Off Copyright Lawsuit: 'The Lyrics Were Written Entirely by Me'. *The Guardian*, 9th August 2022). https://www.theguardian.com/music/2022/aug/09/taylor-swift-files-in-shake-it-off-copyright-lawsuit-the-lyrics-were-written-entirely-by-me.

Standing, G. (2011). *The Precariat: The New Dangerous Class*. London: Bloomsbury.

Stevenson, R. W. (1994). George Michael Loses Lawsuit against Sony. *New York Times*, 22nd June. https://www.nytimes.com/1994/06/22/arts/george-michael-loses-lawsuit-against-sony.html.

Strasser, F. and Randolph, P. (2004). *Mediation: A Psychological Insight into Conflict Resolution*. London: Continuum.

Sun, M. (2023). Madonna Calls Speculation about Her Appearance 'Ageism and Misogyny'. *The Guardian*, 9th February. https://www.theguardian.com/music/2023/feb/09/madonna-age-appearance-look-grammys-2023-ageism-misogyny.

Sussell, A., Peterson, C., Li, J., Minino, A., Scott, K. A., and Stone, D. M. (2023). Suicide Rates in Industry and Occupation – National Vital Statistical System, United States, 2021. *MMWR Morbidity and Mortality Weekly Report*. CDC, 15th December, *72*(50): 1346–1350.

Suttie, I. (1936). *The Origins of Love and Hate*. Harmondsworth: Penguin.

Taylor, T. (2021). What Actually Went Down during The Smiths' Lawsuit? *Farout*, 1st June. https://faroutmagazine.co.uk/the-smiths-breakup-lawsuit-marr-morrissey-rourke/.

The Straits Times. (2024). *K-Pop idols Yeonin, Felix Apologise for Japan Linked Content on S. Korea's National Day*. 19th August. https://www.straitstimes.com/life/entertainment/k-pop-idols-yeonjun-and-felix-apologise-for-japan-linked-contents-on-south-korea-s-national-liberation-day.

Thomas K. W. (1976). Conflict and Conflict Management. In M. D. Dunnette (Ed.), *Handbook of Industrial and Organizational Psychology* (pp. 889–935). Chicago: Rand McNally.

Thorne, M. (2013). *Prince*. London: Faber & Faber.

Thorpe, V. (2023). Primal Scream Musician's Son Says Band's 'Tough Love' Isolated Father before Death. *The Guardian* 10th June. https://www.theguardian.com/music/2023/jun/10/primal-scream-musicians-son-says-bands-tough-love-isolated-father-before-death

Tjosvold, D. (1985). Implications of Controversy Research for Management. *Journal of Management*, *11*, 19–35.

Totton, N. (2006). *The Politics of Psychotherapy*. Maidenhead: Open University Press.

Tzu, S. (2009). *The Art of War*. London: Pax Librorum.
Uncut. (2015). Black Crowes' Rich Robinson: 'The Band Has Broken Up.' 16th January. https://www.uncut.co.uk/news/black-crowes-rich-robinson-the-band-has-broken-up-325/.
UK Music. (2024). *Diversity Report*. https://ukmusic.org/wp-content/uploads/2024/06/UK-Music-Diversity-Report-2024.pdf.
Vaag, J., Bjerkeset, O., and Sivertsen, B. (2021). Anxiety and Depression Symptom Level and Psychotherapy Use among Music and Art Students Compared to the General Student Population. *Frontiers in Psychology*, *12*, Article 607927.
Vaag, J., Giæver, F., and Bjerkeset, O. (2014). Specific Demands and Resources in the Career of the Norwegian Freelance Musician. *Arts & Health: An International Journal for Research, Policy and Practice,* 6(3), 205–222.
Van Deurzen, E., (2001) *Existential Counselling and Psychotherapy*. London: Sage.
Van de Vliert, E. and Kabanoff, B. (1990). Toward Theory-Based Measures of Conflict Management. *Academy of Management Journal*, *33*(1), 199–209.
Virus, P. (Director). (2021). *Freakscene: The Story of Dinosaur Jr*. https://pro.imdb.com/title/tt14781332/?rf=cons_tt_btf_cc&ref_=cons_tt_btf_cc.
Vuchinich, S. (1990). The Sequential Organization of Closing in Verbal Family Conflict. In A. D. Grimshaw (Ed.), *Conflict Talk: Sociolinguistic Investigations of Arguments in Conversations* (pp. 118–138). New York: Cambridge University Press.
Wall, A. (Director). (1998). *The Brian Epstein Story*. BBC. https://www.imdb.com/title/tt0200503/.
White, C. (2020). *Influential Voices Discuss Fight against Racism and Prejudice*. ITV News, 25th June. https://www.itv.com/news/2020-06-25/itv-news-black-lives-matter-panel-discuss-fight-against-racism.
Whiting, C. (2007). *Poor Bloody Infantry 1939–1945*. Staplehurst: Spellmount.
Wills, G. and Cooper, G. (1988). *Pressure Sensitive: Popular Musicians UNDER Stress*. London: Sage.
Windsor-Shellard, B. and Gunnell, D. (2019). Occupation-Specific Suicide Risk in England: 2011–2015. *British Journal of Psychiatry*, *April*(1), 1–6.
Wyman, B. (1990). *Stone Alone*. New York: Viking.
Yam, M. (2011). *Everyone Loves Our Town: A History of Grunge*. London: Faber & Faber.
Yarn, D. H. (Ed.). (1999). Conflict. In *Dictionary of Conflict Resolution*. San Francisco: Jossey-Bass.
Young, J. W.(1960) *A Technique for Producing Ideas*. Colombus, OH: MacGraw Hill Education.
Your Child Team. (2011) *The Realities of Sibling Rivalry*. University of Michigan Health System Resources. https://www.michiganmedicine.org/health-lab/realities-sibling-rivalry.
Youth Music. (2024). *The Sound of The Next Generation Report*. https://www.youthmusic.org.uk/resources/sound-next-generation-2024?gad_source=1&gad_campaignid=1699547186&gbraid=0AAAADshpglXMjbRI-ijndDWv5paJOQIo&gclid=EAIaIQobChMIstHI7o3bkAMV55FQBh0B-DVfEAAYASAAEgJtrPD_BwE.

Zara, C. (2012). *The Tortured Artist: From Picasso and Munroe to Warhol and Winehouse: The Twisted Secrets of The World's Most Creative Minds*. Avon, MA: Adams Media.

Zizek, S. (1989). *The Sublime Object of Ideology*. London: Verso.

Zubizarreta, R. (2006). Practical Dialogue: Emergent Approaches for Effective Collaboration. In S. P. Schuman (Ed.), *Creating a Culture of Collaboration: The International Association of Facilitators Handbook*. Hoboken, NJ: Jossey-Bass/Wiley.

Zubizarreta, R. (2014). *From Conflict to Creative Collaboration: A User's Guide to Dynamic Facilitation*. Minnesota: Publish Green.

Index

Note: Page numbers in **bold** refer to information in tables.

For Product Safety Concerns and Information please contact our EU representative GPSR@taylorandfrancis.com Taylor & Francis Verlag GmbH, Kaufingerstraße 24, 80331 München, Germany